CANADIAN PIE

ALSO BY WILL FERGUSON

FICTION
Spanish Fly
Happiness^{TM}

MEMOIR
Coal Dust Kisses: A Christmas Memoir

TRAVEL
Beyond Belfast
Hitching Rides with Buddha
Beauty Tips from Moose Jaw

HISTORY/HUMOUR
How to Be a Canadian (with Ian Ferguson)
Why I Hate Canadians
Bastards and Boneheads
Canadian History for Dummies

AS EDITOR
The Penguin Anthology of Canadian Humour

AS SONGWRITER
Lyricist on the songs "Con Men and Call Girls, Part One,"
"When the Circus Comes to Town,"
and "Losin' Hand" on the Tom Phillips music CD *Spanish Fly*

WILL FERGUSON

CANADIAN PIE

VIKING
CANADA

VIKING CANADA

Published by the Penguin Group

Penguin Group (Canada), 90 Eglinton Avenue East, Suite 700, Toronto, Ontario, Canada M4P 2Y3
(a division of Pearson Canada Inc.)

Penguin Group (USA) Inc., 375 Hudson Street, New York, New York 10014, U.S.A.
Penguin Books Ltd, 80 Strand, London WC2R 0RL, England
Penguin Ireland, 25 St Stephen's Green, Dublin 2, Ireland (a division of Penguin Books Ltd)
Penguin Group (Australia), 250 Camberwell Road, Camberwell, Victoria 3124, Australia
(a division of Pearson Australia Group Pty Ltd)
Penguin Books India Pvt Ltd, 11 Community Centre, Panchsheel Park, New Delhi – 110 017, India
Penguin Group (NZ), 67 Apollo Drive, Rosedale, Auckland 0632, New Zealand
(a division of Pearson New Zealand Ltd)
Penguin Books (South Africa) (Pty) Ltd, 24 Sturdee Avenue, Rosebank, Johannesburg 2196, South Africa

Penguin Books Ltd, Registered Offices: 80 Strand, London WC2R 0RL, England

First published 2011

1 2 3 4 5 6 7 8 9 10 (RRD)

Copyright © Will Ferguson, 2011

Page 383 is an extension of this copyright page

Manufactured in the U.S.A.

LIBRARY AND ARCHIVES CANADA CATALOGUING IN PUBLICATION

Ferguson, Will
Canadian pie / Will Ferguson.

ISBN 978-0-670-06472-4

1. Ferguson, Will—Travel. 2. Canada—Description and travel. 3. Japan—Description and travel.
4. Northern Ireland—Description and travel. I. Title.

PS8561.E7593Z462 2011   C814'.54   C2011-904611-3

Visit the Penguin Group (Canada) website at **www.penguin.ca**

Special and corporate bulk purchase rates available; please see
www.penguin.ca/corporatesales or call 1-800-810-3104, ext. 2477 or 2474

CONTENTS

INTRODUCTION

I remember the exact moment I realized I was Canadian, would always be Canadian, that there was no opt-out, no do-over, no cure. It occurred outside the country, on the far side of the world, in fact. We often have to go away to find out who we are.

In my case, I was fresh out of university with a shiny new bachelor's degree in fine arts—and let me tell you, the corporate headhunters on Bay Street were knocking down m' door! Resisting the many lucrative job offers lobbed my way, I signed on with the JET Programme instead.

JET is a working exchange between Japan and the Western world, the goals of which are to (a) enhance English education in Japan (you probably noticed the marked improvement in Japanese English-language ability after my tour of duty in the mid-1990s) and (b) broaden the nation's outlook by making Japan more culturally sensitive and internationally attuned (ditto). The JET Programme sought to do this by bringing in hundreds upon hundreds of young, would-be Anne Sullivans selflessly intent on rescuing Japan from its Helen Keller–like, island-mentality insularity. Yes sir! A thousand years of richly layered Japanese context would melt away in the face of our fearless brigade of twentysomethings armed, as often as not, with fine arts degrees and hailing from such widely varied culture milieus as the United States, Canada, Great Britain, Australia, and New Zealand. "Internationalization," as it turned out, required the drinking of great quantities of beer. Hard work, broadening an island nation's world view. It was also how I came to be posted on the lovely Amakusa Islands, in the warm semi-tropical waters south of Nagasaki.

With a stunning lack of judgment, the Japanese Ministry of Education had entrusted me to shape impressionable young minds on these islands. I was hired (through a clerical error on their part, I'm assuming) to teach English at local high schools, where I routinely explained away my poor spelling as "Canadian usage." *("Sure, you can put two r's in Febuary, if you want to spell ... like an AMERICAN!")*

In the next town up, there were two other exchange teachers: Dave, from the U.S., and Fiona, from England. We became friends almost by default, and would often squander our salaries over late nights at noodle shops and Japanese pubs. It reminded me of a set-up to a gag: *An American, a Canadian, and a Brit walk into a bar ...*

The three of us got on well, even if we did disagree on the comparative virtues of baseball, soccer, and hockey. Or, as I put it, baseball, soccer, and a real sport. Alas, our three-way transnational friendship came crashing down after one particular night of *yakitori* and beer. When it came time to divvy up the tab, Fiona—as the English are wont to do—was short of cash, so Dave—American and generous to a fault—pulled out a 10,000 yen note, about $100, and said, "Don't worry, you can pay me back later." (I did the Canadian thing, where you pat your pockets as though looking for an imaginary wallet until someone else takes care of it.)

A few days later, Fiona dutifully stopped by Dave's apartment and, finding him out, slipped a manila envelope into his mail slot. Inside was a music CD that Dave had earlier asked to borrow—along with a crisp 10,000-yen bill. Dave got home, popped the CD out, didn't notice the money, and discarded the envelope ... with the 10,000-yen bill still inside.

Time passed. Paydays came and went, and finally one night Dave asked, "So, when're you going to repay that money you borrowed?" And that's when things got ugly. "What!" said Dave. "You didn't tell me there was cash inside! I tossed a hundred bucks in the garbage." He insisted she repay him the 10,000 yen on the spot. Why should he lose out? he asked. Why should he be penalized for helping a friend? Why should his kindness cost him a hundred bucks? Dave the American argued in terms of justice and restitution. Had he any Stealth bombers at his disposal, I have no doubt he would've called in an air strike. Fiona replied in terms of legal principles. She *had* returned the money, and in doing so had fulfilled her social obligation. Once the money was in his apartment, she could no longer be held accountable. The fact that Dave had bailed her out, and was now the poorer for it, made not a whit of difference. She'd settled her debt. The rest of it was out of her hands, quite literally.

The invective flew fast and furious, until, as the neutral third party, I was forced to intervene. The compromise I suggested ... Ah, but you already know what I suggested, don't you? If you, dear reader, truly are Canadian, you will no doubt have already come up with the same solution. Why doesn't Fiona repay *half* the money? Why doesn't she give Dave 5000 yen? That way, they're both out the same amount. We all lose, so everybody wins. It's the Canadian way! Right?

Well, my proposal did unite them, but not quite in the manner I'd intended. There was agreement, all right; they thought the compromise I put forward was both utterly daft and completely stupid. "What the hell kind of solution is that?" roared Dave. "She still owes me my money! Why should I lose anything? I did her a favour!"

To which Fiona roared back, "I returned the money, all of it. I owe you not a penny more!" She then levelled her gaze on me. "What sort of silly logic is this?" she demanded to know.

"Canadian logic," I said weakly. "It's why we've never had a civil war. Or an empire."

At which point—and it really was quite touching, seeing them come together like that—Dave and Fiona, American and Brit,

shook their heads in perfect unison, rolled their eyes, and muttered
"Canadians."

This was a big moment for me.

I grew up in the backwoods of northern Alberta, in a former
fur-trading outpost on roughly the same latitude as Churchill,
Manitoba—but without the cachet of polar bears. "Closer to the
Arctic Circle than the American border!" we liked to boast, though
I'm not sure why that was such a point of pride. Still, I've always
felt I emigrated to Canada, to that distant *southern* nation. So, to be
recognized as Canadian while abroad was strangely validating, even if
"Canadian" was being used here in the pejorative.

Pollster Michael Adams summed it up nicely: "Canadians feel
strongly about their weak attachments to Canada." When a contest
was held to come up with a Great Canadian Metaphor, on par with
"as American as apple pie," the winner, famously, was *"as Canadian as
possible, under the circumstances."*

When I was young, I remember a popular recasting of the classic
Don McLean anthem, one that put the lyrics into more Canadian-
friendly terms:

Bye, bye Miss Canadian Pie
Drove my Ski-Doo to the Rideau
But the Rideau was dry
Mes amis were drinkin' Molsons and rye.
Singing, this will be the day that I die … eh?
This will be the day that I die

There's a certain lightness in being Canadian. Lightness … and
light-heartedness, too. And what we may lack in depth we more than
make up for in breadth. The rich layers of island cultures—those of
the Japanese, the English, the Québécois—are, as often as not, defined
more by what they *exclude* than include. But the broader, pan-ethnic
civic nationalism that Canada has come to embody is all but unique in
the world precisely because it looks *outward,* throws a wider net. Even

a nation as diverse as the United States is still defined by a staunch sense of American values "worth dying for," of an "American way of life." Who is a true-blooded American, who isn't? Not surprisingly, America has become an increasingly polarized, fractious state. (It must be so exhausting to be American, the sheer weight of it.)

Canada is built on fault lines as well—linguistic, regional, cultural—but it's not fatally fractured. We remain a Land of the Second Chance, a Kingdom of Lost Causes, where the scattered remnants of history regroup to try again. From First Nations to New France, from the arrival of displaced Loyalists to the return of exiled Acadians, from the Vietnamese refugees of the 1970s to the influx of New Canadians today, our nation has provided a forum for reinvention. It's a Big Tent, this country.

In fact, one of the original titles of this book (note the deft use of segue) was "Big Tent Canada." Another was "The Kingdom of Lost Causes." Still another title that was tossed about was "Cracker Jack Beaver," a reference to a mini-bar forage described later, rejected for predictably dour reasons. (We wouldn't want innocent children Googling this book only to be inundated with websites about Cracker Jack.) My personal favourite, though, was "Very Cool, With Trees," something explained at the start of the Canadian Lives section.

None of these titles suggested the slice-of-this, slice-of-that nature of *Canadian Pie*, though. That's right. This is the part of the introduction where I tell you what's in the book that you've (presumably) just purchased. Why do introductions do this? I have no idea, but I'll be damned if I'm going to break with tradition. The material in *Canadian Pie* covers fifteen years of wanderings and musings, of musings and wanderings, often at the same time. It includes essays on the lost art of crank calls and tips on how to get someone to pick blueberries out of a muffin for you. There are "lost" radio scripts of a Maritime soap opera, a roundup of large objects beside the highway, and an ode to young love in Old Quebec. An encounter with an aging kamikaze pilot. An interview with a pair of Canadian brothers playing semi-pro hockey in Japan. An appreciation of the unintentional beauty of New

Brunswick's covered bridges. Lessons in how to pick up women (or not). A journey up the rainforest coast of Vancouver Island. And a look back at life as a space cadet at Toronto's CN Tower. Basically, it's everything you could possibly want in a book. Better buy a second copy. I'll wait.

Canadian Pie includes the very first thing I ever wrote, or had published for that matter—a travel article written for Japan's *Daily Yomiuri* newspaper about a Shinto pilgrimage to Kinkazan Island in 1995—and, more recently, my experiences writing for the Vancouver 2010 Winter Olympics Closing Ceremonies. As for that Great Canadian Metaphor™, the one on par with American pie? I solve that as well. You can find it in the section titled The Writing "Life."

And what of Dave? What of Fiona? Well, you'll be happy to know—deliriously happy, I'm sure!—that their friendship, though strained, did survive in spite of my best intentions. And, really, any friendship that can survive the best intentions of Canadians is something worth keeping.

Cheers.

Will Ferguson
October 2011

Other Plans

Life is what happens when you're making other plans.

—*John Lennon*

The Lost Art of Crank Calls

With every technological advance something always seems to get lost along the way.

My children, for example, will never be able to experience the thrill and sense of accomplishment that comes from calling up random strangers and inflicting one's sense of humour upon them. With the advent of call display an entire art form has died, unheralded and unmourned. I speak, of course, of the lost art of crank calls.

I was once a master of this realm. And mine were no simpleminded, one-line gags. No crude pranks of the "Is your fridge running? Well, you better go catch it" variety. No sir. Mine were more akin to—well, poetry, really. Or perhaps performance art. A living Theatre of the Absurd. My sister Lorna and I once sent the entire neighbourhood on an epic round-robin quest by calling one house after another, claiming to be the neighbour next door asking for a cup of sugar. This triggered a chain reaction, a veritable circle dance of confusion. It was a scene right out of Chekhov—except of course Chekhov didn't normally get grounded for a week after one of his plays was staged. At least, not as far as I know. But no matter. There is always a price to be paid for art.

My favourite crank calls were more surreal than burlesque, reaching levels so sublime the victims themselves often never realized they'd been set up. In the phone books of our small town, families were listed by name, number, and post-office mailing address, which allowed me to orchestrate the following Beckett-like scenario:

Unsuspecting Victim: Hullo?

Me: Martin?

Victim: Yup.

Me: Martin Driedger?

Victim: Speaking.

Me: Martin Driedger of Rocky Lane, Alberta? Just outside Fort Vermilion?

Victim: That's right.

Me: Post office box 149?

Victim: That's me.

Me: Phone number 555-6642?

Victim: Yes.

Me: Oh. Jeez. I must have the wrong number. Sorry.

My kid sister and I made calls like this countless times, and not once did anyone ever notice anything odd about the conversation.

The all-time classic crank call, however, was one dubbed "The Electrocuted Repairman." The set-up: a noisy office (provided by my sister typing frantically on a typewriter in the background) and a gruff, faux-baritone voice (provided by me).

"This is the phone company calling. One of our men is working on your line, and he has the primary transformer console open"—note the clever use of jargon to establish credibility—"so you may hear the phone ring once or twice in the next hour or two, but whatever you do, do *not* unplug the phone. And do *not* pick up the receiver. If you do, you'll complete the circuit, and you might very well electrocute the repairman."

We would then immediately call back and let it ring and ring and ring and ring and ring and ring and ring and ring and ring and ring and ring and ring and ring and ring and ring and ring and ring and ring and ring and ring ring and ring and ring and ring and ring and ring and ring and ring and ring and ring and ring ring and ring and ring and ring and ring and ring and ring and ring ring and ring and ring and ring and ring and ring and ring and ring ring and ring and ring and ring and ring and ring and ring ring and ring and ring and ring and ring and ring and ring and ring and ring ring and ring and ring and ring and ring and ring and ring and ring and ring ring and ring and ring and ring and ring and ring and ring and ring and ring and ring and ring and ring and ring and ring and ring and ring and ring and ring and ring and ring ... until *finally*, unable to take it anymore, the person on the other end would pick up the phone and hazard a nervous "Hello?" At which point I'd let out a high-pitched shriek, *"Aaiieeeeeeeee!!,"* and slam down the phone.

Sometimes, if we were on a roll, my sister would call back as the grieving widow. Alas, my sons will never be able to follow in their father's footsteps. Because of call display, the cry of the electrocuted repairman will never again be heard echoing across the phone lines of this fair land.

Still, the future is not entirely bleak. Just recently, I came across an article about a thirteen-year-old boy posing as a high-rolling "cyberspace millionaire" who managed to buy an original Van Gogh and a vintage 1971 Corvette via the magic of online auctions. The lad's crowning achievement? A whopping $400,000 winning bid on Sir John A. Macdonald's bed.

Needless to say, the boy's purchases weren't covered by his weekly allowance. When his identity was revealed he sheepishly apologized and admitted that his mom and dad had revoked his computer privileges "indefinitely."

A tear welled up in my eye upon reading this, for I knew the torch had been passed to a new generation.

Pedigreed Pooches
and Spanish Prisoners

Dear reader, I am the son and/or widow of an exiled Nigerian diplomat.

I am contacting you today because I need to move MILLIONS upon MILLIONS of UNTRACEABLE American! dollars! into the bank account of a complete stranger. That would be you.

This $$$$ was amassed over many years by (take your pick) a dead diplomat, a dead president, a dead general, a general who was also president and is now dead, and/or a dead foreigner who has the SAME LAST NAME AS YOU! which clearly makes you the legal claimant.

All you need to do is allow us to deposit these MILLIONS upon MILIONS of dollars into your bank account and you can keep (take your pick) 10, 30, 45, 80 percent of it as a commission.

It is 100 percent foolproof! There is no risk to you whatsoever. And no cost either—except for a small, minor, trifling, teeny-tiny processing fee. Just a few hundred dollars. Plus an Offshore Clearance Bond, a Release Form from the Central Bank of Nigeria, an Anti–Money Laundering Certificate, a Terrorism Clearance Licence from Interpol, an International Remittance Voucher, a Tax Adjustment Fee—after that the $$$$ is all yours!

But you're too clever to fall for that. Or are you? The Nigerian email scam costs North Americans alone more than $700 million a year. And that's a conservative estimate.

Hard to believe anyone would fall for it, but fall they do. More incredibly still, the scam itself dates back more than four hundred years, to the days of the Spanish Armada. Nigeria's email swindle is simply a modern, updated version of the "Spanish prisoner" con, one that can be traced to 1588, with letters purportedly sent from the desperate offspring of a captured English officer held in a Spanish prison. Money was needed to bribe guards, cover costs. In return? A reward worth millions. Millions, mind!

I learned this while researching Spanish fly. Not "Spanish fly the beetle that causes irritation of the urinary tract," but rather "Spanish fly the fake aphrodisiac sold in men's magazines." The one labelled *Genuine 100% Placebo!* It was for a novel I was writing about con men and swindles.

Authors are constantly asked "Is your novel autobiographical?" These queries about how much of yourself you put into a story are tricky enough as it is, but when the novel in question deals with cold-hearted swindlers preying on innocent people, it can also be mildly off-putting. *"Your characters are liars, thieves, and cheats. I'm assuming that's based on you, yes?"*

True, I *am* apparently related to Arthur Ferguson, the legendary Scottish con man known for selling Buckingham Palace to gullible tourists. I say "apparently related" because it's really just family lore, something we Fergusons like to boast about over drinks.

Why this would be a point of pride may strike some as odd, but the public's admiration of con men, the audacity and creative self-invention that they embody, is very real. I've found that having a grifter in the family tree trumps even the highest echelons of landed gentry. "Your great-uncle was Lord Hoo-Ha of the Purple Garter, you say? Mine sold the Eiffel Tower to Parisian scrap dealers."

My dad, Jack Ferguson out of Radville, Saskatchewan, was suspiciously well-informed about the world of grifters and the inner workings of con games, something that has never been fully explained to my satisfaction. The main character in *Spanish Fly*, nineteen-year-old Jack McGreary, was based (loosely) on my dad. Much like my father, Jack McGreary was raised amid the dust storms and despair of the Great Depression, adrift in a world of grey. And several of the bunco artists mentioned in the novel—men like Suitcase Simpson and Henry the Horse—were people my dad ran with in the Dirty Thirties.

So many ways for a fool and his money to be parted. There was one fellow Dad told me about who used to earn a decent living simply through sucker bets. He'd travel from town to town, hitting the taverns, betting the patrons that he could bite his own eye. They'd throw money into a pot—and out would come his glass eye. They'd groan, knowing they'd been taken. Then he would up the ante, saying "How about double or nothing on whether I can bite my other eye?" "Well," they'd figure, "he can't have *two* glass eyes," and they'd take the bet. And out would come his false teeth ...

These swindles aren't quaint museum pieces either, bits of folklore from the Jazz Age. Somewhere between "Spanish fly" and "Spanish prisoners," I stumbled upon a description of a shortchanging scam as well. This one hit home, because I recognized it immediately. It had been pulled on me! It was back when I was a high school student, working part-time as a clerk at a neighbourhood convenience store in Red Deer, Alberta. On my first shift—my very first shift, mind!—a charming fellow came in and purchased a pack of gum with a fifty-dollar bill. As I handed him his change he said, "Wait a sec, I think I have some coins. No need for you to break such a large bill."

When I cashed out at the end of the night, I was short *exactly fifty dollars*. The money ended up coming out of my paycheque. All these years I'd just assumed I'd screwed up, had somehow rung it in incorrectly, never dreaming that I'd actually been set up.

I won't explain how this scam works—no need to aid and abet any would-be grifters out there. But I will say this. If you ever find yourself behind a till and someone purchases a small item with large tender, and then immediately wants to hand back the change—stop. Close the till. Take a deep breath. Complete the first transaction before dealing with any other requests. Trust me on this.

Addled store clerks aside, the best cons actually rely on a bit of larceny in the hearts of the victims they target. One of my personal favourites in this genre is a classic that dates back to the 1920s, something called "the pedigreed pooch." A fellow strolls into a bar with a puppy under one arm. Orders a drink, slaps a bill on the counter, says, "Keep the change."

The puppy is for his little girl's birthday, y'see. And—having ingratiated himself with his sizeable gratuity—he asks the bartender to watch the puppy for just a moment while he runs to his bookie to place a bet. Got the inside track on a race, y'see. A sure thing, y'see. Easy money. So he leaves the pooch and hurries off to lay his wager.

Soon after, a swanky couple sweeps in, asking for directions to a certain dog-breeding establishment, when lo! their eyes settle on the pooch. A rare Albanian purebred, they proclaim, then immediately offer the barkeep $1000 or more for the puppy. Provided he can give them the papers the pooch came with.

"It's not mine to sell," the bartender weakly replies.

So the well-heeled pair leaves a note instead for the other fellow, asking him to stop by their suite at—name the swankiest hotel in town; that's where they're staying—and offering said grand for the dog.

The first man now returns, looking despondent. The horse race was a sham, y'see. Lost everything. All he's got left in this world is this puppy—and he's going to give it to his little girl. Stifling sobs, he hands the bartender a few crumpled bills for his time, then shuffles sadly toward the exit.

"Hang on," comes the inevitable cry. "Why don't I help you out. I'll buy your dog."

A good con man could squeeze as much as $500 per puppy. Not bad for a litter of stray mutts. Not that we'd ever fall for something like that. No sir. We're too clever to be taken in by such a ruse.

And if you believe that, I have some beachfront property in Nunavut you might be interested in. That, and a $50 bill that needs breaking.

WILL FERGUSON'S FIVE THINGS YOU NEED TO KNOW ABOUT CON GAMES

1. Outlandish Cons Work Because They're Outlandish

We like to think we're too clever to be taken, but the number of suckers in this world far outweighs the number of con artists. So at least some of us aren't quite as clever as we think. One of the reasons for our misplaced pride is the sheer out-rageousness of many con games—convincing someone that a stray mutt is really a prize breeder worth thousands of dollars, say. But these cons work precisely *because* they're so outlandish; they're beyond most people's normal frame of reference. That's why the Nigerian email scam works: most of us don't normally deal with the exiled sons of Nigerian diplomats. I know I don't.

2. Beware of Any Request for Money Up Front

When you strip away the layers of embellishment, most cons are quite simple. They switch one package for another. They convince you that something is worth more than it is, whether it's a beat-up fiddle they claim is really a Stradivarius or a mangy pooch fobbed off as a show dog. One of the most common cons is the "advance payment scheme." The Nigerian 419 scam (named after the section in the Nigerian criminal code that deals with obtaining money through false pretences) is an example of this. In it, you're asked to ante up now for a dazzling payoff down the road. Same thing when someone phones to say you've won an all-expenses-paid cruise or a luxury car—for free! You just have to pay the taxes on it. Up front, of course.

3. If It Sounds Too Good to Be True, It Probably Is

This is the First Almighty Rule in spotting any con, and is a good guiding principle for business people and investors in general. It's a simple defence, really; you just ask yourself "Why?" Why would someone offer a deal so outrageously tipped in your favour? Why would someone stop you on the street with a winning lottery ticket that needs cashing? What's that? They're in the country illegally and can't cash in their winning ticket without getting caught? But why would they approach strangers on a street? Have they no friends, no acquaintances they could go through instead? When an offer sounds too good to be true, there's a reason.

5. Mind the Details

That's where they'll get you. One supposed landscaper made a very good living pruning trees by quoting a low fee "per cutting"—only to charge the homeowners that amount *per branch*, not per tree. When challenged, he would browbeat them for wanting "something for nothing." Likewise, if someone is peddling "100% Authentic Spanish Fly Aphrodisiacs," check that the word "placebo" hasn't been slipped in there somewhere. And if an author promises you "Five Things You Need to Know About Con Games," check to see that there really are five.

How to Pick Up Girls
(or not)

People often ask me why I'm such a twisted and bitter man. "Why so twisted?" they ask. "Why so bitter?" When this happens, I answer with two simple words: "self" and "help."

Granted, my contact with the world of self-help is limited to the purchase of one (1) book. But so traumatic was the effect and so long-lasting the problems it created that I fear my experiences have, like the bound roots of a bonsai tree, permanently warped me in ways I can only begin to imagine.

It was long ago and far away, in those heady, madcap days now known as "the eighties." I was seventeen years old, fresh out of high school but not yet ready for university. I'd secured a rewarding career in the field of minimum wage and had landed a princely (shared) basement apartment, one ripe with the musk of manly aromas. This should have been my "carefree sowing of wild oats" phase, but things weren't going as planned. I had wild oats aplenty, but not many furrows in which to plant them, if you get my drift.

Employing a scientific approach, I sent away for a self-help book entitled *How to Pick Up Girls,* which was advertised in the back of some sort of magazine. *Scientific American,* maybe.

I waited breathlessly for the book to arrive, knowing as I did that it would unlock for me the innermost secrets of the female psyche. In my view, women were a code that needed deciphering, a safe waiting to be cracked. I was sure that all I needed was the right piece of advice, the right sequence of numbers, and the tumblers would fall into place and the doors would swing open.

The faith I put in this mail-order guide was, sadly, a testament to my desperate and dogged belief that the problems I was having vis-à-vis girls were due not to any flaw on my part, but rather to the inscrutable nature of the subject matter.

So. When the book arrived, I barricaded the door and pored over its pages. Almost literally. I was sweating with anticipation at this point.

Well. This book was an eye-opener, let me tell you. It contained a wealth of advice, a plethora of profound insight. Did you know, for example, that women are slaves to subliminal suggestion? It's true. You need only work in a surreptitious allusion to the word "sex" and they'll swoon right into your arms. For example, you don't say "It's nice meeting you." You say, "It'S EXtra nice meeting you." Cunning, eh?

How to Pick Up Girls covered everything you needed to know: body language (hands hooked in your jeans pockets, fingers subtly pointing toward your crotch, sock-stuffing being optional: "If women can use falsies to their advantage, why shouldn't men?" the author asked in fine Socratic style), handy tips (always lick your lips before you approach a woman; women HATE dry lips), recommended venues ("Supermarkets are a great place to meet women. Even the most beautiful woman needs to eat!"), as well as several surefire, guaranteed pick-up lines (something about angels in heaven and rearranging the alphabet to hold it against you). There was even a seven-point program of erogenous zones. You start with the nape of the neck, proceed to the earlobes, and then the elbows, and so on, through a descending checklist of "hot spots," which—and here I quote from memory, double punctuation and all—*"No woman can possibly resist!!"*

Alas, there was a small typo in that last sentence. It should have read "Which every single woman on the face of this planet can resist without even the slightest hesitation."

I failed to pick up anything other than a few strange looks when I went loping through my local supermarket in a predatory manner, lips pre-moistened, fingers pointing (subtly) to my groin, asking every girl I came upon, "Say, can I take you out, maybe buy you an O'Keefe'S EXtra Old Stock?"

Suffice to say, I failed miserably, and without ever getting to the earlobes let alone the elbows of my would-be conquests. So, sharp consumer that I was, I decided to take advantage of the book's *100% Iron-Clad Guarantee!*, mailing it back to the publisher ("Fly By Night Productions out of San Diego," I believe) and requesting a refund. The reply I received—and here I'm paraphrasing for the sake of brevity—was HAHAHAHAHAHA.

Thus ended both my career as a professional ladies' man and my belief in self-help books. Years later, I would get my revenge. My debut novel, *Happiness*^{TM}, was about a self-help book that actually works—and almost destroys the world.

In the meantime, I tried plunging out on my own, unprepared and unadvised, wading into crowded bars where the music was set at floor-throbbing intensity. The conversations inevitably went like this:

"Good crowd tonight."

"WHAT?"

"I said, 'Good crowd tonight.'"

"WHAT?"

"I said—"

"WHAT?"

"I said, 'It'S EXtra hot in here.'"

My roommate, meanwhile, had developed a foolproof technique of his own. He'd amble into the local laundromat and, with a great flourish and in clear sight of the cutest girl there, would prepare to pour Mr. Clean floor wax onto his laundry. The girl would rush over to stop him, he would give her a boyish smile and say, "I thought cleaner was cleaner," and next thing you know, they were in bed together.

It was that last step I found tricky. I had no problem dumping Mr. Clean all over my clothes, and I had no problem looking like a dolt; it was translating this into a night of wild passion that I found difficult.

"Try again," my roommate would urge. "But look more puppy-doggish. Play on their maternal instincts."

Yet when I went tramping back down to the laundromat for a second attempt, the fetching young female at the next washer saw through my ruse immediately. "Is this some lame attempt at meeting girls?" she asked.

"It was my friend's idea," I said. "You're supposed to fall madly in love with me."

And then something remarkable happened. She laughed.

So I kept going. I told her about the book I'd ordered on picking up girls and the advice it had given and the notable lack of success I'd had following said advice. And she kept laughing. She laughed herself all the way out of the laundromat and up to her room, where she invited me in and closed the door, still laughing.

And I thought to myself, *"Someone should write a book about this."*

Me vs. My Wife
(hint: wife wins)

The following is adapted from "Pots and Pans," which I wrote as part of a fundraiser for hospice and related cancer causes. It appeared in *Mixed Messages*, an anthology edited by Paul Knowles with all proceeds going toward research and hospices. Paul didn't want the anthology to be overly grim, so I submitted something on the lighter side. I think this piece actually dovetails nicely with the one that follows it, an "Open Letter to Women" written for *Flare* magazine.

Here's yet another example of the fundamental difference between men and women. I was sprawled out on the couch the other day, eating Pringles straight from the can (I like 'em fresh) and reading an in-flight magazine from trips long past, when I came across the following factoid: "The last $3 bill in Canada, dated 1886 and featuring the portrait of Queen Victoria, was issued by the St. Stephen's Bank of New Brunswick."

Needless to say, I found this absolutely *fascinating*.

"Honey! Listen to this," I called out to my wife as she made supper, mopped the floor, polished the silverware, balanced the chequebook, and changed the oil in the car—all while juggling a pea and a bowling ball.

"Listen to this," I said, a tad more impatiently. "The last $3 bill in Canada was issued in St. Stephen."

"So?" she asked.

So?

We used to live in St. Andrews, New Brunswick. St. Stephen was just up the road. Plus, we're talking about A THREE-DOLLAR BILL. "Don't you find that fascinating?" I asked.

Of course she didn't. But I'll bet if I'd told a guy about this, he would have been agog. And if there was another male anywhere within earshot, he would have leapt into the conversation. "Three-dollar bills? That's a wonderful/great/horrible/terrible idea!" We would've had an intense, heated debate on the matter, could have discussed it for hours and hours, probably over beer. Hopefully over beer.

My wife, meanwhile, wanted to talk about close friends of ours who were apparently going through some tough times. A divorce or something, financial problems maybe, or an illness. I wasn't really paying attention because I was too busy thinking about $3 bills.

Here's another example. My wife and I have this agreement: when one person cooks, the other one washes the dishes. Sounds good, right? Problem is, we take turns, and my wife actually enjoys cooking. Me? Not so much. She'll prepare meals involving at least fourteen separate stages and at least three different sauces. As a result, I end up washing every single pan, plate, pot, and utensil in our house whenever it's her turn to cook. I end up washing dozens of pot lids—more lids than pots. Where's the logic in that? My wife will be rummaging around in our back cupboards, finding pots and pans I didn't even know we had, as though conjuring them into existence just so I'll have to wash them.

We alternate our cooking days as well, which means our menu plan runs something like this:

MONDAY: Spaghetti. TUESDAY: Lemon chicken
with garlic sauce and sautéed mushrooms.
WEDNESDAY: Spaghetti. THURSDAY: Breaded cutlets
with Caesar salad and lightly tossed stir-fried Thai

vegetables. FRIDAY: Spaghetti. SATURDAY: Braised
filet of salmon with hollandaise and a side of yams set on
fire in a dramatic flambé followed by individually peeled
grape tomatoes and glacier-chilled strawberries. SUNDAY:
Spaghetti.

I tell you, if my wife cooks spaghetti one more time …

I'm kidding of course. My wife doesn't make the spaghetti. I do.
My repertoire, as perfected during my days as a single male, includes
Kraft Dinner, Kraft Dinner Supreme (i.e., Kraft Dinner with hot dogs
cut into it), Kraft Dinner with Parmesan Cheese Sprinkled on Top,
Kraft Dinner Deluxe (i.e., Kraft Dinner with really expensive hot dogs
cut into it), and Kraft Dinner Surprise (i.e., Kraft Dinner with Hot
Dogs That Are Way Past the Expiry Date).

Lately, when it's my turn to cook, I've been suggesting that maybe
instead of me making dinner we should go out for—

"Yes!" says my wife, grabbing her jacket. "Let's go!"

At the last restaurant we went to, I ordered the special without
asking what it was. (As a man, I'm trained to make decisions quickly
and without waiting for all pertinent information. It's a gift we have.)

The waiter brought out a plate of spaghetti.

At least I know what to tip in a situation like this: a nice crisp
$3 bill.

An Open Letter to Women (or me vs. my wife, round two)

My friend Kim Izzo, then the features editor at *Flare* magazine, contacted me to ask if I would write an open letter to women on behalf of all men. How could I say no?

Dear Women of the World,

I am writing today on behalf of men everywhere to ask you for a very simple favour: please don't think so much.

I'm not suggesting you should stop thinking *entirely*—I mean, we don't want you to become men or anything—but please, please, please stop reading secret meanings and hidden depths into everything that the men in your life say or do.

Being a woman must be very strange indeed. Sort of like being a spy, I imagine, inhabiting a world of secret code words and allusions, where every gesture, every statement, every look is rife with hidden meaning. A world where "Pick whatever movie you like" really means "I don't care about which movie we watch because I don't feel the same way about our relationship as I used to, which may be because my feelings for you have changed, and even though I still love you, I'm not sure I'm still *in* love with you." That last bit is especially good. I have no doubt that the top semanticists in the world are female.

So please don't think so much. Especially in bed. The bedroom should be a thought-free zone. The passion pit of the boudoir should be exempt from philosophical musings and sex should not involve discussions (or, worse yet, negotiations) of any kind. One should make love like a Zen master: "Do not think. Do."

The problem with thinking, you see, is that it inevitably leads to talking. And talking just leads to more talking. As my sage and wizened older brother once said, "If there's anything I've learned over the years, it's that when a woman says 'We need to talk' it really means 'You have to listen,' and it's not usually to something I want to hear."

Ladies, I plead with you, have your heart-to-hearts with other women, not with men. Men love gossip as much as anyone, true enough, but only if it involves somebody getting naked. (As a whole, men feel that any anecdote can be greatly improved by adding nudity to it at some point.) Rehashing the troubled familial relationships of your Prozac-popping friends isn't gossip, it's third-party therapy and it bores us to tears.

It's not because men are insensitive. It's just that—well, okay, it's because we're insensitive. But we're insensitive for a very good reason. It's bred in the bone, woven into our very DNA: men are problem solvers. We believe in taking action, in striding forth with bold confidence. We believe in coming to immediate and unwavering conclusions. Women, on the other hand, will talk for hours and hours—and days, if need be—without resolving anything. Men want a solution.

As evidence, I submit a word-for-word transcript of a recent conversation I had with a female friend:

"I don't know what it is, Will. I enjoy my job, and yet, I don't feel it's as fulfilling as—"

"Then quit."

"But I enjoy what I do. It's just that—"

"Then don't quit. Are you going to finish those fries?"

Men don't have time for long, meandering discussions about how we feel. Men prefer facts. Forget all that Venus and Mars malarkey, the real difference is this: women are fascinated with minutiae; men are fascinated with trivia. How do you distinguish between the two? Easy. If you could win a bar bet with the information, it's trivia. Everything else is minutiae.

Case in point: on a recent trip to Toronto, I wanted to visit the Hockey Hall of Fame, but my wife wanted us to go shopping. Guess who won?

"But they've got the Stanley Cup," I said. "It's on display. That's like the Holy Grail itself. Did you know that the 1963–64 Toronto Maple Leafs are misspelled on the side of the cup? The engraving reads 'Leaes.' Don't you find that fascinating? Don't you want to see that firsthand?" She did not. She wanted to go traipsing about from shop to shop instead, even though we have perfectly good malls back in Calgary.

"There are stores everywhere," I grumbled. "But there is only one Hockey Hall of Fame."

I don't mind the actual shopping part. It's the endless *thinking* that accompanies it that drives me up the wall. Every single purchase has to be mulled over as though it were a life-and-death decision. (My wife, meanwhile, complains that shopping with me is like going on a bank heist. "C'mon, get the goods and let's go. Let's go, go, *GO!*")

The point being, womenfolk are different from the rest of us. And by "us," I mean "normal people" (i.e., men).

It's the same thing when we go out for dinner. Like many a man, I want only two things from a restaurant: large portions and a waiter that screws up so that I don't have to leave a tip. My wife, on the other hand, wants to mull over her options. She thinks about what she wants to eat. She sits there, in a perfectly good restaurant, and she *thinks*.

Women do this all the time. It's bizarre. They actually read the menu. They study it. They frown at it. They say, "Hmmm." Go into any restaurant in the land and you will see women frowning at menus as their husbands send laser-focused Impatience Rays in their direction.

The waiters don't help. "Would you like more time?" they ask my wife.

"No!" I scream. "We'll order. Don't leave!"

It's no use. Once a waiter vanishes, that's the last you'll see of him till the next geological epoch. My wife, meanwhile, is carefully pondering the pros and cons of raspberry vinaigrette vs. creamed Camembert. The waiter has long since entered the Federal Witness Protection Program and I'm practising my finely honed Impatience Rays when a thought hits me. The Toronto Maple Leafs team name itself is misspelled. It should be "Leaves," right? Not "Leafs." Don't you find that fascinating?

Of course you don't.

A Good Scottish Name

The silence was deafening.

"Patrick? You want to name him *Patrick*?" My father was upset. Very upset.

"Well," I replied, my voice rapidly losing steam. "It was just an idea."

"Patrick," said Fayther, simply and forcefully, "is an *Irish* name."

He made it sound like an affliction. For my father, Scottish Canadian to the core, the very worst thing you could say about someone or something was that they had an "Irish" quality. Fayther—as my sister Gena dubbed him—was a great mountain of a man, with a booming voice and a stare that could melt tar off a roof.

My wife and I were expecting our first child any day, a baby boy, and we still hadn't chosen a name. Terumi is from Japan and we'd already selected our son's Japanese name: "Genki," meaning "lively or full of life." But after that we'd hit an impasse. The list grew more and more fanciful: *Mortimer, Gilgamesh, Hewlett, Packard.* But none of them had the right ring.

We finally settled on Patrick, which is a good strong name, even if it is a wee bit "green."

The way my father reacted, you'd have thought I was trying to name his grandson Paddy O'Leprechaun.

"Give him a proper Scottish name," said Fayther. "Alexander or Duncan or Murdoch. Anything but Patrick."

Names were a sensitive issue around our house. As a teenager, my first big crush was on a girl named Miriam. She was a minister's daughter, which meant I suddenly got *very* interested in the Bible. I began to attend church religiously, in fact. Unfortunately, Miriam's father wasn't a minister of our denomination (i.e., Presbyterian) but rather that of a crazed splinter group of misguided pagans (i.e., Anglican).

When Fayther heard about my shift in allegiance, he wasn't very happy. But when I explained to him over the phone that my interest in Anglicanism was strictly prurient and not in the least bit spiritual, he was proud. It was about a girl, you see.

"Well, then, that's fine. Go to it, son."

Then I made the mistake of letting slip Miriam's last name.

"Campbell?" he sputtered. "You're in love with a Campbell?"

"But—but it's a Scottish name, Dad. I checked."

"Do you know nothing of Scottish history? Do you not remember how the Clan Campbell betrayed the Macdonalds to the English? Do you not remember how the Campbells hunted down women and children and butchered them in the snow? In the cold snow. Do you not remember any of that?"

He made it sound as though it happened just last week. "But Dad," I said, "that was, like, three hundred years ago. I don't think Reverend Campbell was directly involved."

It was no use. Fayther began reciting a litany of lives ruined and friendships betrayed by the Campbells. This went on for weeks and weeks until, in desperation, I tried to bluff my way out of it.

"Dad, guess what? It turns out I was wrong. Her last name isn't Campbell, it's Gamble. As in, Procter-and-."

The funny thing is, Fayther was right. She did betray me, not to the English, but for a boy named Dwayne who had his own car and bigger biceps—what am I saying, bigger. He had biceps. His last name? O'Reilly or O'Toole or some such. Coincidence? I think not.

Here's the odd part. For all his bite and bluster, my father was only *half* Scottish. His mother was from Norway, which makes me a quarter Viking.

It gets even worse. Our dark family secret, the skeleton rattling in the family closet, the worm in the apple, is this: I'm Irish. And so are all my siblings.

My mom's family was from Belfast, which means I have exactly as much Irish in me as I do Scottish. But Fayther refused to accept this. He had four sons and he tried to name each one of them Angus. My mother, calm and cool, would counter with, "Fine, we'll name the boy Angus. Angus Paul." This caused my dad to gnash his teeth and mutter darkly. Fayther hated the name Paul. "It's a feminine name. Effete. Weak. It's ..." and here he paused for full dramatic effect, "... *English.*"

And so, all four of the boys were spared the name Angus.

Fayther had toyed with the idea of converting our surname back to its Gaelic roots: MacFergus. Which is to say, I came within a hair's breadth of being named Angus MacFergus. With a name like that, you can forget about getting a date on a Saturday night. With a name like that you pretty much have to grow a red beard and sit in a bog eating haggis and looking miserable.

"Angus MacFergus," I said. "It sounds like a bull with a bagpipe."

"It's a fine name," said Fayther. "It has the scent of the Highlands about it." (Years later, I would go camping in the Scottish Highlands. I remember the smell. I don't think this was quite the compliment Dad had in mind.)

Mom, meanwhile, was whispering encouragements in my ear. "Name your baby Patrick," she'd say, her voice as smooth as honey. "Or maybe Paul."

Later that evening, exhausted and head still spinning, I turned to my wife and said, "What do you think about Angus? You know, for the baby."

She frowned. "Angus?" she said. "It sounds like a cow."

As noted, my wife is from Japan. There are no hyphens in her identity. She is Japanese, plain and simple. Her parents were Japanese. Her grandparents were Japanese. Her great-grandparents, her great-great-grandparents, and so on, all the way back into the mists of time—and up to heaven if you believe the Shinto imperial myths. For my wife, Canada's mongrel mélange of cultures is endlessly fascinating.

At one point, she sat down with a calculator and figured out the exact percentages. "Our son will be 50% Japanese, 12.5% Scottish, 12.5% Irish, 12.5% Norwegian, 6.25% Czech, and 6.25% miscellaneous."

We looked at each other. "A mix like that," I said. "You realize what this means?"

She nodded.

"He'll be 100% Canadian."

Our son was born a few weeks later. We named him Alexander.

A Small but Powerful Mastermind

I've become really interested in poop lately. Texture, frequency, aroma. This may be the fatigue talking, though. I'm a new father—which is to say, I'm taking part in a sleep-deprivation experiment conducted by a small but powerful mastermind named Alex.

Alexander is only a few months old, and already he rules most of the known world, as befits his namesake. A good kid. Not much of a conversationalist, true, but he doesn't ask for much in return, just our constant attention twenty-four hours a day. Every night he has to be fed and changed, and then immediately changed again (there's something about a fresh diaper that inspires him), and then burped and fed—or is that fed, then burped, I can never remember—before being rocked gently back to sleep.

It's a tiring schedule. I don't technically do any of this; my wife takes care of most of it, but still. I have to hear about it. It's tough being a father.

Now, before you start sending angry letters denouncing me as an insensitive, lazy, good-for-nothing rag of a husband, let me assure you that I am in fact a modern, post-feminist, insensitive, lazy, good-for-nothing rag of a husband. Which is to say, I won't change a diaper unless under direct orders, and even then I expect to be heralded with praise afterwards. (*See:* mopping of floors, ditto.)

Luckily, my wife is from Japan, so her only standard of comparison is Japanese males. Next to them I seem almost saintlike in my devotion. Japanese men, for one, never go into the delivery room; they stay outside in the waiting room smoking cigarettes, as God intended.

In fact, Japanese husbands are barely present at all for the last month of pregnancy. Most Japanese women go back to their family home for the final stretch, leaving their husbands alone to—this is shocking, I know—do their own laundry and feed their own selves. Sales of instant Cup Noodle Ramen spike with every pregnancy.

Unfortunately, I am not a Japanese male. I was expected to go right into the delivery room with Terumi, and I did. Not that I was a mere spectator. I was the designated "coach." It's a trick, aimed at luring men into what is a very messy undertaking. Not "partner," not "helper," not "emotional support caregiver," but *coach*. I bought a whistle and a clipboard and everything.

During labour, my wife and I divided the duties equally. Her job was to push and strain and moan and sweat and cry and glare. My job was to remind her to breathe. "Don't forget to breathe," I'd say helpfully, at which point her eyes would roll back in her head, flames would shoot from her nostrils, and she'd say, in a voice that made the Exorcist sound like Mary Poppins, "I AM BREATHING!! STOP TALKING!" Women can be so touchy.

Making babies is easy, it's the part that comes afterwards that's difficult. And raising a cross-cultural child is even more of a challenge. So, whenever Terumi and I have a disagreement about how we should raise our children, we sit down and discuss the matter in a calm, mature fashion until it is decided that I am wrong and she is right.

Simply put, we're raising our baby Japanese style. No crib, no baby monitor. Alex sleeps next to Terumi, and if he even so much as hints that he's about to cry she sweeps him up in her arms and comforts him. The idea of leaving a baby alone in a room to "cry it out" is something that horrifies the Japanese, who look upon it as something akin to emotional abuse. "The lesson when they are little should be that they are safe, that someone is always there for them, will always protect them." That's the role of parents in Japan during those first formative years. Discipline is added later, mainly by teachers under a school system that—while not the draconian caricature we have of it in the West—is still very much about instilling proper community spirit and a foundational sense of citizenship. I taught English in Japanese high schools and was amazed at how involved the teachers were in their students' lives. When a student got caught speeding on her scooter, the police would call her homeroom teacher first, then her parents.

This works well in Japan, but Alex isn't going to be growing up in Japan. He'll be growing up in Canada, where peer groups rule and schoolteachers don't have the same central role in how children are raised. But try explaining that to my wife. Please.

In the meantime, the sleep-deprivation experiment continues. Even worse, my wife is now expecting ME to get up in the middle of the night to change diapers and report back.

What did I ever do to deserve that?

Father's Day and
the Brothers Hardy

I've been reading the Hardy Boys books to my son Alex. He was eight when we started, he's ten now, and there are approximately 98,000 books in the series, so by the time we finish, I figure he'll be reading them to me.

Aside from their classic literary stylings—"I'm awfully sorry," Chet said apologetically (actual quote that, from Volume #10, *What Happened at Midnight*)—the Hardy Boys books, like all great literature, raise more questions than they answer. Questions such as, What is it about the town of Bayport that attracts smugglers so?

It's often commented upon that in the world of the Hardy Boys the worst one has to face is illegal importers lurking in the shadows ready to evade regulatory government tariffs at a moment's notice, usually with a hearty laugh, head tossed back, fists on hips. There are no financial meltdowns, no random terrorist attacks, no West Nile mosquitoes, no home invasions, no environmental carcinogens, no gang swarmings. Just smugglers.

Less commented upon is the intelligence of said smugglers, especially as they ALWAYS GET CAUGHT. You'd think word would have gotten out by now. Surely there must be some sort of smugglers' grapevine. *"Psst. Whatever you do, avoid Bayport. Pass it on."*

Equally odd is how Frank and Joe Hardy are always rubbing their jaws and trying to figure out what's going on this time around. "All these mysterious comings and goings, what could it possibly mean?"

You'd think that by now every time a scowling man in an overcoat shouldered past them on the street, Frank and Joe would look at each other and immediately say, "Smuggler. Better nab him now."

Alex had this figured out by the third book. "I bet it's the stranger who pushed past them on the street!" he'd say—breathlessly at first, then with less vim on each passing tale.

Reading the Hardy Boys as an adult is very different from reading them when you're ten. As a ten-year-old you say, "Hooray! Mr. Hardy is away again. Frank and Joe will have to solve the case on their own! Again!" Whereas, as an adult, you find yourself wondering about Mr. and Mrs. Hardy's marriage. You start to think maybe there's a reason Detective Hardy is always out of town on business.

For Alex, that doesn't matter. For Alex, the Hardy Boys are all about possibility. The possibility of adventure hidden in the day-to-day details of life. When you're ten, life is an open promise; it's an age when astronaut-archaeologist-cartoonist is still a viable career path. The past is so small, the future so overwhelmingly large.

I remember Alex at age four, rummaging through leaves, searching for lost treasure. These would be leaves I had just raked. Ten minutes before. And there's me, in spite of myself, hoping maybe he'd find some.

Or Alex at age three, sitting on my lap as I read him a story about a little boy who makes friends with a duck and how the little boy visits the duck every morning at the pond and how one day the little boy gets sick and doesn't show up, so the duck leaves the pond and comes to the boy's house and goes up the stairs to the boy's room to cheer him up.

Alex became very quiet, and when I asked him what was wrong he said, "How come, in storybooks, ducks and little boys are friends but whenever we go to the park and I try to say hi to the ducks, they just run away?"

Why?

Because life doesn't work that way. Because there are no friendly little ducks who come to visit you when you're sick and there are no smugglers lurking in coves for plucky youngsters to thwart and there is no treasure hidden in the leaf pile, except maybe what the neighbour's cat has left.

That's not what I told him, though. What I said was, "Well, I think the ducks in the park are a little shy is all. How about some ice cream?"

As a father, one of the hardest burdens you have to bear is the wonderfully heartfelt and wholly unjustified faith your children invest in you. The teenage years are coming, sure enough, and with them the inevitable discovery that far from being a paragon of manly perfection I am in fact little more than a walking compilation of flaws and foibles. But not now. Not yet.

When I took Alex to the Calgary Stampede he was five years old and wearing a hat with a plastic whistle. I wanted my son to see the bull riders and chuckwagon races; I hadn't thought about the calf-roping. By the time the second calf had been yanked off its feet and tied down Alex was in tears. "Make them stop," he said. "Make them stop."

It's a burden and a glory, being a dad. It's the one time in your life when someone really believes in you, really believes that you can stand up in the middle of a grandstand filled with twenty thousand people and say loudly, firmly, in much the same manner as you'd announce it's time for bed and no more dilly-dallying, "This has to stop. Right now! I'm sorry, but I'm the Dad and you have to stop hurting those little cows."

But I can't. I can't stop it any more than I can stop the pain from coming, or the heartaches, or the darkness from falling or the sadder truths from dawning. All I can do, I suppose, is make the landing a little softer.

Canadian Lives

A popular historian. A humorist. A newspaperman with a strong satirical streak. Canada's first female MP. A Department of Indian Affairs
poet. And a mad trapper on the Rat River. Very different lives, yet all
of them Canadian and all of them, in their way, iconic.

We begin with Pierre Berton. I first met Pierre through his nephew,
Berton Woodward, who was my editor at *Maclean's* magazine at the
time. When Pierre died, *Maclean's* asked me to write a tribute.

Pierre Berton:
Shit Disturber

It was one of those summer evenings when the darkness sneaks up on you. The kind of evening when the details dissolve almost imperceptibly until you find yourself reduced to silhouettes and disembodied voices, to spectral stories.

"You see those trees?" he said, referring to the sweep of forest outlined now against the sky. "I planted every one of them. This was just an open field when I started."

I'd been invited to the home of Pierre and Janet Berton in Kleinburg, Ontario, for a night of steak and sushi. Thick slabs of sirloin were thrown onto the barbecue as Pierre poured me a slosh of hooch (to use the proper Bertonian turn of phrase). The sushi, in turn, was wrapped in a light seaweed and steeped in sweet vinegar. It was an odd, yet oddly satisfying, combination.

Pierre was eighty-three at the time, and still on his feet. Tall, indomitable. Janet, in turn, was a wonderfully gracious host: warm, wry, very funny. She had raised eight children while her husband was stabbing away at his typewriter with two fingers. When I asked her what it was like watching those trees grow from a field, she laughed and said, "I didn't have time to notice. I was pregnant the whole time."

Being asked to write a tribute to Pierre Berton is like being asked to explain the Rockies. Where to start? Fifty books. Millions sold. The Order of Canada. The Leacock Medal for Humour. A history award named in his honour. Three Governor General's Awards. I could hardly add to his stature. What I can do, though, is express my gratitude to him. As a writer, as a Canadian, I owe him an immense and abiding debt.

Pierre Berton showed me a Canada that was worthy of passion. Even when I disagreed with his conclusions, I never doubted the strength of his commitment, especially to what should have been a lost cause: Canadian history.

Pierre Berton rescued Canadian history from Canadian historians. Or rather, he rescued it from a certain narrow, academic view of what history should be. He understood that history is a literary form, not a social science. It was not enough to *explain* the past, one had to evoke it. The Klondike. The War of 1812. The search for the "Arctic grail." The self-fulfilling myth of a National Dream. Pierre's writing was grounded in solid research and primary sources, but without ever becoming bogged down. He was many things, but he was never boring.

When I try to read academic books about the Great Depression my eyes glaze over and my head begins to bob toward my chest. But when Pierre Berton writes about the Depression, I can *see* the dust storms rolling in, can taste the wind and raw desperation, can feel the anger, the mounting despair.

Pierre Berton came from a journalistic background, and his early books—*The Comfortable Pew*, *The Smug Minority*—were rousing polemics. He was never a defender of the status quo, and when I mentioned to him that according to the *Canadian Oxford Dictionary* the term "shit disturber" is a Canadianism, he seemed inordinately pleased by this. It was a label he himself wore proudly and one which, I'm sure, he would have preferred to "national icon."

As we sat outside that evening, sawing away at our steaks, I asked him if he believed in ghosts. He thought about this, and said, "No ... but I believe in ghost *stories*." He also shared a piece of advice he often gave to anyone thinking of becoming a writer: "Try to be born in an interesting place." In Pierre's case, it was the Yukon and the faded glories of a gold rush.

He asked me about my own northern hometown, the wide arc of the Peace River, the curtains of auroras that moved on solar winds.

He said, "You never really leave the North, do you?"

One of my all-time favourite books as a child, and one I was even then reading to our youngest boy, Alister, was *The Secret World of Og*. It was probably Pierre's best-loved work, and when I mentioned it to him he said, in the breeziest, most offhanded way you can imagine, "Would you like to see the playhouse?" I almost fell over. This was like being asked if I wanted to see the wardrobe from Narnia or the looking glass from Alice. Suddenly I was six years old again, and giddy. "Really? The playhouse? From Og?"

"Sure," he said. "It's just down the hill."

The story of *The Secret World of Og* begins in a children's playhouse, when a handsaw cuts a trapdoor in the floor and a baby is whisked away into an elaborate underground world of green creatures whose entire language consists of one word: "Og."

Sure enough, nestled near a stand of trees was the very playhouse I'd read about as a child, still standing. "Can't go in," he said. "It's not safe." So I peered in through the window instead, looking for that secret doorway to Og. "There's no trapdoor," I said.

Pierre looked at me. "You do know that it was just a story, right?"

I've decided, in lieu of any evidence to the contrary, that my family and I occupy the same house Pierre Berton used to live in, back when he was in the army. This isn't as far-fetched as it sounds. Our neighbourhood was once part of Calgary's Currie Barracks, and our house was once a military residence. They've added a veranda and tarted it up a bit, but the original frames and floor plan—sturdy, no-nonsense— are still very much in evidence.

"The old Currie Base?" Pierre said. "Hell, that's where I was stationed. It was out at the edge of town, and if we missed the last streetcar, we had to hike up that damn hill."

He shook his head in amazement when I told him that his old army base (a) has been gentrified and (b) is now considered a "central neighbourhood." He described the lanes and the building where he'd once bunked, and it sounded uncannily like our street, our house. So what the heck, as far as I'm concerned, the matter is settled: it's Pierre's house; I just live in it.

The last time I saw Pierre Berton was in Toronto in 2004, when he was being honoured for the publication of his fiftieth book, *Prisoners of the North*. We were supposed to have a drink afterwards— a symbolic drink, as it were, since Pierre was no longer allowed to imbibe. "Doctor's orders," he growled.

Unfortunately, Pierre's health took a turn for the worse and he wasn't able to go anywhere after the event ended. He was in a wheelchair at that point, on his way back to Kleinburg and Janet.

"We'll get together again next time," he said. But there never will be a next time.

I want to carve an epitaph on the mountains, I want to write it on the last light of day: *Pierre Berton lived here. Husband. Father. Storyteller. Shit disturber. Prisoner of the North.*

Dead Politicians:
The Life and Raucous Times
of Eye Opener Bob

When Brindle & Glass publishers released a new edition of *Eye Opener Bob*, Grant MacEwan's classic biography of Bob Edwards, they asked if I would write an introduction. I was happy to. This is an expanded version of what appeared.

Bob Edwards was a genius. There. That's all you really need to know, but that would make for a rather short introduction, so let me also say this: he was a failed genius. Or rather, an *unfulfilled* genius.

Edwards arrived in the Canadian West in the 1890s and set up shop as a one-man newspaper operation, launching *The Eye Opener* a few years later in High River. He was soft-spoken with a slight lisp and a distinct Scottish lilt, not the sort of person you would peg as a hellraiser or firebrand, but brand fire and raise hell he did.

> An editor who started about twenty years ago with only
> 55 cents is now worth $100,000. His accumulation of
> wealth is owing to his frugality, good habits, strict attention
> to business and the fact that an uncle died and left him the
> sum of $99,999.
>
> —*Bob Edwards*

Edwards was a wandering soul, and *The Eye Opener* moved six times between five different towns in its first ten years of operation. Despite this, the paper was a raging, albeit unlikely, success. Circulation soared from 250 to 35,000, though as historian Hugh Dempsey points out, "*The Eye Opener* was not a newspaper, but Bob Edwards' personal platform for social comment and humour."

Edwards fought for minimum wage legislation, old age pensions, provincial rights, increased Canadian curriculum in schools, agricultural co-ops, prison reform, and a system of public hospitalization that would give equal access to all. Health care, he argued, was a basic human right. He opposed the racial restrictions placed on Chinese immigrants and warned Canadians about "the prospect of becoming hewers of pulpwood and drawers of waterpower for the Americans."

He even led a campaign to abolish the Senate, or at the very least reform it, labelling Canada's Upper House an "impotent relic," "a refuge for fallen political prune-eaters," "a haven for the discredited," "a home for pensioners who don't need the money," and "an exhibition of ill-visaged wax-works."

Which is to say, not much has changed over the years. Senate reform, medicare, American ownership: it's all eerily familiar, a hundred years later.

He was also a great admirer of that other prairie hellraiser, Nellie McClung.

> About the slowest way to settle an argument is to get two
> women interested in it.
>
> *—Bob Edwards*

In *The Eye Opener,* Edwards mocked women as mercilessly and with the same unbridled gusto as he did men, but he was also a staunch supporter of women's rights, urging more women to run for political office. "It is our firm conviction," he wrote, "that the blending of women's ideas with those of reasonably thoughtful men will some day bring about an era of common sense." And that, in its essence, was what Edwards believed in, dreamed of, fought for. An era of common sense.

The Canadian West, especially in its formative years, was very much a self-selecting venue. It attracted misfits and outcasts, dreamers and schemers, oddball eccentrics and would-be tycoons. The restless. The lonely. The thirsty—thirsty for something more, something better. Thirsty for life. Thirsty, in Edwards' case, for rotgut whisky and that elusive "era of common sense." The young city of Calgary, where Edwards eventually settled, was a boomtown rife with robust individualism and larger-than-life characters: the undisputed cattle king Pat Burns, the rascally Irish lawyer Paddy Nolan, the thundering, hard-drinking fire chief Cappie Smart—and right in the thick of things, Bob Edwards, social crusader.

> The most distinctive attribute of a large, bustling city are streetcars, crooked gamblers, confidence men, and a 'complacent' police force. Hurry up with those streetcars, will you?
>
> *—Edwards' assessment of Calgary*
> *in its early years*

Bob Edwards wielded truth like a weapon. He abhorred pretension and was more than capable of blowing his opponents out of the water with a barrage of verbal brickbats. When a Presbyterian minister in High River began harassing a local hotel-keeper, Edwards let loose a blast of calumny that is breathtaking even now; he described the minister as one of those "tactless, offensive, conceited, self-sufficient, arrogant young parsons with no experience of men and things, uncultured by travel or reading, with absolutely no knowledge of the world, possessing a highly developed faculty for making themselves ridiculous and obnoxious, troubling the waters of a peaceful village, and sowing discord, having no rational argument in favour of their own existence."

Whew!

You wouldn't want to get on the bad side of Bob Edwards. More often than not, though, he preferred to employ a devastating sense of mockery when taking down the high and mighty:

> We understand—ha ha!—that—haw haw!—R.J. Stuart—
> ah-yaw-haw—ha ha ha!—is going to run oh oh ha ha—for
> alderman—ha ha ha ha ha ha!—Ha ha ha ha ha ha!—ha ha
> ha ha ha ha ha ha ha ha!

How do you recover from something like that?

He even took on the Almighty CPR, a law unto itself in those days. The railway had been treating public safety with a disdain that bordered on contempt, and in response Edwards launched a campaign of "ridicule and awkward truth." Awkward truth, indeed. Edwards' forte, that. *The Eye Opener* began running grisly details of accidents and, when threatened with legal action, responded by reporting on when accidents *didn't* happen, under banner headlines reading NO DEATHS CAUSED BY THE CPR THIS WEEK! and NOT A SINGLE LIFE WAS LOST AT THE CPR CROSSING ON FIRST STREET WEST! Chastened, the CPR began introducing safety measures and controlled crossings.

Throughout his years as a windmill-tilting, dragon-engaging, underdog-defending knight errant, Bob Edwards was only ever successfully sued for libel once, and that was over an obvious spoof. He published an apology and continued on, undaunted.

When cautioned to use the word "alleged" more often, Edwards replied with a news article that ran:

> J.W. Pringar of Cayley, with his alleged daughter, paid High
> River a visit last week. After putting his alleged horse in the
> barn, Mr. Pringar filled up on some alleged whisky which
> seemed to affect his alleged brain.

(The humour here is incredibly deft; note how each "alleged" Edwards employs carries with it a slightly different nuance and a slightly different meaning, suggesting, in turn, infidelity, a stolen horse, cheap moonshine, and a lack of intelligence.)

The Eye Opener offered its readers a wealth of advice—almost all of it bogus, whether it be health tips or points of etiquette and fine dining. A typical recipe, for rabbit stew, begins: "Take a good fat cat and give it a bat over the head in the cellar."

And in keeping with other newspapers, *The Eye Opener*'s "Answers to Inquiries" purported to take questions on a wide range of topics, both gastronomical and scientific:

How do you make a lemon tart?—*Angelina*
They are already tart, Angelina. Ask us something difficult.

Don't you think 'absolutely' a much overworked word?
—*Reader*
Absolutely.

What was the date of the landing of Caracticus on the shore of Britain?—*Anxious Inquirer*
Damned if we know.

What is the best way to straighten out bowed legs in a child?—*Mother*
Can't say, I'm sure.

What is the exact age of Nellie McClung?—*J. T.P. Le Due*
Don't know.

What is the population of Peking?—*Student*
Haven't the slightest idea.

Edwards also published equally bogus, and wildly popular, "Society Notes," which perfectly lampooned the pretensions of Calgary's social-climbing set. The comings and goings—and drunken excesses—of such upstanding citizens as Annabel McSwattie, Mrs. Bucklewhackster, Lottie McGlory, Peter O'Snuffigan, and Mrs. T. Tinglebuster were duly reported in deadpan style, leaving readers guessing as to which events being alluded to were true and which were not.

Some of Edwards' "Society Notes" were at the level of schoolboy humour: "The Okotoks Methodist Ladies' Aid will give a bean supper from 6 to 8 p.m. to be followed by a musical program." Others were not-so-subtle digs at the presumed respectability of the middle class: "Peter F. Ayer, who has been absent from the city for over a year, returned home last week to find himself the proud father of a bouncing boy just a few weeks old." My personal favourite? One from 1922: "Mrs. J.B. Scluff, of Fourteenth Ave W., entertained some of her neighbours informally last Monday afternoon. That is to say, she and her cook had a quarrel on the front porch."

And, in one of the most cutting examples of political satire penned in Canada, Edwards once ran a "transcript" of a debate in the House of Commons, in which the Members of the Opposition raise the matter of a high-ranking inspector in the Liberal government, a man who, it's been proven beyond a shadow of a doubt, has killed his mother-in-law, chopped her into pieces, laced her remains with strychnine, and fed them to the wolves. He then sold the pelts back to the government for a profit.

The Liberals brush aside the Opposition's questions as irrelevant. "The honourable member is surely aware that the department lays down no hard and fast rules as to what kind of bait shall be used in the case of wild animals on whose pelts a bounty is paid by the government … It seems a pity that the honourable members do not obtain more exact information on which to base their charges against the government."

"But the minister killed his mother-in-law and fed her to the wolves!" the Opposition shouts. "Surely such a monstrous piece of business should be looked into. Will the government take steps to remove the inspector from his position?"

The government refuses, stating that the inspector's work within the department has been exemplary and that any pelts he sold were done so in perfectly good faith. The prime minister himself eventually rises to scold the Opposition for besmirching the inspector's good name and to protest against the House's time "being frittered away in this manner." It's as laugh-out-loud funny today as it was when Edwards wrote it in 1907, and sadly, just as true.

Beyond the razor slice of his political satire, Edwards was also capable of being remarkably playful and light-handed at times. He even penned a verse or two:

She frowned on him and called him Mr.
   Because in fun he went and Kr.
So out of spite the next good night
   The naughty Mr. Kr. Sr.

After sitting through an especially effusive funeral eulogy, one that managed to elevate a recently deceased alderman from the realm of mere politician to that of statesman, Edwards mused: "Now I know what a statesman is; he's a dead politician. We need more statesmen." It was probably his best-known quip.

The aphorisms of Bob Edwards are on par with those of Ambrose Bierce, and indeed, one could easily recast many of Edwards' sayings as definitions, akin to those in Bierce's *Devil's Dictionary*. I've done so with just a few of Edwards' observations, as an example:

Illusions: the grand ideas we have about ourselves.

Delusions: the silly ideas other people have about us.

Lawyer: someone who gets two men to strip for a fight and then runs off with their clothes.

Marriage: two people promising at the altar with perfectly straight faces to feel, think, and believe for the rest of their lives exactly as they do at that minute.

Highbrow: a person whose education is generally beyond his intelligence.

Cynicism: the art of seeing things as they are, instead of as they ought to be.

The philosopher Santayana may have warned that "those who cannot remember the past are condemned to repeat it," but it took Bob Edwards to enter a plea on behalf of the common man. "If it's all the same to history," he wrote in the aftermath of the First World War, "it need not repeat itself anymore."

Over time, Edwards' prairie fame spread across North America and as far away as Great Britain. A New York literary journal hailed the "clear judgment and common sense" of his writing and held up a theatre review he'd written as a "specimen of dramatic criticism that might well serve as a model for some of our more pretentious critics in the New York press." In the British papers, Calgary was referred to, by way of explanation, as "the place where *The Eye Opener* comes from."

Applause has made a fool of more men than criticism.
                                                              —*Bob Edwards*

The tragedy of Bob Edwards was that he failed to live up to his larger literary talents. In the pages of *The Eye Opener* he penned brilliantly comedic tales about such characters as Peter J. McGonigle, an irascible but oddly charming horse thief and boozehound who was the fictional editor of the equally fictitious Midnapore *Gazette* and who was constantly being thrown in and out of jail, and Albert Buzzard-Cholomondeley of Skookingham, England, a wonderfully inventive British remittance man whose letters home, trying to inveigle further funds from his gullible parents, stand with the best of Stephen Leacock. But Edwards was also an alcoholic and a binge drinker who would go on week-long benders that ended with him in Calgary's Holy Cross Hospital being treated for delirium tremens. It was his battle with the bottle that ultimately undermined him.

> One of the worst stings of defeat is the sympathy that goes with it.
>
> *—Bob Edwards*

In his final few years, Edwards tried his best to stay sober. He married the aptly named Kate Penman, settled down, and even ran for the provincial legislature—as an independent, natch. By then his health was already failing. He attended only one session of government and made just a single speech in the legislature.

Robert Edwards died on November 14, 1922, and was buried in Calgary's Union Cemetery at the alleged age of fifty-eight. (Alleged because there's a discrepancy between the date of birth Edwards had given and the dates inscribed at his grave.) His widow tucked a flask of whisky and a couple of copies of her late husband's newspapers into the coffin. And thus, Bob Edwards was laid to rest alongside his greatest strength and his greatest weakness.

> Meanwhile, the meek are a long time inheriting the earth.
>
> *—Bob Edwards*

Mind the Gap!
Stephen Leacock and the
Invention of Canadian Humour

The following is adapted from an introduction I wrote for the Penguin Black Classics edition of Stephen Leacock's *Sunshine Sketches of a Little Town*.

Analyzing humour, it's been said, is a lot like dissecting a frog. You may learn something about anatomy in the process, but the frog itself usually dies.

Stephen Leacock, the funniest writer Canada has ever produced, managed to do the near impossible: he defined the very essence of humour—and did so without killing a single frog. The root of all comedy, he wrote, "lies in the deeper contrasts offered by life itself; the strange incongruity between our aspirations and our achievements."

Imagine a town where the leading citizen is a 280-pound illiterate saloon keeper. A town where the elections are rigged and the leaders are blowhards. A town where a dumb-luck barber stumbles into money—and is immediately heralded as a financial wizard. A town where a community fundraiser is considered a success because it lost only twenty dollars. A town where the local Tory candidate urges his supporters to "vote and keep on voting till they make you quit." A town that burns down its church for the insurance money.

Now.

Imagine that this same town has come to represent everything that is gentle and idyllic in the Canadian soul, and you'll appreciate just what Stephen Leacock has accomplished with *Sunshine Sketches of a Little Town.* The fictional Mariposa, for all its shortcomings, all its flaws, truly is idyllic. There is an innocence that permeates Mariposa, a lack of cynicism that is absolutely disarming. It's a town inhabited almost entirely by eccentrics, where something as innocuous as a government census is cause for grandstanding civic pride and finger-wagging huffery. A town of false fronts, in every sense. A town where boats sent to rescue passengers from a sinking steamer have to be rescued themselves—by the very vessel they were trying to save. A town where the heroic cry of "Women and children first!" is put forward mainly as a way of testing the lifeboats. (As Leacock's narrator explains, "What was the sense, if it should turn out that the boat wouldn't even hold women and children, of trying to jam a lot of heavy men into it?") Nowhere is this "strange incongruity," this wellspring of humour, more deftly—more lovingly—depicted than in the little town of Mariposa.

Leacock's own life embraced incongruity, and he often embodied the very contradictions he wrote about. Raised in the "genteel poverty" that comes from being the offspring of a remittance man (those disgraced misfits and second sons, sent off to the colonies and supported by funds from Olde England), Leacock was a backwoods would-be aristocrat. His father was a morose English exile, ill-suited to being a farmer, who abandoned his wife and children when Leacock was in his teens. But Leacock attended some of North America's finest schools, earning a Ph.D. in economics and political science from the University of Chicago before joining the faculty at McGill University in Montreal. Robertson Davies suspected that it was the deep running tension between Leacock's background (upper crust, elitist) and his reality (colonial, hardworking), between head and heart essentially, that defined Leacock and made him a humorist. Tension, after all, needs to find a release somewhere.

Leacock's first book, and single biggest money-maker, was not a work of humour. It was a textbook entitled *Elements of Political Science,* which was translated into eighteen languages and became required reading in more than thirty American universities. At the age of thirty-seven, Stephen Leacock toured the British Empire as a Rhodes Scholar, giving rousing speeches in support of the imperial status quo. By the age of thirty-eight he was the head of political science and economics at McGill.

This early success allowed him to buy a rustic slice of heaven in Orillia, not far from where he had grown up: thirty-three acres on Lake Couchiching in a secluded inlet he'd discovered while sailing years before. Ruins of a brewery were hidden among the maple trees, and a grassy shore sloped down to waters teeming with fish. Leacock dubbed it the Old Brewery Bay, "a name that could rouse a thirst as far away as Nevada," and with his brother Charlie he built a temporary shelter, not much more than a lean-to shack, down near the water's edge.

It was at Lake Couchiching that Leacock relaxed, gardening and fishing in his wrinkled jacket and equally wrinkled tie, a crumpled gentleman in rumpled clothes. When he sailed into town, docked his vessel, and walked through Orillia in bare feet, he was occasionally mistaken for a tramp.

He might well have grown old as an academic, marinating in a world of tenure and tweed, summering in Orillia and teaching in Montreal, but in his fortieth year Leacock's career took an unexpected turn. He'd been publishing short comedic pieces in various magazines, more or less as a hobby, when—ever the economist—he thought, Why not increase the return on labour expended? Why not gather these pieces up and submit them to a publisher, maybe earn a bit of extra cash? With a certain naïveté, he sent his collection of humorous sketches to the same company that had published his textbook. Surely if they were interested in economic theories of capital, they'd also be interested in publishing his little spoofs. Nope. Feeling a bit miffed, Leacock decided to publish the book himself, and so it was that a cheaply printed chapbook entitled *Literary Lapses* appeared in 1910. The same year that Mark Twain died.

Stephen Leacock had dropped a small acorn into a very large lake—and harvested a tidal wave. A distinguished British editor who happened to be visiting Montreal picked up a copy of Leacock's chapbook for the voyage home. As soon as he arrived in England, he wired Leacock an offer.

The success was immediate. A second collection appeared the following year, and Leacock the humorist quickly surpassed Leacock the academic. American reviewers loved his light, literary style, which they considered very British. The British, meanwhile, hailed him as an important new "American" voice. He was neither. He was both. He was, in a word, Canadian.

With his literary income now tripling that of his university salary, Leacock faced a hard choice. One of his fellow professors at McGill had warned him against publishing humorous stories, fearing it would damage Leacock's reputation. Forced to decide between one career path and the other—between economics and humour, between the hallowed irrelevance of academia and the crass joys of commercial literature—Leacock chose ... both. In much the same way that he divided his time between Montreal and Orillia, he would divide his life between the classroom and the popular press, between the university and Old Brewery Bay, between the ivy-clad and the sun-dappled, so to speak.

If there was any doubt where Leacock's allegiance ultimately lay, though, he made it clear. "Personally, I would sooner have written *Alice in Wonderland* than the whole *Encyclopedia Britannica.*"

Leacock would become the most celebrated and successful author Canada has ever produced, and he loved the attention. A natural-born ham, his classes were popular as much for his theatrical presence and rambling humour as for his ability to distill complicated ideas into easily grasped summaries. When he swept into a classroom and took command of the podium, his students said it was as though "a gust of wind" had entered.

He once almost killed a man with laughter. It was during a public lecture; a fellow in the audience started laughing so hard he passed out and had to be rushed away. The man survived, though, much to Leacock's regret. "My fortune would have been made," he said wistfully. "Think of the headline: MAN DIES LAUGHING AT LEACOCK!" Damn rude of him to have lived.

Stephen Leacock was a grab-bag of contradictions: an academic who held academics in disdain, a defender of social justice who was also a staunch imperialist. He admired Jefferson, yet exalted the British monarchy. He loved money, but couldn't stand wealth. He was scathing in his assessment of the capitalist class, but was just as caustic about the muddle-headed left. ("Socialism," he noted, "would work only in Heaven, where they don't need it, or in Hell, where they already have it.") Leacock described himself as "a liberal Conservative, or, if you will, a conservative Liberal with a strong dash of sympathy for the Socialist idea, a friend of Labour, and a believer in Progressive Radicalism." It was enough to make your head spin.

He penned—quite literally; working with ink and nib—more than sixty books over the course of his remarkable career, including works of literary biography, Canadian history, and social commentary. Prolific to the point of promiscuity, he once had three different books appear in the span of seven months. When asked the secret of being a successful author, Leacock famously replied, "You just jot down ideas as they occur to you. The jotting is simplicity itself—it is the occurring which is difficult."

Over the years, Leacock's ramshackle shanty on Lake Couchiching grew, piecemeal and pell-mell, with rooms and whole wings added every which way. Chicken coops and greenhouses, woodsheds and other additions, would appear one year only to be torn down or refitted the next.

Leacock tried to turn his property into a profitable hobby farm, but failed to grasp the economic principle that the cost of transporting one's produce to market should not exceed the amount *received* for said produce. As a farmer, Leacock was an excellent professor.

"Expectation greater than realization." He jotted this down in his notebook in reference to one of his failed fresh-vegetable schemes—unwittingly paraphrasing his own definition of humour. (What is life itself but a note in the ledgers that reads "Expectations greater than realization"?)

Mariposa has been presented as an idealized version of Canada, but there are other ways to connect the dots, and hidden in the constellation of Mariposa is another portrait, that of the author himself. Stephen Leacock was very much a Leacockian character. And Mariposa, with its eccentric tics and blithely unresolved contradictions, has a personality oddly reminiscent of its creator.

In his bulky racoon coat and tattered academic robes, with his ill-fitted watch chain and permanently loosened tie, Leacock generally looked as though he'd gotten dressed by crawling through a clothes hamper. Even the nickname his students gave him, "Leaky Steamcock" (a moniker he did not find particularly amusing), could have been lifted right out of *Sunshine Sketches*.

He once sent the following request to a university librarian: "I wish you would send me a copy of G. Ball's *Mathematical Recreations* (?),—if it is called *Mathematical Recreations*, and if it is G. Ball. If not, please send me the book I am trying to think of." It was the sort of thing Leacock might have put in one of his stories.

True, he had a volcanic temper and was known for firing his entire household staff in a fit of pique, but—and this is very much a Leacockian *but*—he would inevitably end up hiring them back the next day ... and at higher pay, something you could easily imagine the thundering Judge Pepperleigh doing in *Sunshine Sketches*.

Although hailed as "the Canadian Mark Twain," Leacock never had the sweep of Twain's narrative scope. He only ever wrote two novels—*Sunshine Sketches of a Little Town* and *Arcadian Adventures with the Idle Rich*—and even those are more a series of linked stories than proper novels. But he had a wonderful ear for dialogue and was superbly skilled at creating polished, self-contained scenes and evoking character with a few sure strokes—talents more theatrical than novelistic.

Indeed, Leacock's great love was, in a very real sense, the theatre. He married an actress, after all: Beatrix Hamilton, from Toronto, who was performing in New York when Leacock asked her to be his wife. He considered trying his hand at commercial theatre as well, but never quite took the plunge. He did write several theatrical spoofs and various "playlets" that appear in his humour collections, most notably in *Behind the Beyond*. He was, as his students and audiences would attest, a grand performer. And during holidays at Old Brewery Bay, he would often write short plays for his guests to perform. But we must not consider Leacock "an unfulfilled playwright" any more than we might think of him as "a failed novelist."

He was a master of his realm: the perfect vignette, the quick spoof, the gentle poke to the eye delivered with a chuckle so warm you could only think, "Why yes! A poke to the eye is just what I needed." As a humorist—as a pure, undiluted, and unrepentant humorist—Leacock was second to none. Robertson Davies considered him a genius. And Robertson Davies was right.

Sunshine Sketches of a Little Town first appeared as a newspaper serial, and it shows—in the best possible way. Quick anecdotal tales with richly interconnected characters, they were originally commissioned by an editor at the *Montreal Star,* whose only stipulation was that they be "typically Canadian." Typically Canadian? They would prove to be *definitively* Canadian.

The sketches ran from February through June 1912, and grew out of the stories Leacock liked to tell around the dinner table in Montreal about the small town in Ontario where he spent his summers. Stephen Leacock didn't invent Mariposa. He simply embellished Orillia.

"Mariposa is not a real town," he declares with a breezy insincerity. "On the contrary, it is about seventy or eighty of them. You may find them all the way from Lake Superior to the sea."

But the "sinking" of the *Mariposa Belle* was almost certainly taken from an incident that occurred on Lake Couchiching when the steamer *Longford* ran aground on a sandbar. (Once the passengers were evacuated, the *Longford* floated free … and continued merrily on its way.) Orillia's Anglican church *did* burn down (though hopefully not for the insurance money) and the local hotel owner *was* a man of enormous girth.

Leacock changed most of the names, but the half-hearted pseudonyms he assigned were as transparent as a thin coat of paint. You wonder why he bothered. Orillia's undertaker, Bingham, was now named Gingham. Jeff Shortt the barber was now Jeff Thorpe the barber. Jim Smith, Orillia's beefy hotel owner and saloon keeper, became Josh Smith, Mariposa's equally beefy hotel owner and saloon keeper. And Canon Greene, Orillia's beloved church rector, was caricatured (unfairly, many thought) as the Rev. Drone. Even the name "Mariposa" wasn't invented, but was taken from that of an earlier settlement which had once existed nearby. Orillia's Mississaga Street became Missinabi Street. Hatley's General Store became Netley's. And so on.

The barber in question, who had chatted so freely with Leacock whenever he shaved him, now found himself forced to apologize to his customers. "How in hell was I to know he would put these things in a book?" A lawyer in Orillia threatened to sue Leacock for libel, but Leacock insisted, years later, that the threat had been made only "in fun." The editor of *The Orillia Packet and Times* also mentioned "mutterings about libel suits," but nothing ever came of it.

Bruised small-town pride aside—and small-town pride is so easily bruised—the humour in *Sunshine Sketches* is never mean-spirited, never vindictive. Leacock was always tolerant of, indeed quite enamoured with, the constancy of human foible. No moral high horse (not in his humour at least). No withering takedowns. No vivisectionist-style satire. Just irony, affection, and an understanding that none of us are perfect, that we are all of us susceptible to flattery, afflicted with blind spots, secretly convinced of our own inner nobility, our buried talents, our true callings.

In Mariposa, your point of view dictates what you see. It's an observer-affected universe, where perspective is everything and reality is all in how you look at it, where the *Mariposa Belle* grows larger and grander the longer you live there, and where the foyer of a Paris opera house pales next to the gaiety and buzz of Jim Eliot's drugstore.

Biographer David M. Legate has said that "although he brought fame to the town, Leacock was never popular in Orillia," but the accuracy of that statement has been disputed, and Leacock certainly wasn't run out of town after *Sunshine Sketches* appeared. Far from it.

Some have suggested it wasn't the book but the lifestyle that the more respectable citizens objected to. In prohibitionist times, Leacock was anti-temperance. In the "dry" town of Orillia, Leacock was "wet," and at Old Brewery Bay the booze ran freely. Mimicking the pronouncements of the temperance ladies who were the bane of his existence, Leacock took his own stance, declaring, "The sale of whiskey should be rigidly restricted to those who need it at the time when they need it, and in the quantity they happen to need." When guests arrived, Leacock's standard greeting was, inevitably, "Will you have a drink?"

As the years went by, Leacock spent more and more time in Orillia, soaking up the sun, tending his garden, and boating along the shimmering waters of his own personal Eden.

He eventually decided to replace his patchwork of a summer house with a proper mansion. A major undertaking, but Leacock, ever the shrewd economist, had a cunning plan. He assured the young architect he hired that they could save money by building the new house with the material from the old house.

There was a long pause. The architect looked at Leacock. "You want me to build a bigger house out of a smaller house?"

Leacock paid for the extra materials.

And good thing that he did. The result was a handsome home overlooking Old Brewery Bay with a wide veranda and oak panelling throughout.

When he passed away in 1944, Stephen Leacock was remembered as Orillia's "most distinguished citizen," and that's saying something, because Orillia has a knack for producing iconic national figures:

Sam Steele of the Mounted Police, songwriter Gordon Lightfoot, the unsinkable Stephen Leacock—Orillians all. (Leacock, Lightfoot, and Steele: how's that for an all-Canadian triumvirate?)

If there was any resentment about the way Leacock lampooned Orillia, it seems to have since dissipated. A medal for humour is awarded annually in Leacock's name, and his home at Old Brewery Bay is now a national historic site. And if there were any lingering doubts, they were laid to rest in 1995 when volunteers came together in full force over a single weekend in September to help rebuild Leacock's boathouse, that lakeside building where the author had done so much of his writing. The event had the sunshine air of an old-fashioned barn raising, and people don't show up in the thousands to honour the memory of someone they dislike. (Though, if it were a proper Leacockian tale, it would have ended with the boathouse sliding into the bay.)

In many ways, our image of Canada as a small town, sleepy and innocent, was invented here, on the shores of this lake. Steeped in gentle delusions and coddled in sunlight and summer lullabies, Leacock's Mariposa is both the source of and template for a particular Canadian myth. The Myth of Canada as "The Mariposa of Nations."

Leacock dedicated *Sunshine Sketches of a Little Town* to Canada as a whole, describing the nation as "a land of hope and sunshine." Winter doesn't exist in Mariposa, and the sunshine sketches are exactly that: sketches made in the season that is not winter.

But it's also important to note that Leacock's little town is rooted in a very specific time and place: an Anglo Ontario community, an outpost of Empire, blissfully unaware of the fact that it exists at the end of an era, in a world about to be destroyed forever by the horrors of the Great War. A town sleepwalking toward a larger nightmare. In the death of Judge Pepperleigh's son in the South African War and the photographs of Canadians marching off—but not returning—we find an unintended foreshadowing of this. Tellingly, the book itself ends with a eulogy.

Mariposa may have been just a dream, but it was a collective dream nonetheless. It was a dream we once shared, and perhaps still do. A dream nurtured not because it is real, but because we want it to be real. And that is the strangest incongruity of all: although based firmly on a real place and real people, Mariposa itself never really existed.

The house that Leacock built at Old Brewery Bay is an improbable sight today. It's akin to stumbling upon an English estate in the Canadian woods. Befitting this incongruity, the house manages to be both grand and modest at the same time. The veranda has an expansive view of the bay, and there's a wine cellar and a billiard room, but the house itself was never ostentatious and it never lost that sparse, summer-home, under-furnished feeling it always had.

The property fell into disarray after Leacock died. Vandals ransacked it, hoboes slept in it. The sun porch collapsed, the garden grew wild with weeds. At some point a ghost moved in, though whose ghost exactly is still a point of debate. But thanks to the efforts of a reporter named Pete McGarvey and other like-minded citizens, Leacock's home was eventually rescued and restored, and is now open to the public.

Leacock's presence is palpable. His desk, books. The view from the veranda. And among the items in the library: a folder he'd labelled "Letters From Damn Fools." Even now the mirror in the living room is set at an angle so that one can keep an eye on the staff in the next room, something that Leacock added.

Outside, a summer haze lies low along the water. It mutes the sun, reducing the lake to pastel colours and blurred borders. I am here with Elizabeth Kimball, Leacock's niece and the author of *The Man in the Panama Hat*, a memoir about her famous uncle. Elizabeth's mother was Stephen's younger sister.

"What did he look like?" In her memoir she answers that question in the following manner: "Like a teddy bear that has been left out in the rain ... Like a soldier who has fought through every battle of the Hundred Years' War ... Like a mischievous child, just before he bursts the paper bag full of water ... Like a safety-pin cushion, and a very old one, at that."

Elizabeth is turning ninety, still sharp, still funny. She has that same strong Leacockian jaw, and like her uncle, she is a natural-born raconteur. She tells me tales, tall and otherwise, of her various uncles and aunts, of the swarms of cousins, and the holidays they spent at the Leacock summer home. "Uncle Stephen had a great hospitable spirit. He loved to have the family around him." But she hasn't glamorized her memory of Old Brewery Bay either. The water was murky and cold, the mosquitoes were as ferocious as "Bengali tigers."

We make our way down to the reconstructed boathouse, and she points to a nook beside it. "This is where I swim." The use of present tense is revealing. "The rocks are a little slimy, so I have to sort of pull myself out into deeper water first." For her ninetieth birthday, Elizabeth will be taking her sailboat out on Lake Ontario.

At the boathouse, she turns and looks back at the house with the grand veranda and the sweeping views. Even with memories of mosquitoes and the shivering cold swims of her youth, she misses the place. "It was always summer when we came here."

On March 18, 2011, Elizabeth Kimball passed away at the age of ninety-eight. She is greatly missed.

Best Canadian/
Worst Canadian

Canada's national history magazine, *The Beaver*, once asked me to write about a historical figure I admired. Later, they asked me to nominate a "worst Canadian" for a feature they were running. I've combined the two here, back to back, for your perusal.

Maybe it has something to do with the way I grew up. I was raised by strong women: my mother, Lorna Bell, riding herd on half a dozen kids (more when you counted foster siblings and assorted strays who found refuge in our messy home), and my grandmother, Lily Bell, a retired schoolteacher who rolled her own cigarettes and spiced her tea with brandy.

I never believed women were delicate buds. Nor did I see them as moral agents descended from heaven. Which is why I've always felt slightly uncomfortable with such early feminist leaders as Nellie McClung and Emily Murphy (who, family legend unverified by fact, suggests I'm related to, her maiden name being Ferguson; a tenuous claim indeed. As with the con man Arthur Ferguson, we basically claim anyone up to and including the former Duchess of York as kin.)

Emily Murphy may have led the crusade to have women declared "persons" in the eyes of the court, and Nellie McClung may have spearheaded the fight to grant women the vote, but what truly fuelled their passions—and those of many other suffragists of that era—was the belief that women had a "moral mission," a greater purpose in life, a higher Christian calling.

Two schools of feminism took shape in those early years. Maternal, or "separate sphere," feminism saw women as society's moral guardians with a special civilizing mission distinct from that of men. Equal rights feminism, however, sought social and legal equality for women as a worthy goal in and of itself. And though often downplayed today, dark nativist attitudes lay just below the surface of much of the maternal feminism movement. The same women who wanted the vote for white Anglo-Saxon women all too often wanted these same rights denied to Asian males.

Which is why Agnes Macphail (1890–1954) is such a refreshing presence. In 1921, Macphail became the first woman elected to the Canadian House of Commons, as a member of the U.F.O. (United Farmers of Ontario). And though sticklers can pull out quotes by Macphail that suggest otherwise, it is clear that she was very much an equal-rights feminist.

"What do women want?" asked Macphail. "I think women just want to be individuals, as men are individuals—no more and no less."

During a 1924 debate about divorce laws, a male MP declared, "There has always existed and there always will exist in women, an inborn weakness, a marked inferiority … Woman is looked upon—and with reason—as the angel of the home, as a gentler being than men."

To which Agnes Macphail rose and replied, "When I hear men talk about women being the angel of the home I always, mentally at least, shrug my shoulders in doubt. I do not want to be the angel of any home; I want for myself what I want for other women—absolute equality. After that is secured, men and women can take turns at being angels."

Ironically, Agnes Macphail fulfilled many of the predictions posited by maternal feminism: that women would have a "civilizing" effect on the national discourse. She fought for prison reforms, better health care, workers' rights. She lobbied for old-age pensions, disability allowance, agrarian reforms, hospital insurance, and student bursaries.

Once, when she arrived at the Kingston Penitentiary to investigate conditions, officials tried to turn her away, telling her that prison was "no place for a lady."

"I'm no lady," Macphail shot back. "I'm an MP."

Throughout her career, federally and later in the Ontario provincial legislature, Agnes Macphail fought the good fight. Her humour and determination, her quick wit and social conscience, resonate now more than ever. Agnes Macphail was—and still is—a hell of a good role model.

———

The poet Duncan Campbell Scott (1862–1947) had a knack for killing Indians. His purple verse is littered with the bodies of Natives who died gruesome and romantic deaths. And throughout the carnage, Scott bemoans the twilight passing of Canada's "tragic savages," that "weird and waning race."

No wonder. Here's a statement made by the director of Indian policy during that period: "The Government will in time reach the end of its responsibility as the Indians progress into civilization and finally disappear as a separate and distinct people, not by race extinction but by gradual assimilation."

The bureaucrat's name? Duncan Campbell Scott.

Scott was Canada's senior administrator of Indian policy from 1913 to 1932. Under his watch, Native ceremonies were outlawed, their communities were barred from making legal claims against the government, and they were not permitted to leave reserve property unless they had a pass. "The Indian in himself had no title to the soil demanding recognition," wrote Scott in 1914, "nor, in his inferior position as a savage, had he any rights which could become the subject of treaty or negotiation." This from the head of the Department of Indian Affairs.

As a poet and as a bureaucrat, Duncan Campbell Scott represents the two extremes of how Canadians have dealt with the First Nations: romanticizing them ridiculously on the one hand and marginalizing them callously on the other. Often at the same time.

The Mad Trapper of Rat River: Anatomy of a Photograph

When Mark Reid, editor of *The Beaver* (since renamed *Canada's History Magazine*), was putting together a glossy coffee-table book titled *100 Photos That Changed Canada*, he asked me if I would like to contribute. He sent me a list of photographs to choose from, and I eventually narrowed it down to two: the first, a photo taken during the Great Flag Debate of 1964—the year I was born—featuring an early prototype of our maple leaf flag; the second, a grim portrait of a dead trapper. The following is an expanded version of this second essay.

Consider the photograph on the facing page a Rorschach test.

When you look at it, what do you see? A madman? A murderer? Or a tormented soul? The Mad Trapper of Rat River remains a blank canvas even now. Just about the only thing we know about him is that his name was not Albert Johnson; that was given to him early on and in error.

They called it the "Arctic Circle War," a forty-eight-day pursuit through the howling depths of winter across some of the harshest terrain on earth, and one that ended with a shootout on the Eagle River on February 17, 1932.

Albert Johnson, as he was known, had drifted into the North and

taken up a hermit-like existence
along the Rat River. When he
began encroaching on Native
traplines the Mounties sent a
pair of officers out on dogsled to
talk to him, a routine check that
would trigger a chain of events
leaving one officer dead and two
others wounded.

When the Mounties ham-
mered their fist on Johnson's
cabin door, he refused to open
up. So they went back and got a
warrant (this is Canada after all),
returning several days later. This
time they were answered with
gunfire. Johnson fired a bullet
into one officer's chest, and
though the officer survived—

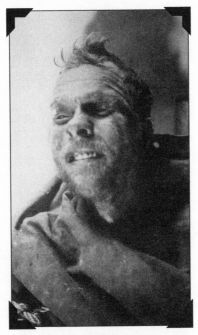

Albert Johnson, the Mad Trapper,
after death, Northwest Territories

barely—the war had begun. The Mounties retreated and then returned
in full force, special constables at their side. They proceeded to blow
up Johnson's cabin with dynamite.

As the smoke cleared, they could see Johnson's body lying amid
the smouldering ruins. They waited. And waited. Nothing. After
several hours, they moved forward. At which point Johnson rolled
over and fired a single shot. It hit a Mountie in the heart, killing the
officer instantly.

The man known as Albert Johnson now fled into the wild. He
wore his snowshoes backwards, scaled canyon walls, kicked down
avalanches to cover his trail, and ran behind caribou herds, mixing
his tracks in with a thousand churned hoofprints. At one point, two
officers, following two separate trails, met each other face to face going
in opposite directions. The greatest winter trackers in the world, the
Loucheux Indians and Mounted Police of the Far North, couldn't

keep up with him. For three weeks they chased apparitions and ran in circles.

Panic spread ahead of Johnson as women and men abandoned isolated cabins and crowded into trading posts. Newspapers as far away as Europe picked up the story, following the events as they unfolded, up there, beyond the curve of earth in that elemental domain of ice and snow. The Mad Trapper of Rat River had become the world's most famous hermit.

Wilfrid "Wop" May, a legendary bush pilot and former World War I flying ace, was now called in to help, marking the first time in Canadian history that police used aerial tracking in the pursuit of a criminal. This arctic manhunt was also the first time in Canadian history that two-way radio was used in the field. Technology was catching up with Albert Johnson, a single man pitted against the concentrated efforts of the RCMP, Indian trackers, aerial surveillance, deputized trappers, radio relays, dog teams, dynamite, and gunfire. It was an eerily silent pursuit, as well. During the entire chase, from the first confrontation at his cabin to the final barrage on the Eagle River, Johnson never spoke a word.

Wop May had earlier flown a mercy flight to deliver serum during a diphtheria epidemic to the remote trading post of Fort Vermilion, Alberta. He'd flown with a co-pilot in an open-seat plane through minus-forty weather. He now joined the hunt for Albert Johnson, not in an open-seat plane this time, but through freezing winds nonetheless. May pursued Johnson over mountain ranges and above blizzards in conditions he would later describe as the most fearsome in his career—and this was a man who had tangled with the Red Baron.

As Wop May flew in fresh supplies and tracked Johnson from the air, the noose slowly began to tighten. Johnson's trail was becoming ragged, his stride uneven, his footsteps faltering. This cheered his pursuers on. They didn't know it then, but, unable to make a fire for fear of being spotted, Johnson was now eating frozen squirrels and living on snow.

With Wop May circling above, Albert Johnson was finally cornered on the frozen Eagle River. All told, they put seventeen bullets in him. Even after he fell they kept firing. Wop May landed on the river, walked across, and stared into the dead man's eyes. Pale blue. No answers.

"Johnson's lips were curled from his teeth in the most terrible sneer I've ever seen," May recalled. "It was the most awful grimace of hate I'll ever see—the hard-boiled, bitter hate of a man who knows he's trapped at last and has determined to take as many enemies as he can with him down the trail he knows he's going to hit … I was glad he was dead. The world seemed a better place with him out of it."

Johnson was photographed and fingerprinted and buried without a past in a graveyard in Aklavik. It had taken four gun battles, 150 miles of Arctic, and more than a little luck to stop him. Yet we never learned the why of it. Why he fired. Why he ran.

His fingerprints matched none on record, here or in the States. They found some ammunition and a dead squirrel on him, along with a sizeable amount of cash and some gold dental work in a jar. Not his gold dental work.

He remains nameless—or rather, *unnamed.* No birth dates, no family records, no history beyond that of his arrival in the North and the chase that followed. We have only a story of motion and the end of motion, and the only date we can really pin on him is February 17, 1932. The day he died.

Was May right? Is the death grimace in that photograph the sneer of an unrepentant sinner? A photograph of evil? Or of mental illness? Cabin fever run amok? Is this the photograph of a heartless killer or a lost soul? Or both?

The Writing
"Life"

When I'm asked what the best thing about being a writer is, I always say, "The hordes of love-starved women who are constantly throwing themselves at you wherever you go." The worst thing? The fact that these aforementioned hordes of love-starved women are completely imaginary.

That they don't actually exist aside, these literary groupies are still a major perk of the job. Other perks include "working in your underwear" and "scratching yourself whenever you like." Try doing that in your typical office environment. The following essays cover the breadth, the width, and—yes—the depth of the writerly life, from book-tour blueberries to the Fine Art of Not Writing.

Early Influences
(or why I'm such a twisted
and bitter man, part two)

I grew up surrounded by comic books, courtesy of a mother who loved *Pogo* and three older brothers whose tastes in literature ranged from the merely gruesome to the spectacularly gory, much of it in the blood-splattering sword-and-sorcery vein. No *Velveteen Rabbit* or *Wind in the Willows* for me; *Pogo* aside, my childhood was drenched in tales of *Conan the Barbarian* and others, in both pocketbook and comic form.

These novels had muscular, manly titles like *Conan the Destroyer, Conan the Usurper, Conan the Ubiquitous, Conan the Ambidextrous*— and so on, the gist of their message being that, at any time, in any place, a demonic creature is liable to leap from the shadows and pull your entrails out through your spleen. (This is where I first learned the word "entrails." And "spleen.")

One of my earliest memories is of cowering behind a clutched pillow, sheets smelling faintly of urine, while my brother Ian regaled me with the latest tale of demons and usurpers. My older brothers have never quite forgiven me for cutting out an order form for X-ray specs from a first edition of *Conan the Barbarian #1*, which they insist would probably be worth a million bucks by now save for my act of vandalism. (The X-ray specs didn't even work. All they did was create a hazy double image that looked vaguely skeletal. Hardly worth the million dollars we forfeited.)

Comics aside, the book that made the biggest impression on me was about neither sword nor sorcery. It was an old hardcover children's book with a comfortingly musty scent, the pages all but falling out. I found it exiled to the back of the bookshelf, pushed behind the Conans and Krulls. A simple tale, called *Stone Soup*. It was the story of—well, a con man, essentially: a charming beggar who, refused food, asks a housewife for a stone with which to make soup. Soup from a stone? Intrigued, the lady allows him to boil some water in a pot. He lets the stone simmer awhile, tastes the water, decides it needs a bit of salt. Then a pinch of pepper. Some onion. A couple of carrots, a little bit of beef stock … and so on. By the end, he has his soup. The housewife is mightily impressed. She even gives him some bread to go with it, and the beggar leaves, belly full.

I loved the cheerful gall of it, the sheer cleverness. That, and the fact that no one was disembowelled and then throttled with their own entrails at any point in the story. Years later, when I found myself writing about swindlers selling love potions to hapless rubes, I knew where my fascination with con men came from: X-ray specs and stone soup.

I grew up in a former fur-trading post in northern Alberta (Fort Vermilion, pop: 841). It wasn't exactly bustling with activity, so when word spread that a bookstore—an actual bona-fide bookstore!—was about to open, I almost burst from the sheer joy of it. I was in junior high by then and trembling with anticipation.

Sure enough, a brand-new, double-wide trailer appeared in front of the Hudson's Bay store. The sign read MARANATHA BOOKS. Now, I didn't exactly understand the meaning of the word "Maranatha," but it sounded vaguely futuristic.

"I bet they have lots of sci-fi," I said, speaking breathlessly to my friend Kevin. "Stories about time travel and robot armies! Asimov, Bradbury. I bet they've got 'em all."

Kev and I skipped school in order to be at the bookstore the very moment it opened. Giddy with excitement, we walked inside …

Oh, there were novels, all right. Novels aplenty. Christian novels. Christian novels about Christian kids doing Christian things. There was non-fiction as well, mainly Christian self-help, radiating sunshine and rainbows from their covers. One entire section of the store was labelled "Happiness." And there were Bibles, too. Boy were there Bibles. Stacks and stacks of Bibles, with not an Asimov or a Bradbury in sight.

The kindly gentleman who manned the till smiled at us in a benevolently Christian sort of way, but it was no use. Our hearts had already shattered. It was like some sort of horrible prank; it was worse than having no bookstore at all. Not that it mattered. A few months later, Maranatha Books closed down.

And somewhere between Conan and stone soup, between comic books and Bibles, between happiness and its many disappointments, the germ of a writer was born. *Cue the hordes of love-starved women!*

Book Tours
and Blueberry Muffins

It seemed like a reasonable enough request. "The blueberries," I said. "Can you pick them out of the muffin for me?"

The publicist, a pleasant and relentlessly well-organized young woman, blinked.

We were in a car on our way to Kitchener-Waterloo for a TV interview, and had just driven through Tim Hortons to pick up coffee and muffins for the road.

When she handed mine over, I said, with a heavy sigh, "Can you puh-lease pick out the blueberries."

"Oh," she said. "I misunderstood. I thought you asked for blueberry. I can get you a plain muffin instead."

"No," I snapped. "I like blueberry muffins. What I don't like is blueberries. Can you PLEASE pick them out for me?"

I was on book tour, you see. Six cities. Nine days. My fourth tour in as many years, and I knew full well that the unwritten role of a publicist is to Indulge the Author, just as surely as the unwritten role of the author is to Torment the Publicist.

There are many ways to torment a publicist: you can refuse to do interviews, you can show up late, you can whinge, you can moan. You can even demand they pick blueberries out of a muffin for you.

What a lot of new authors don't realize is that writing a book is only the first step. Now you have to go out and flog the damn thing. ("Flog" in the promotional sense, though there's often the "dead horse" feel to it as well.) Authors, having spent months, years even, huddled over a keyboard, are now expected to wobble forth atop a unicycle juggling copies of their book, trying desperately to get the attention of a blissfully unaware media.

Never mind that the single most boring sentence in the English language is "Mr. Jones will now talk about his book"; the promotional tour is a rite of passage, much like the running of the bulls—but with more casualties.

At first, book tours seem like a wonderful, all-expenses-paid break from the solitary hunt-and-peck existence of the writerly life. When you're on tour, you jet into a different city every night. You get to have wine with every meal and can order up room service for breakfast every single day—all on someone else's tab. But the novelty of wine and room service soon wears off. Damp toast and cold eggs. Long dull taxi rides from one airport to another. *If it's Monday, this must be Ottawa . . .*

I'm not complaining. Many books don't get toured at all, and in today's precarious world of publishing, any author who gets sent on a cross-country media whirl has no right to complain about anything. It's exhausting, but it's also deeply flattering. An entire fleet of people, from publisher to publicist to marketing team, are hard at work trying to sell your ideas—your *words*—to the general public. The only acceptable emotion any writer lucky enough to get toured should be allowed to express is gratitude. Ah, but writers are a notoriously prickly and insecure group, and there's something about running the gauntlet of interviews—two-minute wham-bam on-air hits followed by interminable call-in shows and ear-numbing phoners—that tends to bring out the very worst in people. And of course, when I say "people," I mean "me."

Long stretches of monotony punctuated by sudden self-conscious bursts of self-promotion—it's not the most dignified way to reach an audience. And even then you're jostling for position with other writers, other snake charmers, with musicians and magicians, mountebanks and medical quacks, all hungry for a piece of the promo pie, all sparring with tight-lipped smiles in greenrooms across this great land of ours.

The media is indeed the master, and greenrooms—as the waiting areas are known—are strange places, indeed.

After a while, TV greenrooms begin to blend into one another. The same guests seem to circulate, reappearing again and again with a déjà-vu predictability. There's always a chef, oozing charm. There's a singer, heavily mascaraed and shellacked with bulletproof hairspray. Or maybe a band: Cape Breton fiddlers or angry urban hip-hoppers usually. And there is always—always—a B-grade American actor who has some sort of role in some sort of upcoming made-for-TV movie. Everyone fawns over the B-grade American actor, and the B-grade American actor always wears a sour expression.

Amid this odd microcosm, this one-room sociological experiment, sits a writer. He's in the corner, holding his book on his lap, as welcome as an insurance salesman at a cocktail soirée.

Some hosts have actually read your book; they come prepared. They have peremptory Post-it Notes marking specific passages and a list of questions to ask. These hosts are almost always women. Others, mainly men, mainly guys, mainly wacky morning-show radio hosts, are cheerfully uninformed about who you are. They don't know and they don't care. And when it comes time to interview you, they just flip your book over and read your bio directly from the back cover.

"Welcome back. We're here today with ... Where's the name? Let's see ...Wilf Erguson, author of—whoa!—*Bastards and Boneheads.* Where'd you get a title like that?"

This isn't necessarily a bad thing. After all, hosts who haven't read your book haven't had a chance to form a critical appraisal of it either. These are the hosts who praise your book the most highly. ("Our guest today is the author of—what was it?—*Canadian Dummies for History.* No? Close enough. Anyway, it's a great book! Fantastic! I recommend it 110 percent!") Whenever you hear a radio host pouring effusive praise on a book, you can bet a week's wages that he hasn't even cracked its spine, let alone read the first page.

In the U.K., I was once interviewed on BBC Radio by a host who not only hadn't read my book, or even the back cover, but hadn't even managed to get all the way through my name. He'd been expecting the novelist Will Self to show up. A tad awkward, that.

"You're not Will Self then."

"Um, no. A completely different Will."

"Oh. I see."

Stranger still, by a weird twist of fate I found myself sitting beside Will Self at a publishing dinner the very next night. This was the first and only time I ever met the man, which made my conversational opener all the more ill-advised. On being introduced to him, I said, "Hey! I was just mistaken for you!" This elicited a somewhat perturbed look on Mr. Self's face followed by a discernible shift away from me at the table.

It's not the interviews that grind you down when you're on a book tour, though. It's the waiting. That's what grinds you down.

Here then, is my confession. Although I'm always surprised—and genuinely appreciative—of any exposure the media gives a touring author, I *hate* being the writer in the greenroom. I really do. I hate being the guy with the book. When you're the writer in the greenroom, you're always the least cool person in the room. The chef is loud and gregarious and speaking in a staged Italian accent. Unless he's a French chef, in which case he'll be speaking in a staged *English* accent. The singer is flirty and radiant. The band is noisily scarfing down bagels with both hands. (I once watched in awe and admiration as the Barra MacNeils polished off an entire buffet just before heading out, on stage, live. Some of them were still chewing as they walked out.) The B-grade American actor really is a prima donna—at least by Canadian media standards. But the writer? When you're the writer in the greenroom, not even the singer will flirt with you. When you're the writer in the greenroom, the other guests' eyes glaze over when you tell them what you do. It got so bad that I took to lying whenever anyone asked.

"Why am I on the show? I invented a lethal dartgun that can kill a cheetah from 140 paces."

"Really?" they say, eyes lighting up.

"Yes. And then I wrote a book about it."

"I see." Their eyes immediately begin glazing over.

This is where the publicist comes in. Among the many and varied responsibilities that fall upon him or her (though it's almost always a her)—that of coordinator, chauffeur, troubleshooter, babysitter—the publicist acts as a sort of "triage therapist," leaping in once the shooting stops to assuage wounds and stroke frail authorial egos. Which is to say, they lie an awful lot.

"You were wonderful," says the publicist as she whisks you from one disastrous TV interview to the next. "Don't worry about the nosebleed, you were fine. No one noticed."

Publicists collect author anecdotes the way Sicilians collect vendettas, and certain writers clearly stand out. Some of the stories are amusing, some are affectionate, some are rife with seething calls for divine vengeance. Some authors are infamous for being lewd, some for being petulant, some for being pouty. One is even renowned for his flatulence. Some authors treat publicists as personal servants, some treat them as confidantes. One well-known author, a woman who wrote a children's book no less, took the publicist on a drunken pub crawl at the end of the day. "She was great," said the publicist. "But man, what a hangover."

I have no idea where I fit in. For all I know, publicists right now are sitting around a smoky bar swigging gin and muttering, "I had Wilf Erguson last week. God, what a nightmare."

You see, I was only kidding about the blueberries. I was having a larf, was poking fun at the type of diva authors that publicists hate, but incredibly the publicist took me seriously. Her face was set in diplomatic stone, but her eyes betrayed a barely concealed contempt as she looked, first at the muffin, then at me.

"You want me to pick out the blueberries," she said. It was a statement, not a question.

"Kidding!" I said. "Just kidding!"

"I see," she said, voice even, gaze steady. "Very funny."

Once we were out on the highway and heading for the TV station, I asked the publicist what she would have done if I hadn't been kidding, if I had in fact been dead serious in my request.

"Well," she said with a weary sigh, "I suppose I would have started picking."

The day after this story ran, a FedEx package arrived at my door. It was from the publicist in question. Inside were a dozen blueberry muffins and a pair of tweezers, along with a note that read, "Here you go, Will! Knock yourself out."

Stranger still, the tale of the blueberry muffin has gone on to become something of an urban legend in publishing. I was back on tour again just recently, with a publicist I hadn't worked with before, and when I asked her if she'd ever had any difficult authors, she said, "Not really." But then she lowered her voice and said, "I heard there was this one author who made his publicist pick blueberries out of a muffin ..."

Mini-Bar Ninja

Have you seen Cracker Jack lately? What the hell happened? This iconic caramel-peanut-and-popcorn snack used to come in its own special box with incredibly cool toys you built yourself—working hydro-electrical generators, that sort of thing. Now they're packaged in a bag, like common chips, and instead of a toy they come with a little square of paper that has an "interesting fact!" printed on it. Because we all know how much children prefer interesting facts to toys.

I found Cracker Jack in a hotel mini-bar basket, one of those wicker-bowl horns-o-plenty that sit atop mini-bar fridges, offering sustenance and hope to weary travellers as they stagger in, drop their bags, and say, "Wasn't I just here?"

The bag of Cracker Jack contained the following Interesting Fact—and you know it's true, because this is Cracker Jack; they have a fleet of fact-checkers working 24/7: *The beaver is the only mammal that never stops growing.*

I was so taken aback by this, I had to sit down.

The beaver is the only mammal that never stops growing. The ramifications are enormous. For starters, it means that if you were to hook up an elderly beaver to life support and just keep it alive, you would eventually grow this massive … gigantic … creature. A buck-toothed, web-toed Godzilla of the North.

Now. Call me a dreamer if you will, call me a romantic if you must, but that's how I like to think of Canada: as this giant, improbable, overgrown aquatic water rat, sprawling across half a continent. Hotel mini-bars bring out the patriot in me.

And if nothing else, I've become a connoisseur of mini-bar baskets. A ninja master, if you will, a stealth-like expert on this perk of the expense-account traveller. (Only people who are on expense accounts, or those who've been drinking—or those who are on expense accounts who've also been drinking—ever raid a mini-bar. Who else would be willing to open an $18 jar of cashews, price per cashew $4?)

This embarrassment of riches, with the treats fanned out for your appraisal, entices lonely travellers with its very predictability. There's always a Toblerone, the inevitable bag of M&Ms, the half-tin of Pringles, the pack of Dentyne gum, and—of course—the cashews. Cashews are the gold standard of hotel offerings. When you approach the mini-bar, a shaft of light falls from heaven and illuminates the cashews. I'm not sure who decided they should be served shrink-wrapped in mason jars of the sort your grandmother used to pickle beets in, but no matter. A book-publishing VP once walked me through the Mini-Bar Food Chain. "You always start at the bottom and work your way *up*, beginning with the Pringles, then moving on to the M&Ms, then the Toblerone, and finally, around midnight, you figure what the hell, I'm going for it … and you crack open the cashews."

Mini-bar baskets may *seem* to be the same wherever you go, but they aren't. As I've discovered, if you look closely there's always at least one item that they would only think to include in that particular city. In Vancouver, vacuum-packed salmon. In Calgary, beef jerky. In Saskatoon, a complimentary sampler jar of the city's eponymous jam. In Toronto, I once found a financial magazine neatly rolled beside the basket. Presumably, this was so I could check my investments over breakfast. In Ottawa, it was a free patronage appointment. (That's *Senator* Ferguson to you, bucko!)

Okay, so I made that last one up. But it's true that there's always that one quirky item in any mini-bar basket, which comes in handy when you wake up discombobulated in a strange room. Just check the mini-bar basket. *"Where am I? Let's see. A selection of Twinings Teas? Gotta be Victoria ... "*

When I arrived at the hotel in Montreal last time, I discovered—tucked in discreetly among the wares—a small packet of condoms. Condoms, mind you. In the mini-bar basket. You could almost hear the shrug. *"What? This is Montreal, you never know ... "*

By the time I reached St. John's, I was dying to find out what site-specific gift the Hotel Newfoundland had seen fit to slip into my selection of goodies. I arrived at the hotel under a wet Atlantic gale, checked in, and headed straight for the mini-bar. And there—tucked in, just as discreetly—was a single tube ... of ChapStick.

Clearly, "protection" has a different meaning in Newfoundland than it does in Montreal. The sad thing is, at my age, the ChapStick came in handier. I actually *used* the ChapStick.

Even if it didn't come with an Interesting Fact.

"So How's the Book Going?"

Deadlines are like a strange dog on an unfamiliar road.
—*playwright Eugene Stickland*

A writer with a deadline is a terrifying sight, more so when the writer in question is the one in your own mirror. That haunted look. Those bloodshot eyes. The whiff of fear, the facial tic of despair, the rank body odour of desperation.

With writers, the correct question is never "How's the writing going?" but rather "How is the NOT writing going?"

Not writing is the easiest thing in the world to do. And that's what an author means when she says she's "working" on a book. Working means "not writing." Working means reading, working means "research." Working means taking long diversionary walks. Working means perusing newspapers with an unnaturally intense interest. It means everything and anything except the actual act of writing.

At present, I am "working on" a travel book, a memoir if you will, about a long walk I took across Northern Ireland. Seemed like a good idea at the time. Even better, the trip itself provided an excellent alibi for not writing, because I was "in the field" and "on the road," gathering insights and harvesting anecdotes. It wasn't travel, it was research! That wasn't a pint in a Belfast pub, that was research! And I'm hoping Revenue Canada sees it that way too.

The differences between travel writing and, say, fiction, are comparable to different types of sculpting. To write fiction is to work with clay; you build something *up*—from a single character, perhaps, or an image, a scent even. It's the art of addition. Non-fiction, and travel writing in particular, is like working in marble or granite, chipping away at everything that doesn't fit. You start big and cut it down, reducing the weight of possibilities, deciding what matters, what doesn't. Any travel destination might conjure up any number of vastly different books, even from the same author. Focus on one throughline instead of another and the book will suddenly veer off, leading you in startlingly new directions. Or over the edge of a cliff. Travel writing is the art of selective subtraction. It's clay vs. marble. Building up vs. paring down.

I lugged home boxes and boxes of material from Northern Ireland, along with more than thirty hours of tapes I'd recorded during my trek, plus five fat notebooks, stuffed full, along with maps and reams of travel brochures, tatters of random paper, scribbled scraps of profundity and cryptic asides—they're piled in the corner of my office even now. But much to my amazement and chagrin, they have refused to sort themselves out. They have refused, Sorcerer's Apprentice–like, to leap from said boxes and fly into waiting, conveniently cross-referenced files.

It took me several months just to come up with a title. More than a few people suggested "The Marching Season," in reference to Northern Ireland's annual parades, but that struck me as flat and more than a bit obvious. I'd wanted to call the book "Death by Sausage," but was worried people might mistake it for a culinary tour of sorts or, even worse, an Agatha Christie–type mystery.

While I wrestled with the title (the wrestling of titles also being an excellent reason for Not Writing) the book itself had stubbornly and—it must be said—ungratefully refused to write itself. It lies buried somewhere in those boxes of paper, breathing, waiting for me to unearth it. I don't need a word processor, I need a pitchfork. I need a secretary. I need a plan. I need—a coffee, that's what I need! So off I go. Writing is all about priorities.

Hours later, I return from Second Cup, having read with unnatural interest a report on the recent fluctuations in NASDAQ shares (I don't have any stocks or investments, per se, but you never know), only to find that my book has still not magically assembled itself.

I have no time for anything else now. I must write. There's no time. That's my new motto. I'm a walking Burton Cummings riff: *I got got got got no time.* My wife and I have two children, aged seven and twelve, who need attention the way hamsters need food pellets. But I have no time to help. I can't run that errand, pay that bill. I have no time. No time! I'm writing a book, dammit!

The original deadline—the one I so cheerfully agreed to when I signed that contract, lo those many months ago—has long since passed. In an alternative universe, the publisher is preparing for a spring release; catalogue copy is being fine-tuned, prose is being polished, typesetters are standing by. But considering that my "book" still consists primarily of loose, unfiled papers—and oh, how tempting it is to simply upend those boxes on my editor's desk and say, "There you go! It's a little rough, but I think you've got enough there to work with"—it seems a bit premature to be ordering champagne and caviar.

Not that Canadian book launches involve champagne and caviar; it's more likely to be President's Choice cheese cubes and screw-top wine—but still. Faced with an inexplicably looming deadline, I asked for a year's extension. A year, mind you. And the publisher agreed. The bastards!

That was a year ago.

Okay. So enough fooling around. I'd better knuckle down, get going, light the proverbial candle at both proverbial ends, keep my nose to the grindstone, roll up my sleeves, grab the bull by the bootstraps. And though I'm too busy to shower or shave, I am, oddly enough, never too busy to drop everything and regale friends and family members, and even the occasional passerby, with exhaustive explanations about how busy I am. (I'm something of a philanthropist that way.) And if a newspaper editor suggests I stop everything to write an article titled "So How's the Book Going?" I will gladly take on the new assignment. Why? Because I'm an idiot, that's why.

An author, a very famous author, once stated he loved deadlines. He liked "the swooshing sound they make when they go by." So true. I just wish I could remember who said that. I'd stop and look it up, you understand, but I've got no time. I'm working on a book.

Spanish Fly
and J.C.

Here's a handy tip for young, impressionable writers out there that you may want to jot down: If you repeatedly call someone a bastard in print, you should not identify yourself as the author of such if you run into said person.

I wrote this piece for *The Walrus*. Since then, Toronto's annual BookExpo has come to an end, the latest casualty of the digital age, replaced by conference calls, online promos, and e-catalogues. A sad day for swag lovers everywhere.

BookExpo is all about buzz. At least, that's what they tell the authors.

From the groaning Grinch-that-stole-Christmas-type tote bags people were hauling around the Toronto Convention Centre, I'd say the real point is swag: both accumulation of and distribution to. Advance reading copies of fall books (ARCs, as they are known) are pressed on people like religious tracts being handed out on street corners, and toys and trinkets and every manner of tie-in giveaways line the aisles.

Douglas Coupland was signing boxes of Kraft Dinner. Dave Bidini was signing hockey pucks. So I figured I needed a gimmick, too. A giveaway. Hence the packets of aphrodisiacs labelled SPANISH

FLY: 100 PERCENT GUARANTEED PLACEBO EFFECT! that the publicists
were handing out. This was to promote a novel about grifters peddling
pseudo love potions in the 1930s, and I'd originally wanted to include
a small amount of powder—baking soda, say—in each of the packets,
until someone pointed out that perhaps distributing a mysterious
substance in a crowded public event was not the best idea. (Though
I have to say, a CSIS raid on BookExpo, complete with rappelling
ropes, drug-sniffing dogs, and anthrax-hunting agents would have
gotten us excellent media.) We decided to put condiment-sized packs
of Sweet'n Low in the Spanish Fly envelopes instead.

It was just as well, because one of the conference's star authors was
a former prime minister. Jean Chrétien was in attendance that year to
promote his forthcoming memoir, *My Years as Prime Minister,* a book
named with the same creative flair that marked his term in office.

Mr. Chrétien, still spry, jumped up on a small podium in front of a
packed audience and casually swatted down the one political question
that flew his way as though it were a mildly pesky mosquito—"Hey,
I am here to sell books"—and declared he was looking forward to
travelling across Canada on book tour, meeting people and shaking
hands "because it's in the contract."

I was heading back to the Convention Centre hotel afterwards,
thinking about what the mini-bar basket might yield, when I spotted
someone coming toward me. It was Bill Richardson, whom I'd known
during his days on CBC. I hadn't seen Bill for a couple of years, and
we were chatting in the hallway when around the corner swept Jean.
He was accompanied by his publisher, along with several young men
in blazers whom I assumed were some sort of security detail. The
entire entourage would have passed us by—Chrétien was moving so
fast everyone had to run to keep up—but his publisher spotted me
and stopped the others. She brought them over, asked, "Have you met
before?"

We hadn't. Mr. Chrétien said hello and we shook hands. I
considered telling him that I had a book coming out at the same time
he did, that we would indeed be going head to head. But I didn't want

to intimidate him—this was only his second book after all—so instead I said, by way of identification, you understand, "I'm the guy who wrote *Bastards and Boneheads*."

His smile disappeared.

Why I chose that book, I don't know. It's an earlier work based on a system I'd developed for classifying Canadian leaders as either "bastards who screwed Canada" or "boneheads, who just screwed up." It had circulated in Ottawa for years; I figured if he didn't know who I was, he might still recognize that particular title.

He did. Though not quite in the manner I had hoped.

He pinned me to the wall with a steely stare and said, "Oh yes. You're the one who's been having fun on me in your ..."—he paused to come up with just the right word to describe what it is I do—"... your *writings*." He said "writings" but clearly meant "illiterate scribblings."

Apparently, calling someone a *bastard* has a different nuance in French than in English.

"Is it too late to apologize?" I asked.

"Did it sell lots of books for you?"

"Um, yes actually, it did."

"Well then ..." he said, and he moved on to shake Bill's hand.

One of the men accompanying the former prime minister stepped toward me at that point. "Mr. Ferguson?" he said, and I thought, *Okay, here we go*. But no. He didn't want to pepper-spray me into submission or throttle me *à la le petit gars de Shawinigan*. The man in the blazer was, of all things, a fan. "Read *Bastards and Boneheads*," he said. "Enjoyed it." Then, with a wide grin and a stage whisper, "It's all true."

And off they went, with Jean striding forth and the others hurrying again to keep up. And as I watched Mr. Chrétien leave, so upbeat, so full of promise, all I could think was, "The poor guy. He has no idea what a cutthroat business publishing is." I can only hope he managed to generate some buzz.

In Search of the Great Canadian Metaphor (or why you should never trust a poet)

I offer the following as a cautionary tale. This is what happens when you attempt to pen something insightful at two in the morning after one too many beers.

Alison Gzowski at *The Globe and Mail* had asked me to contribute a short essay on Canadian culture, post-*Survival*, as part of a larger "round table." Seemed straightforward enough. I was on the road at the time, but hey, no problem, as long as I emailed it in before Monday, everything would be fine.

I was in Halifax that weekend, and on Sunday evening I was out with a group that included Montreal poet Carmine Starnino, who brushed aside my repeated protestations about having "a piece due tomorrow."

"I really have to call it a night," I pleaded. "I've got to get back to my room to write this thing for the *Globe*."

"Relax," said Carmine. "How many words do they want? Two to three hundred! That's it? We'll help you write it, don't worry. So finish your beer so we can order more." That sort of thing.

At the end of the night, Carmine staggered off to bed, his promise to help me ghost write the *Globe* assignment long forgotten. I ended up typing madly in the wee hours in one extended burst of desperation, a task made all the more difficult by the fact that I could no longer focus my eyes on the screen (whether this was due to a lack of sleep, or a surfeit of alcohol, or—as I suspect—a combination of both was hard to say). But I did get it in on time. Barely.

I have now used more words explaining the article than there are in it. Here's how it ran, along with the *Globe*'s original intro.

Beyond *Survival*: The Food Court vs. the Caravan

Thirty years after Margaret Atwood drew the link between Canadian culture and the survival ethic, *The Globe and Mail* asks writers what the new Canadian paradigm might be. Here is author Will Ferguson's response.

If our history teaches us anything, it is this: Canada has always beaten the odds. We're a land of the lost cause and the dogged second chance.

But what began as a collection of leftovers and letdowns has evolved into something more, something better. An inclusive, confusing place, where everything is in flux and nothing is nailed down.

The image most often used to describe this strange new reality is that of the mosaic. Canada is presented as a grand tapestry of shards, arranged just so, the coloured glass fixed into place. It's an attractive image, one that suggests a larger plan, a greater scheme, into which various disparate pieces somehow fit together like the pieces of a jigsaw puzzle or the panes in a stained-glass window.

But cultures do not exist in isolation. They clash. They collide. They jostle for position. They fall in love. They fall out of love. They feud. They fret—and they influence one another in subtle and profound ways.

A mosaic, after all, is just one step away from becoming a museum piece. It's time we discarded this image once and for all. Just as we've moved beyond mere survival, we must also move beyond the brittle beauty of the mosaic. Canada is not a mosaic. It's a circus tent, a cross-roads caravan of jugglers and blindfolded tightrope walkers that defies both gravity and common sense.

At its best moments, Canada is a market. One filled with jumbled stalls and cultures colliding: chaotic, messy, and very much alive.

At its worst, Canada is a food court. A climate-controlled, hermetically sealed, shopping-mall food court: clean and commodified, with the cultures of the world reduced to fast food.

All that remains to be seen is which version will ultimately emerge as our new national metaphor: the market or the food court, the circus or the shopping mall.

William Shakespeare, Great American

Good morning. I'll wait for you to take a sip of coffee first so you can spit it dramatically across the table when you read this: William Shakespeare was an American.

It's true. Years of research, often late into the night, have led me deep into a conspiracy of global proportions. Simply put, the British swiped Shakespeare. They've taken credit for the Bard of Avon, altering his works to make them more "English" and less American.

Romeo and Juliet? The original title was "Romeo and Debbie." It was set in the Bronx, and contained that now classic scene wherein the young love-struck maiden gazes down from her ivy-clad balcony and utters those wistful, immortal words, "Hey! Who the hell's down there?" To which our bold young swain replies, "It's me! Don't shoot."

Truly, love is a bullet which doth pierce the breast of even the most unlikely people. Only an American could come up with such imagery.

Other examples abound, such as "Bill Shakespeare's Summertime Laugh Fest" (otherwise known as *A Midsummer Night's Dream*), in which the impish Puck concludes, "These mortals, stupid or what?"

Hamlet's soliloquy? The one that's usually read in a plummy British accent: "To be or not to be, that is the question / Whether 'tis nobler in the mind's eye to suffer the slings and arrows of outrageous whatever"? Well, here's the newly restored version, as translated back into American English by none other than Prince Charles himself:

Frankly, the way I see it,
At this point in time, the gist of the matter
Is whether I should just lie down under all these hassles
And let them walk all over me,
Or whether I should call it a day and say, "Hey, I get the
    message,"
And do myself in.

Brilliant. Absolutely brilliant. I think we would all agree that this is a much improved version. You may also recall the king's jester, Yorick, as in Hamlet's "Alas, poor Yorick! I knew him, Horatio, a fellow of infinite jest." Well, his name wasn't Yorick. What kind of name is Yorick? His name was Frankie, and the passage originally went, "Hey guys! It's Frank! Alas, he's not looking so good, if you get my drift." (Other evidence indicates that the jester's name is in fact a misrendering of Richard, as enunciated in the American vernacular, "Yo! Rick!")

But even here, Shakespeare does not rest on his laurels. "Laurels," he says, "who needs them?" He went on to write great works of poetry as well, which include such immortal lines as—and I quote—"Hey nonny, nonny, nonny, hey nonny, nonny, no." What can I say? The man was a genius! There's even evidence that this was originally done in a country-and-western style: "Hey nonny nonny nonny, the wife ran off with my truck."

Not all the mysteries surrounding Shakespeare have been solved, however. There is still the question of Shakespeare's identity itself. The latest theory is that William Shakespeare's plays were not written by William Shakespeare, but by someone else *with the same name.*

Other mysteries remain as well. Extensive academic research has failed to discover the identity of the mysterious woman to whom

Shakespeare mysteriously dedicates his mysterious collection of love sonnets. The note at the start reads simply, and mysteriously, "These poems are dedicated to my great-aunt, Martha P. Braithwaite (*née* Shakespeare) of Newark, New Jersey, 428 Main Street, #102." What are we to make of this? Who is this mysterious Miss "B"? Where does she live? How can we find her? Sadly, these questions may never be answered. Their secret lies hidden in the depths of time.

Shakespeare also wrote for television sitcoms. He was an American after all, and the sitcom is a quintessentially American art form. (Although Shakespeare himself preferred to call them "situational tragi-comedies.")

I've gone through ancient quill-pen television scripts deep in the archives of various studios and have found many examples of Shakespeare's early work in television. For example, originally, at the end of each episode of *Family Ties,* everyone dies. But this caused some casting problems and the studio executives decided that, rather than have everyone die at the end of each episode, they would instead "learn a little bit about themselves and become better people for it."

It's all there. Murders, codpieces, bodkins, messengers, sword fights, long footnoted speeches—you find them throughout the early drafts of such television shows as *Little Harlot on the Prairie, All in the Family That Ends Well,* and, of course, the now classic *I Love Titus Andronicus,* in which Desi Arnaz finally acts on his repeated comedic threats to put out Lucy's eyes and cut off her tongue.

Unfortunately, nervous television executives were worried that Shakespeare's deft touch might be misunderstood by the general public. They ordered the scripts rewritten, the British gentrified what remained, and the English language is poorer for it. Alas, alack. And so on. Hey nonny nonny no.

A Poetic
Interlude

In my Christmas memoir, *Coal Dust Kisses,* I wrote about my quest to create the Ultimate Haiku, incorporating the strict requirements of a 5-7-5 form and a seasonal reference in its purest Zenlike essence. After years of hard work, often late into the night, I came up with ...

SEASONAL REFERENCE
a haiku by Will Ferguson

First, five syllables
And then seven syllables,
And now, back to five.

Elm Street magazine would later invite a select group of literary luminaries—Red Green, Ed the Sock, Seán Cullen, and myself—to commemorate Canada's newly created position of "national poet laureate" with a bit of verse. Reflecting on the solemn dignity of this, I chose as my form the understated elegance of the limerick.

There was a young lad, bureaucratic
Who longed to write forms in iambic.
To Ottawa he went,
With poetic intent,
And now pens verse so dense (in accordance with regulation 27-58, Sub-Section 47a, paragraphs 9 through 11) you can't stand it.

The Kingdom of Lost Causes:

Canadian Travels

On early maps of Canada, Portuguese explorers added the words "very cool, with large trees." And as much as I like our national motto, "From Sea to Sea"—which anyway really should be "From Sea to Sea to Sea" to include the Arctic—I think the Portuguese description would have made a better slogan. Other early descriptive notations made by explorers include "Terrible, With Snow" and "A Land of Fog and Bog," but these don't have quite the same welcoming aspect as "Canada: Very Cool, With Trees."

The following section covers some of my travels in this too-big land of ours, beginning with a couple of longer pieces: a journey by logging camp supply ship up the rainforest coast of Vancouver Island, and another to Friendly Cove in Nootka Sound. These were part of an ongoing project of mine to travel all of Canada's coasts, something that has taken me from the Alaskan panhandle to Newfoundland's Avalon Peninsula and up to the coast of Labrador, and which will eventually (I hope) take me through the Northwest Passage and along Arctic shores as well. My own version of *A Mari Usque Ad Mare ... Ad Mare.*

I've been doing this for more than a decade, though, and it will probably take me ten years or more to complete—at the very least. So I thought I'd submit a preliminary report, as it were, from the west side of Vancouver Island.

Next time, I think I'll tackle a country with less of a coastline. Switzerland, say ...

Voyage
of the *Uchuck*

The rainforests of Canada's Pacific Northwest form a narrow ribbon of land along the outer edge of Vancouver Island. These are temperate rainforests—cool, moist, and exceedingly rare in the world.

The rainfall here is measured in metres. And the towering evergreens of these forests—the cedars, Douglas firs, Western hemlock—follow a two-thousand-year life cycle. A single tree will stand living for a thousand years and then dead for another five hundred (though still teeming with other life) before toppling to the forest floor, where it will take another five hundred years to decay. The forest is heavy with these fallen trees, great spongy whales of biomass. "Nurse logs," as they are known. There are more living organisms in a single rainforest nurse log than there are people on earth. Millipedes, ferns, moulds, moss, fungi—they number in the billions. Moss grows in thick carpets, tendril roots appear, and slugs and salamanders, small birds and burrowing insects, all help churn the mulch. It's one big, earthy compost heap.

In the temperate rainforests, everything grows on everything else, a seeming paradox known as "dynamic equilibrium." They say that these forests are so fertile, so *fecund*, that if you have sex outdoors a Douglas fir will grow in the wet spot. Okay, they don't actually say that. But they should.

This amazing fertility belies the tentative nature of Canada's rainforest, though, because beneath these layers and layers of biomass, the topsoil itself is exceedingly thin. And the self-sustaining cycle of life consuming life—of new trees sprouting from old, of death, decay, rebirth, and regrowth—is ancient, but easily broken. These rainforests, seemingly so vast, so impenetrable, are in fact very fragile. Which is why logging remains such a contentious and scrutinized industry.

I am here neither as a booster for nor a critic of the livelihood of timber. I'm not here to make excuses for the clear-cuts or the erosive effects of the lumber industry, nor am I here to stab a righteous *j'accuse* finger at anyone. I'm drawn here, not by a political agenda, but by a landscape and a coastline unique in Canada. I am searching for the wild. And it isn't hard to find.

I cross the interior of Vancouver Island on a hinterland highway out of Campbell River in a rented car driven with impunity (as you do) across washboard surfaces and muddy shoulders over to the rainforest side of life. And as I wend my way alongside pooled lakes and in and out of hidden valleys, ELK CROSSING signs give way to warnings about logging trucks. Gravelled access roads fan off on either side as amphetamine-powered logging convoys ramrod through like freight trains with failed brakes, their bundles of pick-up-stick logs bouncing wildly.

It's a rugged, defiant landscape, one of dead-drop cliffs and knife-edge peaks, of sudden unexpected vistas. And the road is "double yellow" most of the way, too; there are very few of the dotted Morse-code messages that allow passing. Every corner is blind, each twist of asphalt a gamble.

At one point I pull over to stretch my legs and crick my neck—to escape that odd bubble-like existence that comes with being inside a car—and as I walk down to a sandbar littered with driftwood for a scenic pee a black bear ambles by, all shoulders and rump, not ten feet from where I'm standing, the speed of my urination increasing markedly as he passes. I wait a very long time to exhale.

Now, I've had my share of what are euphemistically dubbed "wildlife encounters." I was almost mugged by a gang of moose at L'Anse aux Meadows on the northern tip of Newfoundland. (It was rutting season, and the dominant male thought I was eyein' one of his wimmin. You can see much the same behaviour at any country-and-western bar.) I've had encounters with bears before—though never with quite the proximity and blasé insouciance of the one that ambled past me on the road to Gold River—but nothing prepares you for the shadows that slink through the forests of Vancouver Island.

When you reach Lady Falls you have entered the rainy leeward side of the Island, where mossy branches are draped in green beards. The air feels heavier, moister—and this climatic divide, running straight down the spine of Vancouver Island, is almost tangible; I'm sure you could chart it in the deepening shades of green that appear.

Whereas on the eastern side Douglas firs predominate, on the Pacific side it's Western hemlock, with stately red cedars standing apart and slightly aloof. Lady Falls, caught in the middle, has both trees equally entrenched. I park beside the road and follow a hiking trail up through the dusk, a leg-straining path that leads to a darkening view of falling water. The falls tumble down in a mist of white noise, a great deep breath of cool water. Night is descending.

As I retrace my steps I hear—*something*. A muffled noise behind me. When I turn around—the noise stops. I snatch up a thick stick, hit it hard against a tree, but the sodden wood has the texture of Camembert and the stick falls apart when it hits, making only a dull wet thud. Silence. I walk more quickly now—so quick it might better be described as "fleeing"—and it's only when I get back to the bottom of the trail that I notice the warnings Parks Canada has posted. Cougars have been sighted along this path—*today*.

Cougar. Mountain lion. Puma. A large carnivorous cat by any other name would be as skin-crawlingly terrifying. I grew up in a village on the edge of the boreal forest and I'm not easily spooked by noises in the underbrush, but this was no imaginary boogeyman. This *was* the boogeyman.

Vancouver Island is home to the highest concentration of cougars in the world. It also, not coincidentally, has the highest number of attacks on humans, many of them fatal. Cougars inhabit Vancouver Island the way ghosts inhabit our subconscious, lying in wait, purring …

Cougars kill people. They pounce. They attack—in a very unsportsmanlike fashion, it must be said—from behind, sinking in their teeth and then dragging their prey into the bush to be gnawed upon at their leisure. Never mind that you're in more danger of dying from drinking bad milk than from being attacked by a cougar—milk doesn't rip your flesh from your bones before it kills you. Only a few years ago, a cougar was caught and tranquillized in the parkade of Victoria's Empress Hotel. *"Spot of tea with your crumpets and bloodshed?"* On Vancouver Island, the wild is always near.

I drive away, heart racing, tires all but squealing, back onto the road to Gold River, where the highway—both symbolically and physically—comes to an end. Gold River is a "planned community," called out of the wilderness like a small-scale version of Brasilia or Canberra. It's a town that lives and dies on the price of lumber, which gives it a fatalistic boom-and-bust air, but the streets are leafy and well-wooded and the mountains are at your back door. Imagine a cozy suburb dropped into a primal forest and you have an idea of both the incongruity and the appeal of Gold River.

At the Ridgeway Motor Inn Café, truck drivers and loggers are gathered around a cabal of coffee cups, discussing the mill closure and rumours of its resurrection. Casually, and just in passing, you understand, I bring up the subject of, oh, cougars and such. "Those warning signs they post, those aren't serious, right?"

Looks are exchanged. "Listen, friend," says one of the men from beneath the brim of a well-worn cap. "You're in cougar capital. You see a warning sign, you take it serious. Up in Port Alice, cougar chased down a tugboat captain riding his bicycle down to the dock. Cat outran him, took him down. Was mauling the guy good, had its teeth right in him, was chewing off the poor bugger's face, would'a killed him too, if a mill worker hadn't driven by. The worker had to pound the cat with his tool chest before it would let go. And right here—in Gold River—a cougar pulled a Mountie off his horse."

A Mountie? *Off his horse?* Jaysus.

"But you'll be fine," the man beside him assures me. "Just don't go walking along trails alone. Or at dusk."

The others agreed. "Avoid areas with lots of water, as well, where the younger males hang out."

Doing a quick tally, I realize that during the hike to Lady Falls I was (a) alone, (b) hiking, (c) at dusk, deep in the forest, where (d) there was lots of water and (e) a great bloody warning sign posted and (f) I probably deserved (g) to die.

So I bring up the noise ha ha I heard in the woods earlier. I was so scared ha ha—and you're going to find this just as funny as I did—that for a moment I actually thought I was being stalked by a cougar ha ha.

But instead of ringing with hearty laughter, the room goes deathly still.

"That was a cougar all right."

I swallow. "And if I encounter one ..." My voice is sounding oddly distant.

The advice comes in a flurry: "Stand tall. Be brave. Fight back. Look right at him. But not, you know, *at* him. Don't make eye contact—that's considered a threat. At the same time, whatever you do, don't turn your back on him, not for a second! Cougars always come at you from behind. They'll grab hold of the scruff of your neck and try to break your spinal cord. Get away, but don't run, because that'll trigger a chase response. Try to look big, but don't go making noise with a stick or anything stupid like that, and"—here was the single most ridiculous tidbit—"whatever you do, *don't show any fear.*" Sure. I'm facing a puma in the middle of the woods and I'm going to maintain my suave sense of sang-froid. All I can say is, let's hope cougars are repelled by the scent of human urine, because wetting my pants as I run shrieking like a little girl constitutes pretty much the only defence I have.

I thank them for their advice, head up to my room, and deadbolt the door—just in case, you know, the cougars up here have somehow evolved thumbs.

Gold River is twelve/thirteen/fourteen kilometres and/or miles from the headwaters of Nootka Sound. It depends entirely on whom you ask. If you want to start an argument in any coffee shop in Gold River, just wonder aloud how far it is to the dock; the conversation will quickly descend into factions, with some insisting it's thirteen kilometres, others that it is "absolutely" fourteen, others that it is "no more" than twelve, and still others speaking in miles and even feet.

The road south from Gold River runs alongside a dramatic river-cut canyon, past waterfalls that waft water across the road, misting the windshield.

Hitching a ride with me is Tom Pater, the "district area representative" for the western swath of the Island. He's on his way back to Kyuquot. During the night the motel manager had slipped a note under my door that read "Tom needs a ride to the dock. Can you take him?" No last name, just Tom.

Tom is a pleasant fellow, soft-spoken, slightly weathered. He tells me his surname right up front. When we arrive at water's edge, the MV *Uchuck III* is already docked and waiting as the crew hurries about moving the last of the provisions on board. The *Uchuck* is a narrow ship, and smaller than I expected, with a trident of poles that rise up like masts. These are the winches and derricks used for swinging pallets of supplies from dock to shore.

Alberto Girotto comes out to greet us. "Come aboard, I'll introduce you to the crew." Alberto is the *Uchuck*'s land-based operations manager, meaning he stays on shore and juggles logistics. He's young, fast-talking, and quick-walking. I have to scurry to keep up as he strides along the gangplank.

Wooden crates. Rows of oil barrels. Loose coils of rope. "Ship was built in World War II," says Alberto. "A minesweeper." The *Uchuck* has since been refitted to carry cargo, but signs of her wartime origins are evident in the superfluous strength of her hull—two inches of solid wood on a one-inch liner, bolted onto oak frames, practically armoured—and in the thickness of her porthole glass. Alberto taps it with a knuckle as he passes. "Same up in the wheelhouse. Almost bulletproof." The glass was meant to withstand the type of blasts a minesweeper might stir up and it makes me feel very secure.

Alberto is co-owner of the *Uchuck,* along with Captain Fred Mather and Fred's son Sean. "We're a working freighter, but we take passengers as well." *Walk-on freight,* as it's known. "We'll take forestry workers, fishermen, even recreational kayakers—and their kayaks. We lower 'em into the water with the derrick, with the kayakers sitting right there in their kayaks."

Today's run will take us to the far side of the Island, to the remote community of Kyuquot, far beyond the reach of roads. I practise pronouncing the name, "kah-YU-cut," so that it'll roll off my tongue in a suitably smooth fashion. It feels as though I'm running away to sea.

In quick succession and with a flurry of handshakes, Alberto introduces me to the rest of the crew: the chief engineer, the deckhand, the first mate, and Donna the cook. "Captain's up in the wheelhouse," Alberto says. "Make sure you stop in and say hi. He'd love to talk to you." (*See:* irony, unintentional uses of.)

"I definitely will," I say, imagining a salty sea-dog character who peppers his vocabulary with phrases like "Thar she blows" and "Aye, she's a wild sea tonight."

Alberto steps back onto the dock as the ropes are cast. The horn blares, a loud reverberating trumpet call announcing our departure, and the *Uchuck* slides free. I stand on the upper deck, fists on hip and face full of wind, a nautical, sun-creased look in my eyes. I can feel the low throb of the engines through the deck and I catch a manly whiff of diesel. There's a snap in the air, and as my jacket billows like a sail, I think, *"This is the life."*

The *Uchuck* follows the long, steep-sided fjord of Muchalat Inlet, where the rainforests create a curtain of green along the water. The trees here grow on impossibly steep angles—verticals rising out of verticals. A cumulous mist rolls down, filling the valleys, catching the early morning light. We leave a shimmering trail of silver in our wake.

I climb the stairs to the wheelhouse to speak with Fred Mather, a square-jawed, solid-looking man. Walking in uninvited, as is my style, I attempt to strike up a salty, sea-dog, nautical-type conversation. "So what does this do?" I say, placing a hand on a brass sea-dog-type piece of nautical equipment.

"Don't touch the brass. You touched the brass. Don't do that." Then, under his breath: "Now I'll have to polish it." Polishing brass is, I gather in my indubitable journalistic way, high on the list of duties that sea captains like to avoid. I take note: *Touching of brass. Best to avoid.*

The wheelhouse of the *Uchuck* is an elegant arrangement of bronze and mahogany, with round portholes and smooth wooden panels. The equipment, raided from older decommissioned ships, gives the *Uchuck* a dash of style. Not bad for a working freighter.

"So," I say, leaning in, pen poised over notepad, accuracy—as always—of paramount concern. "Is this a boat or a ship?"

"You're touching the brass again," he says.

"Ooops, sorry." I suspect Captain Fred isn't really listening to me—you'd almost think he had better things to do. "So," I say. "Ever run into a *Perfect Storm*–type wave? The kind that could flip a boat like this upside down?"

"Ship," he says. "It's a ship. And no, when the swells get too high we tie her up and hide. The Outer Passage especially, it gets dangerous. Groundswells can reach fourteen metres with ten-metre waves on top. We don't take any unnecessary risks."

"But c'mon. Weren't you ever tempted to hit full throttle and run right up through it instead, yelling '*Aarrgrh!!*' like they do in the movies?"

"No."

Okay, then.

I hang around the wheelhouse for a while, mainly because the view is so expansive up here, and Captain Mather eventually warms to

my presence—or at least comes to tolerate it. His guard lowers, ever
so slightly.

"You want to know the best thing about this job?" he says,
addressing a question I haven't technically asked. "It's always different.
It seems the same, but every stop, every day, every trip is different. On
some it's blowing rain, others are misted over. Sometimes the sun is
out, shining on the water …" He looks at the landscape sliding toward
him, at the valleys that open onto water. "Every day is different." And
the name *Uchuck,* he reminds me, is from a Native word meaning
"healing water."

Later, as we thread our way through a maze of smaller islets,
some little more than tufts of trees above the waterline, a scattering of
seabirds lifts off, taking wing as the sun breaks through. It's all one can
do not to break into applause.

The *Uchuck* stops at logging camps and fish farms along the
way, where men with hair gloriously uncombed and jeans glazed in
dirt come down to greet us. They look like castaways stumbling out
of the woods: workers on the edge of nowhere, breathing clean air,
grinning wide. Ropes are thrown to shore. The ship bumps up to
the dock, supplies are unloaded. Tie up, cast off: a catch-and-release
ritual played out at each stop. Barrels of fuel and flats of beer are
unloaded, and empty containers are swung up and onto the deck in
return. At one point, a mud-spattered all-terrain vehicle in need of
repair is hoisted on board in one smooth motion. If you ever need a
mattress moved to a second-floor apartment, these are the guys you
want to call.

I spot black bears moving along the tide line at one point, just
a desperate stone's throw from where the men are unloading. When
I point them out to Shayne, the *Uchuck*'s deckhand, he remains
unperturbed.

"Up here, bears are like racoons," he says. "More a nuisance than
anything."

Except, of course, that no suburban dweller ever has to worry
about being mauled and left for dead by a racoon.

Shayne shrugs. "Okay, so they're a little more dangerous than racoons."

We pass the alluvial fan of the Tsowwin River on one side and the windy notch of Blowhole Bay on the other, where a chink in the mountains funnels dangerous winds. Planes have been sucked down here, lives lost. Ahead, at the end of the inlet, we can see the tumble-down sawmill community of Tahsis, wedged in at the headwaters. We turn and enter an even narrower channel along the north end of Nootka Island—it feels as if we're scraping either side—and the town of Tahsis, with its rum and fisticuffs reputation, slips out of view.

High cliffs give way to an isolated dock at Ceepeecee. The name sounds as though it's derived from a Native word, but in fact, says Tom Pater, "it's a transliteration of CPC: the Canadian Packing Corporation. There was a sardine-packing plant here back in the 1920s. There hasn't been a fish plant at Ceepeecee for years, but the name has remained."

From Ceepeecee, we skirt the mouth of Zeballos Inlet, where a historic gold-mining town lies tucked out of sight. And suddenly, manicured lawns and clean white buildings, wildly out of place, mark a religious retreat at Esperanza. A good choice of locale, that. God must seem to hang on every breath of mist out here.

We stop in at a fish farm anchored in an inlet—a floating aquatic ranch, with fences and pens—and then later pass an entire colony of sea otters, dozens of the creatures, floating free, bellies up. They consider us with a look of collective bemusement as we pass. Prized for their pelts, sea otters were once hunted to extinction along the B.C. coast, but they've since been reintroduced, and though still rare, are surprisingly common along the *Uchuck*'s route. Otters have always struck me as the teenage slackers of the animal kingdom. Maybe it's the couch-potato posture, but I can perfectly imagine a small television perched on their tummies, bags of Doritos on hand.

Donna the cook, the only female member of the *Uchuck*'s crew, is a former bank teller from twee Victoria. She's been with the *Uchuck*, full-time now, for four years. She also controls the coffee pot, which means I spend a good part of the day in her vicinity.

"I was worried at first," she says, about signing up as cook, "because I'd never really worked with guys before. And these aren't just guys," she adds with a laugh. "They're *guy* guys. The first couple of months they were polite and everything, having a woman around. But that didn't last long."

"The crew gets along well?"

"They get along better than bank tellers, I can tell you. The guys here pull pranks on each other all the time, but it's funny, there's this unwritten code: You never mess with someone's coffee, their food, or their bed."

"No short sheets in the bunks or salt in the sugar bowl?"

"God no!"

Shayne walks through just then, coffee cup in hand. "Donna is the one in charge around here," he says, stealing something from the pantry. "Not Fred."

"Don't listen to him," she says. "He's just the dock dork."

"Deckhand," he says, calling back over his shoulder. "Correct term is deckhand."

She laughs. "Whatever you say, Poopsie!"

"Shayne!" he yells. "The name is Shayne."

Donna, chatty and affable, has a personality very unlike the Captain's, yet she describes the allure of the journey in almost identical terms.

"The voyage is always the same—but different. Every time. When the sun is out and the water is calm, it's beautiful. When it's stormy, there's a beauty to it too. It's like a different landscape each time, depending on the weather and the season." Outside, the water is shot through with splinters of silver. "Did I mention," she says, more to herself than anyone, "did I mention I once worked in a bank?" It's almost as though she's trying to remember a past life, and I suppose in a sense she is.

We are entering an alley of quick-running currents, a "continuous surge" known as the Rolling Roadstead. It is here that the *Uchuck*, long and narrow and prone to rocking, earns its stormy-weather nickname "the Upchuck." Donna closes her cupboards and (literally) battens down the hatches as the ship begins to bob like a cork in a bathtub.

Ridges of stone, low along the water, create cross-hatched currents and boiling waves, and the sea is churning like a washing machine set on agitate. The entire Pacific Ocean is behind these waves, pushing them into the coast. Long swells, sudden drops—they rise and fall in a queasy procession, creating a drunken swagger in one's steps, a lurching in one's stomach. It's as gentle, and as nauseating, as a lullaby that goes on too long.

"When the swells get too high," says Fred when I stagger in, "it's actually easier to swing all the way out, into open ocean, rather than follow the shore."

"And today?" I ask, gills green, stomach turning.

"Not too bad. I've seen worse."

I stumble back down the stairs, cling to a table. At Rugged Point, the Rolling Roadstead ends, and we angle inward, past Union Island, an exposed outcrop of stunted spruce trees.

"Natural bonsai," says Tom, as I join him on deck. He seems to have surfed out the Roadstead with nary a hiccup.

"Windswept," I say.

But windswept doesn't begin to describe Union Island. "Wind-tormented" would be more accurate. *Wind-punished.* The pines are twisted in near agony and the bedrock beneath them looks like bone rubbed bare. "The trees here have bark like sheet metal," Tom says approvingly. "In winter, the prevailing southeasterlies blast through. We get six or seven hurricanes a winter, with gale-force winds."

Past Union Island, we finally enter Kyuquot Channel, and the winds become muted. The *Uchuck* makes a final call at the Chamiss Bay logging camp. The day is bleeding away, the sun is swollen and red. A sky the colour of red wine. Islands transubstantiating into silhouettes.

And then …

On a small outcrop a house appears, perched on a nub of rock. Another island comes into view, another house, then another. And as we slip through a narrow strait and enter the leeward side of a large island: lights on either side. We have reached the clustered archipelago of Kyuquot, population 349 (350 now that Tom is back). It feels like a village on the edge of the map, at the end of the world. Mowachaht homes are clustered together on reserve land, with the rest of the community scattered across nine different islands, Walter Island being the largest. Kyuquot is a "Venice of the backwoods," where salt-water channels are the roads and the buoyed traffic signals are for boats, not cars.

The *Uchuck* docks and the walk-on freight disembarks, filing out along shell-strewn planks and past the village's General Store/Post Office, which is balanced above the water. Kyuquot is a village built largely on stilts. Stilts and piers and jerry-rigged, ad hoc docks, many of which seem to be held together only by binder twine and a cavalier disregard for the laws of gravity. They create a cat's cradle along the shore. It's a wonderfully ramshackle, arbitrary sort of place, with most of the homes little more than cabins—some well-kept and tidy, others just shacks, collapsing inward on themselves in slow motion, soft and soggy.

"We'll run you over to the other side," Captain Mather tells the passengers, and we drag our rucksacks down wobbly stairs and then onto a flat-bottomed boat that *putt-putts* across to the Mowachaht side of the strait. On the other shore, we climb more rickety stairs to a spacious home—"the B&B" as Mather calls it—where we'll be spending the night.

Having divided up the rooms and exchanged the usual pleasant-ries, most of the passengers crawl off to bed. But some of us are still restless and a bit stir-crazy after the long boat ride, so we walk back down to the dock instead to watch the last streaks of sunset.

I head off alone, following a rutted muddy path behind our B&B and emerging at the Kyuquot schoolyard. Night is coming in from all sides, but the echoing sounds of volleyballs—serve, set, and spike—are ringing inside the gymnasium. Two Mowachaht girls, junior high students bored with volleyball, are sitting on the swing set outside, kicking at gravel. They are (begrudgingly) taking care of their cousin, a round-cheeked six-month-old with wondrous big eyes and a marvellously runny nose. When I ask them if there's a store nearby, or someplace I can get a bite, one of them points to a second trail. "Down on the Rez, sure. Store's open still."

"It's not," says her friend.

A sullen silence in lieu of argument passes between them, and then the first girl says to me, "Store's open late tonight."

"It's not."

I descend through the falling dark into the reserve, and sure enough, the store is closed. It seems to be in someone's house and I consider pounding on the back door, but I'm not sure what the protocol is in such cases, so I forgo munchies and wander about a bit instead. Communal dogs everywhere. Kids hanging out. Glowing squares of light. Muffled laughter, faint voices. *What a great place to call home.* Across the water from me, the *Uchuck* is asleep, pulled in and tethered up snugly for the night. Pinpoints of light glide past: a boat, moving between buoys. Stars are spilling out from behind the moon.

If God is ever going to tap you on the shoulder and say, "Well, what do you think?," this would be the time. The tap on the shoulder never comes though, and I trudge back up to the schoolyard instead.

"Closed," I say, as I pass the girls, still sitting listlessly on the swings.

"Told you."

Morning comes far too soon. Shivering with yawns, bleary of eye and stale of breath, we lug our bags back down to the pier and are ferried back across to Walter Island where the *Uchuck* is waiting, engines rumbling, ropes taut, eager to get moving. But I'm jumping ship here at Kyuquot.

During the journey out Tom Pater had suggested I take the mail plane back instead, giving me another day in Kyuquot. "I'll talk to the pilot and see if you can't hitch a ride back to Gold River" is how Tom put it. Inveterate freeloader that I am, how can I resist? Thumb a ride with a pontooned seaplane? That's the sort of thing that gets you a spot in the Hitchhiker's Hall of Fame.

I get a hug from Donna and he-man handshakes from the crew and I wave from the dock as the *Uchuck* eases away. The ship squeezes through Kyuquot Narrows and then disappears into that endless arrangement of island and sea ...

From the pier, I walk into a sleeping community only now waking up. Smoke trickles from stovepipes, wood-burning breakfasts on a slow simmer from the smell of it. Homes are strung along the edge of Walter Island like laundry on a line, and paint-peeling fishing boats lie overturned on the shore.

Tom has invited me to drop by for tea, but when I find his cabin the lights are still out and no smoke is uncurling from the stovepipe, so I tiptoe away—and as I do, a bald eagle drifts by, wings wide, directly across the path. Had I reached out, I could have run a hand along it as it passed. The eagle reels away, low across the water, and then arcs up into the sky. I lose it in the sun.

Inspired, I decide to walk the length of Walter Island, out to the very tip, to the Narrows. Pointing myself in the general direction, I follow a path behind the buildings, one that weaves through stands of cedar trees, thick spills of green, great splays of fern. The path is layered with cedar needles, and the forest floor feels spongy underfoot.

A salad of rainforest smells. Peaty aromas, ripe with promise. I am especially happy to discover that the pathway is draped with slugs. Slugs fascinate me, existing as they do somewhere between solid and liquid. The slow momentum, the nebulous shifting mass. Poke one gently with your finger and it will harrumph grumpily within its mucous membrane, phlegmatic in every sense of the word.

Birdsong in the trees above. The shrill cries and scolding replies. The cough of crows, the cackled laugh of ravens. If sea otters are the couch potatoes of the animal kingdom, birds are the chatterboxes, filling the air with aviary gossip and endless exclamations points. *"She didn't! She didn't?! She did she did she did! She did she did she did!"*

The path I'm following runs past jumbled derelict fishing shacks and old piers that are decaying slowly, inevitably. In Kyuquot, the buildings are either rainforest pliant or driftwood dry. Mossy and fern-festooned, they aren't so much homes as nurse logs inhabited by humans. Moss grows thick as peach fuzz on the window frames, and the doors rot from the bottom up.

Past an old schoolyard scattered with rusted barrels and tarpaulins, the forest ends and the shore appears. I follow a spear of stone down to the end of Walter Island. Waves, stewed with seaweed, rise and fall. Driftwood lies jumbled like bleached bones. And, coming in across scattered islands: the scent of open ocean.

As I pick my way along the shore a boat plows past, pushing a swell of water in front of it like dough before a roller. A woman on board waves at me, pointing down. "Charlie!" she shouts.

Sure enough. There she is.

I'd almost tripped over her without realizing. Miss Charlie, the most famous seal in Kyuquot, sunning herself among the lichen-stained rocks of a shallow pool. She squints up at me, whiskers drooping, barely able to muster the strength to open one eye. Then, with a sigh, she rolls over, slips away. I follow her raindrop shape under the water to where she resurfaces farther along the shore. She finds another sun-warmed pocket of water to loll in awhile and I leave her to her leisure, turning back, retracing my steps past the old schoolhouse and sawmill to the General Store. The path runs past a shed where a very determined young boy has painted, in large letters: NO GIRLS ALLOWED! A clubhouse of some sort, I suppose. No girls, indeed! Then, beneath that, in smaller letters: *except Kirsten.*

And, I'm assuming, Charlie.

Tom is awake and the kettle is on when I stop by his pleasantly mildewy home. He introduces me to Susan Karya, who has dropped in as well. The daughter of a Finnish fisherman, she has a healthy

Scandinavian look about her. "I saw you at the Narrows," she says with a wide smile. "That was me on the boat."

"It was Susan's father, Esko, who found Charlie," Tom says as he pours the tea. "Charlie's like the neighbourhood dog. She makes her rounds and people give her fish. She's very contented. Loves octopus."

"To play with?"

"To eat."

This is a land where the racoons are bears and the neighbourhood dog eats octopus.

"Charlie's a harbour seal," says Susan. "Dad rescued her. She was an orphaned pup. Mom raised her in a bathtub. Charlie grew up with us. I remember Dad taking her away to return her to nature. It was very sad. He took Charlie way, way, way out into open sea, and said goodbye … She was waiting for Dad when he got home. She beat the boat back."

Charlie will be turning forty soon, which is old for a seal. She's slowing down. Often, she'll simply ride the tide up the shore and then allow the water to slip away from under her. Then she'll bask there, half-asleep in the warmth, until the tide comes back in and rolls her free.

"Still," says Susan with a laugh. "Every year, come mating season, the urges return and she begins pining for Dad. Oh, she's in love with him all right! It's very sweet. She'll follow him around, batting her big brown eyes at him. Poor Dad, he's really embarrassed by it."

A sad tale of unrequited love, that one. *The old man and the seal*, as it were.

"When we were children, our parents would take Charlie with us on picnics, and she would swim with us. We would hold onto her and she would tow us through the water. Then she'd get tired and flop up on shore and Mom would feed her milk from a bottle." Susan laughs at the memory of it. "Mom would even warm the milk up first, like you would for a baby. Then she and Mom would have a little nap together. She's really cute when she's dry and fluffy. Charlie, not Mom." Another easy smile, another laugh.

When the Kyuquot whaling station closed in the 1920s, many of the Norwegian and Finnish workers employed there stayed on. Whalers became fishermen and a small outpost of Scandinavia took shape on Walters Island, once the traditional wintering home of the Mowachaht people, who now live across the strait. These two communities— Scandinavian and Native—together form the archipelago village of Kyuquot. It's a village that operates by its own unstated rules, to its own rhythms, its own internal clock. "Kyuquot is the closest you will ever come to a working anarchy," says Tom.

The hundred or so people living on Walter Island, commercial fishermen and their families mainly, get along well with their Mowachaht neighbours on the mainland, I'm told. Mainland?

"Where you stayed last night."

"By the school?" I say. "I thought I was on an island."

"Well, technically, yes—you were on *Vancouver* Island. Which we refer to as the mainland."

I swallow. Once again I'd been walking along trails, alone, at dusk. "Any, um, cougars?" I ask.

Tom nods. "The woods are full of them, especially this time of year. The young males are now on their own, hungry, confused. They haven't established their territories yet, they're not sure what's prey and what isn't. In '94—"

"Ninety-two," Susan says quietly. She already knows what Tom is going to say.

"A little boy was killed by a cougar, taken right in the schoolyard. It was evening, he was playing with his friends. There was an event going on in the gym. Adults everywhere. The school caretaker ran out, killed the cat right there, but it was too late." Tom looks into his cup of tea. "It was rough on the whole community."

I think about my recent walkabout on Walter Island, deep in the forest. "But on the islands over here, on this side. It's safe, right?"

Tom leans in and says three words I do not particularly want to hear: "Cougars can swim."

That afternoon, Tom takes me on a hike to the back of Walter Island, to that even wilder, uninhabited Pacific side, and as I flail about in the underbrush he strides on ahead with a surefootedness that borders on bravado. Blowdowns have toppled this way and that, adding sharp diagonals to a forest of verticals. Obstacle after obstacle on the trail. Tom points out clustered colours in the bushes as we pass—huckleberries, winterberries, salmonberries—the very names burst with flavour.

We reach a rocky ledge on the far side of the island, and in front of us the Pacific Ocean curves into the distance like a giant convex lens. As we step out of the shelter of the forest, the wind knocks us back on our heels. Tom gestures to a twisted ladder of metal lying to one side, bent now like origami. "BC Hydro," he says. "They set up a tower to test wind velocity, to see if this island would warrant a generator."

The buckled metal says it all.

"*Kyuquot.* The name means 'place of many winds.' And we get wind from every direction."

It's just not commercial wind, is all. At Kyuquot the gusts constantly shift, they buffet you this way and that, they roar in then suddenly die down. Not steady enough for power generators, not predicable enough for development. There is no money in these winds. There is only wind.

The wealth here is not to be found in the air; it lies lower, at the bottom of escarpments like the one we're standing on, in the border between land and sea.

"This region was the Fort Knox of the Pacific Coast," Tom tells me. "All along here you'll find *dentalia*—it's a small, tooth-shaped shell. Among the First Nations, the shells acted as currency. This area was one of the main sources, and the people here were very wealthy. The dentalia from Kyuquot was passed from nation to nation, village to village, up and down the coast, all the way to California—and even inland, across the plains, as far as Arizona. You'll still see it used on the ceremonial dress down there, as a way of 'wearing one's wealth.'"

Tom turns his head, hears something in the wind. "Mail plane's coming," he says. "We better get back."

In by sea, out by air. Pontoons slapping across the waves, and then— lifting off, into air. I'm wedged in with the mailbags, looking out the window as the islands of Kyuquot recede.

The pilot, and president of Air Nootka, is a man by the name of Grant Howatt, and he handles his Cessna 180 with the sort of easy confidence you want in a pilot. Grant runs scheduled mail runs to Kyuquot, and flies Native band leaders, sport fishermen, and hunters in and out. If there is anyplace else on earth he'd rather be, it doesn't show.

Below us, along the shore, black bears amble about in their big-bummed way; we're low enough to see the waddle and sway of their hips. Whitecaps are rolling in along empty beaches. A landscape that rises straight out of the ocean, Atlantis in reverse. Flying along it is like tracing the contours of a map. And I think to myself: *This is where my country begins.*

"Keep your eyes open for whales," Grant shouts as we follow the coast of Vancouver Island back toward Gold River.

But I see something even better than whales. It's the *Uchuck* herself, cutting across the waters of Nootka Sound, plying her trade, heading for home.

"The Wind
from All Sides"

This is the story of stolen bones and Spanish gardens, of northern conquistadors and the clash of empires. But most of all, this is the story of a wooded cove on a rainforest island, deep within the fjord of another, larger, island. Boxes within boxes. This is the story of a specific place: Yuquot cove, on Nootka Island, in Nootka Sound, Vancouver Island.

A small hook of land, Yuquot was labelled on imperial maps as "Friendly Cove," a name that would take on unintentionally ironic overtones when it became both the epicentre and flashpoint of an international geopolitical power struggle. And yet—Yuquot is barely known today.

Perhaps it has to do with the real estate of it—*location, location, location,* as they say—out here on the far side of the Island. The Pacific Northwest was one of the last major coastlines in the world to be charted by Europeans, and the first to arrive was Captain James Cook, who sailed into the deep cleft of Nootka Sound in 1778 with his ships the *Discovery* and *Resolution,* unaware that he and his men were entering the soggy embrace of what was in fact a vast island. Among Cook's crew was a young midshipman named George Vancouver, who would later chart the coast of the larger island in meticulous detail, realize it was water all the way 'round, and eventually give his name to this great nurse log moored off the continental coast. But we're getting ahead of our story ...

Captain Cook was the greatest explorer of his day, and this would be his last hurrah. Called out of retirement by the King Himself, Cook was charged with unravelling a Northwest Passage through the Arctic islands, a prized and fabled shortcut to Asia. Unlike previous attempts, however, Cook decided to come at it from the other side, the Pacific side, through the back door so to speak.

On his previous journeys of discovery, Cook had racked up an impressive list of firsts: he'd discovered the Hawaiian Islands, and charted the eastern shores of Australia—claiming it in its entirety for Britain. (You gotta love explorers. *"By raising this flag, I hereby claim ownership of this entire continent!"* A bit like a flea claiming the elephant it happens to land upon.) Cook had circled New Zealand and crossed the Antarctic Circle, had dodged Maori arrows and icebergs. But the Pacific Northwest proved a greater challenge than even he'd expected, and he came limping into Nootka Sound in a less than heroic fashion, on board storm-damaged ships and in search of safe harbour. A quiet corner where he could repair his masts before pushing on. He found much more.

A flotilla of hardwood canoes surrounded the British ships. Instead of being attacked, though, Cook and his men were welcomed by Chief Maquinna and the Mowachaht with pageantry and chanted songs. Cook's men replied with some tunes on a French horn and a couple of jigs, and when Cook gestured ahead and asked what this land was called, he was told *"Nutka itchme"* ("Go around that way"). From which came the name Nootka, a misunderstanding on par with Cook's earlier and apocryphal naming of the kangaroo—from an Australian Aboriginal phrase meaning "I don't understand."

The Mowachaht at Yuquot, the small cove whose name means "wind from all sides," were part of a larger network of political alliances and Native trade routes. They were more than able to accommodate Captain Cook and his men. Indeed, the Pacific Northwest was the most culturally and linguistically complex area in all of North America; in Nootka Sound alone there were fifteen distinct cultural groups, each with their own lineage, territory, clans, and castes—as well as a highly developed sense of ownership. When Cook sent his men out to cut grass for the goats on board, they soon found out, as Cook dryly noted in his journal, that "there was not a blade of grass that had not a separated owner."

Nor was it simply land or property that was strictly controlled. Water routes, fishing sites, even certain songs and styles of clothing were owned by specific people. It was a hierarchical society, with the *taises* ("hereditary chiefs") at the top, *taiscatlati* ("nobility") and *meschimes* ("commoners") below, and slaves at the bottom. Even within the chieftain class there were at least three separate rankings, plus shamans, who could heal the sick and predict the future, master carvers (who formed a separate subclass of their own), and finally, the elite whalers. The whalers were more a secret society than a social class, semi-mystical, somewhat haughty, held in awe. The shamans might call the whales closer to shore, but it was the whalers who headed out onto open seas. In canoes. To hunt whales.

The mind boggles. The whalers of Nootka chased down humpbacks and grey whales alike, spearing them first with toggle-headed harpoons that trailed sealskin buoys. The whalers would follow these buoys, paddling hard, avoiding the thrash of the tail, and when the wounded whale resurfaced they'd be waiting, spearing it again and again until the whale grew too tired to dive. One of the hunters would then swim across and sever the whale's tail tendons. A lance would end it, and another band of swimmers, working quickly, would sew the mouth shut to keep the whale's body afloat. (If it filled with seawater, it would sink.) Towed back to shore, where a celebration awaited, the whale would be carved up, the blubber boiled, and the oil skimmed.

People willing to pursue whales on open sea in wooden canoes aren't easily intimidated. Cook paid for every blade of grass. And while the captain repaired the *Resolution*'s foremast with Douglas fir, a lively trade developed between his men and Maquinna's: iron and brass, knives and chisels, even metal buttons and nails—all for sea otter pelts.

Sea otters are sociable animals, often floating together in "rafts" of a hundred or more, and unlike other sea mammals, they have no insulating layer of blubber. To stay warm and waterproof they rely instead on the sheer thickness of their fur. It's the thickest, most luxuriant fur of any mammal—and the English sailed away with a wealth of pelts in the hold. These would later be sold for a fortune when Cook's men reached Asia. Cook himself never made it, though. Having failed to find a Pacific entrance to the Arctic, he turned his ships south, for the sunnier climes of Hawaii, where he was later chopped down—and then chopped up—by disgruntled islanders. It was one of the hazards of the job.

No matter. Word was out, and ships began to flood in, jostling for position in Nootka Sound. Pelts purchased with $100 in trade goods at Nootka Sound could be resold for $8000, a hefty markup that, and one that triggered a full-scale, sea-borne stampede. Nor was it only fur that was flying. Logging was soon underway, with the first trees shipped to China as early as 1786—a date that marks the start of the logging export industry in what would one day become British Columbia.

This was Canada's "Pacific First Contact," and it's important to note that it was the Europeans who were the nomads. The First Nations were well-rooted, moving between summer and winter villages in what amounted to "pre-fab" homes: longhouses with planks that could be removed from their frames and then reassembled elsewhere. The Europeans, on other hand, had—quite literally—been blown in. The ships that followed Cook were referred to by the First Nations as "floating islands" and their captains as *"tiyee awinna"* ("travelling chiefs"). The whites themselves were referred to as "people lost at sea."

With Great Britain, Russia, and even the young upstart American republic making competing claims to Nootka Sound and Friendly Cove, the Spanish Empire decided to reassert its authority, sending warships north to deal with these interlopers from other nations trespassing on what Spain considered its territory. This was "their" coast after all, from Mexico to Alaska.

Two American vessels and a British ship flying a Portuguese flag of convenience were moored in the bay. The Spanish promptly seized them, stripping them bare and towing two of them back to California as "legal prizes." More ships kept arriving, though, including one with Chinese workers hired to build a trading post for a particularly brash British trader. The Spanish commander was enraged. He took the crew and workers prisoner, arrested the captains, and built a fortress on an outcrop of rock beside Friendly Cove. The Spanish built a second fort soon thereafter and established a year-round colony, protected by cannons and warships, with a governor's house and a Grand Hall, a barracks for the men, a hospital, a bakery, gardens ripe with vegetables, and paddocks of cattle. They didn't pay for every blade of grass. This was not the proto-mercantilism of Cook, this was old-school conquistador imperialism.

Yuquot would be occupied by the Spaniards for six years. It was the farthest reach of the Spanish Empire in North America. It also signified a remarkable intersect of history. On the farthest reaches of Canada's Pacific coast, in a land they had scarcely begun to chart, the great imperial powers of Europe—Spain in its twilight, Great Britain in its ascendancy—prepared for battle.

Only a round of last-minute diplomacy averted what would have been a world war, and no fewer than three separate international treaties on Nootka Sound were signed. One such attempt at resolving the impasse was made by George Vancouver, now a captain in his own right, who'd been sent to "fill in Cook's map" and who now met with his Spanish counterpart, Juan Francisco de la Bodega y Quadra.

It was, at one level, a battle of the place names, with Vancouver hurrying to chart the coast before the Spanish could. (Like Adam in the Garden, the Europeans seemed to believe that they could take dominion over a land through the very act of naming it.) Captains Vancouver and Quadra dropped anchor at Friendly Cove and, amid flagons of fine wine and great slathers of flattery, eventually decided to "share" the trade rights of the region. This is what happens when you let hard-nosed negotiators drink too much. In the spirit of friendship, Vancouver even offered to call it "Quadra and Vancouver's Island."

The Spanish Empire, overextended and bogged down in South America, would eventually retreat from Canada's Pacific Northwest entirely, leaving little more than a smattering of Spanish names and a handful of relics behind. The fortress at Friendly Cove was dismantled, the Spanish flag lowered and the British flag raised.

Tensions at Friendly Cove had been stewing for years. American traders had fired on Native communities and Native chiefs had attacked English ships over insults and boorish manners. (The Mowachaht had a refined sense of what constituted proper decorum, something the ragtag sailors actively ignored.) It came to a gory climax in 1803, in the dying days of the sea otter trade, when the Mowachaht, under another Chief Maquinna (a different Maquinna had welcomed Cook; it was more a hereditary title than a name), launched a surprise attack on the *Boston,* an American trade vessel. It was more massacre than battle. The Mowachaht warriors killed two dozen men, cutting off their heads and dumping their bodies overboard. Only two crew members of the *Boston* were spared: the ship's sailmaker, John Thompson, and a nineteen-year-old blacksmith and armourer named John Jewitt, whose forehead was split open with an axe during the attack. When Jewitt regained consciousness, the deck was slick with blood and the killings had, thankfully, ended.

Jewitt and Thompson were ordered to run the ship aground at Friendly Cove, where it was looted and then burned. They would spend the next two years as slaves of Maquinna before finally being rescued. Jewitt hammered out blades for whaling harpoons, Thompson built sails and rigging for the Nootka canoes. Jewitt's account of their time among the Mowachaht remains one of the most gripping and richly informative documents in early Pacific Coast history. He learned the Mowachaht language, and took (reluctantly, he insists) a young Mowachaht bride. The Spanish gardens, he noted, were now running wild. A few onions, some peas, a small patch of turnips—overgrown.

This is what brought me to Nootka Sound: the story of Cook, of Maquinna, of Vancouver and Quadra, of the armourer John Jewitt, his capture and confinement.

Unlike Cook in his storm-damaged ships, or Vancouver in his party boat, or Jewitt on a blood-slicked deck, I would reach Friendly Cove neither in luxury nor as a captive, but on board a water taxi piloted by a Mowachaht skipper named Max. And not once, during the whole trip, did he try to massacre me.

Max Savey's water taxi can seat twelve, but I'm the only passenger this day—aside from Max's eldest son, Michael, a good-natured teen who's come along for the ride.

Max has a suitably wind-creased face and salt-and-pepper hair that he wears long and swept back. He grew up in a logging camp farther north—"a tough little town, that one," he says with a smile— and his ship is named *The First Citizen*.

"It's a boat, not a ship," he says. "Used to be called *The Isabelle*. I bought it in Campbell River, had it trucked in. They say it's bad luck to rename a boat, but those are just superstitious people saying that."

And anyway, as Michael points out, it's not as though Max renamed it the *Titanic*. I give a nervous laugh as the engine hacks and coughs like a smoker over breakfast. Max steers us out into the deeper waters of Nootka Sound.

He's been running his water-taxi service for eight years. "Nothing like it," he says. "Best life there is, especially when you're born and raised on the water like me."

As *The First Citizen* cuts across choppy waters, hitting every incoming wave head-on it seems, we pass Resolution Cove, where Captain Cook stopped to mend his mast with Douglas fir.

"You only ever hear one side of it," Max says when I ask him about Chief Maquinna and the massacre of the *Boston* sailors. "You need to hear our side of the story. A lot of what's said is exaggerated."

"The Mowachaht didn't kill those twenty-five sailors and line their heads up on the deck of the ship?"

"Well, yeah, they did. But it's been exaggerated."

I'm not sure how one exaggerates twenty-five heads lined up on a deck, but I don't get a chance to pursue it.

"Whale," he says, pointing at one wave among thousands. "D'you see it?"

I don't. Of course I don't.

"There it is again. Grey whale." But strain as I might, I espy no grey whales, only grey waves. I suspect he may be pulling my leg and I half expect him to say, "Mermaid at four o'clock. You must have seen *that.*"

"Should come back in summer," says Michael. "There's a big camp. Kids from all over. We have a salmon barbecue." He looks ahead at the water rolling in. "It's good."

"I'm third-generation residential school," says Max. "Up till I was nine, all I knew was my Native tongue. Then they took me away, and we got the strap if we spoke our language. You lose your language, that's a large part of who you are. After I'm gone, it's gone."

"It?"

"The language, the customs. The memories of it."

I turn to his son. "You don't speak …" My question trails off.

Michael gives me a big, toothy grin. "Nope."

In the 1880s, church-run residential schools began removing children from their families with the stated goal of cultural assimilation. It broke down societal ties at their most basic level, parent and child, and the after-effects of this hundred-year experiment are echoing across communities even now. Anthropologist Diamond Jenness, a respected figure in the study of Native cultures, described the residential school system as "an abject failure." That was in 1947. The last residential school in British Columbia didn't shut down until 1984.

The "Friendly Cove" of Yuquot was coming up quickly on our right.

"Any cougars?" I ask. "At Friendly Cove?"

"It's an island," he says.

"But cougars can swim, right?"

He shrugs. "I suppose."

We arrive at low tide, beneath a looming pier that will require a ladder to scale. Near a monument marking the site of the Spanish fortress sits an eagle, shoulders hunched, guarding the entrance to the cove. He should have a cigarette dangling from the side of his beak, I think.

Max bumps the boat up alongside the barnacle-encrusted pier, cuts the engine. "I'll wait here," he says.

Above us, on an exposed knuckle of rock, a government lighthouse and a few tidy white buildings are arranged like a giant game of Snakes and Ladders. Across from the lighthouse, the pebbled beach arcs toward forest. Two more houses sit off to one side, boats pulled up on shore. Only a single Mowachaht family still lives at Yuquot, once the historic homeland of the nation.

"This was once the capital of the entire coast," says Max.

Archaeological findings at Yuquot date the Native settlement back more than 4200 years. People were living here before the pyramids were built, before Moses led his followers out of Egypt.

"My grandma used to have a home here," Max says as he ties up his boat. "Used to be a whole line of homes, all the way down."

Following a rickety climb up the ladder, Michael makes his way toward a house to visit a friend or a cousin—I wasn't sure which, maybe a cousin of a friend—and I head toward a church, stark white against the evergreen, its steeple rising up in clean straight lines.

I enter on a whispered and wary "Hello?" It's quiet inside, and musty, the interior a mix of stained glass and Native art. Fluid carvings of killer whales and ravens, coaxed out of rainforest wood by master carvers, adorn the altar.

Back outside, shoulders as hunched as any cigarette-dangling bird, I walk through a sputtering rain to the windier side of the cove where whitecaps are being driven in. I stagger at times, pushed and pulled by multidirectional winds, my ears filled with white noise until I reach the dark curtain of forest at the other end.

A path leads to an old graveyard.

Crosses: leaning this way and that, tumbling into benign neglect, their right angles sinking into mossy green. The woods are dark and wet. The branches drip with condensation and the path is layered with pine needles. The entire forest appears to be perspiring: cold vapour beading on leaves, trickling down bark in rivulets.

But even here, in the forest, the sound of the sea is ever-present. Rolling in, rolling out. Long sigh in, long sigh out.

I come at last to a freshwater lake that had been hidden from view. Reeds stand in their own reflection. Rain pocks the surface. Lake and sea and falling mist—the very landscape seems liquid.

On the far side of this lake, a wooded grove. In this grove, a different kind of church, one marked more by an absence than a presence. On this small islet, beside this small lake, once stood a Native whaler's shrine, a holy site that predated the arrival of Christianity here by a thousand years—or more. A shrine so secret that even John Jewitt, who spent several years among the Mowachaht, taking endless notes, never knew of its existence.

Great ceremony went into the preparations for a hunt. Fastings. Ceremonial baths. Prayers and incantations. The whalers would scrub their bodies raw with hemlock boughs and bathe, first in clear-running streams and then later in the sea itself. They lived apart prior to a hunt, and at this hidden shrine, they performed intricate purification rituals.

The shrine is gone. And with it a wealth of carved effigies and a collection of human skulls, which were venerated in much the same way Catholics venerate the bone-shard relics of saints. Gone, all gone. Looted in the name of archaeology. Packed up in 1904 and shipped to the American Museum of Natural History, where the items taken were carefully labelled, photographed, and then put in storage. It sits there still, in the basement: the Yuquot Whaling Shrine.

The empty islet in Friendly Cove remains a reminder of things lost, of things stolen. A reminder that our national narrative doesn't begin with the arrival of European ships on the horizon.

Max was right: we only ever hear one side of any story. There are other stories in play, parallel histories hidden in the forests, moving through the reeds. I sit awhile, listening to the wind and sea.

The rain has turned to mist and the mist has begun to lift. I retrace my steps, through the forest and along the shore, back toward the pier, where I can see *The First Citizen*, loosely tethered, engine idling, waiting for me to leave.

Yukon Gold

My son Alex was in grade five or six when the *Twilight* craze really caught on. Vampire romances! O boy! Alex was as excited as anyone—at first. But his excitement quickly dimmed, and he never even finished the first book in the series. When I asked him why, he said, "I thought it was a VAMPIRE romance. But it turns out it was a vampire ROMANCE."

When they survey people about their dream jobs, "travel writer" often tops the list. As someone who started out in travel writing—in newspapers, magazines, guidebooks—I find this odd. Travel writing can be a hard slog in every sense. I'm not complaining. It beats working in a pickle factory, as they say. But still, I suspect the public at large romanticizes travel writing because they see it as "TRAVEL writing" when it's actually "travel WRITING." As noted later on, the travel is easy, it's the writing that's hard. (*See*: "So How's the Book Going?" in The Writing "Life" section.)

That said, one of the best gigs I ever had was with *Maclean's* magazine. The editor had approached me about writing a series of cross-Canada travel essays. Working on the principle that it's harder for them to fire you if your name is in the title, I decided to call the column "Will Ferguson's Canada." It ran for two years and twenty instalments, and took me from the Yukon to Newfoundland, from Thunder Bay to

Tadoussac. I even managed to convince *Maclean's* to cover the cost of a helicopter ride above the barren lands of Churchill, Manitoba. (I slipped it in with my other receipts, between "taxi ride to the airport" and "lunch.") Writing that column was great fun, even if it did, you know, involve a lot of writing.

Here's a selection of some of those travels, beginning with a trip to the Yukon when Alex was younger and including an essay on covered bridges I wrote for the *Ottawa Citizen* and another about a girlie bar in Saint John that I wrote for the *Telegraph-Journal*.

Gold! We leapt from our benches,
   Gold! We sprang from our stools.
Gold! We wheeled in the furrow,
   fired with the faith of fools ...

Robert Service, "Bard of the Yukon" and self-described "versifier," could rarely be accused of understatement. But Service's exclamatory ballad "The Trail of Ninety-Eight" was in no way an embellishment, capturing as it did the sheer giddiness of the gold rush fever that swept through North America after a discovery in a remote corner of the Yukon. Gold! lying as thick as slabs in a cheese sandwich. Gold! in the Klondike. Gold! along a pair of small creeks renamed, with a flourish, "Bonanza" and "El Dorado."

Leaving our homes and our loved ones,
   crying exultantly, "Gold!"

It was a form of contagious insanity, and it sent those inflicted on a wild stampede headlong into one of the most unforgiving terrains on earth. The headlines of the day said it all: "Gold! Gold! Gold! Gold!"

There was no "trail" of Ninety-Eight, not in the singular. There were *trails*. The stampeders, whom the press romantically dubbed "Argonauts," pushed north along several ill-defined routes in the winter and spring of 1898. Some fought their way up the B.C. interior; others—suckered by shady promoters—attempted to travel overland from Edmonton. Hundreds more went snow-blind and mad trying to cross glaciers and ice fields. The most direct route, though, and the most popular, was by ship up the Alaska panhandle, where you would disembark and then drag your supplies over either the Chilkoot or White Pass into the Dominion of Canada. From there you'd have to build a raft or small boat and sail down the Yukon River to the Klondike.

They were young, for the most part, these argonauts. Restless men in their twenties. But there were women among them as well, and children. There were former mayors and ex–bank presidents, aristocratic Brits and faux French counts, prize boxers and American fugitives, rich men and poor. They moved in dishevelled columns, a massive, undisciplined army trudging northwards. Of the estimated 100,000 who set out, fewer than 40,000 ever made it.

The first ragtag travellers arrived only to find that the best claims had already been staked by prospectors living in the region. No matter. The journey itself had been a test of character, and there was still gold to be made "mining the miners." At the marshy confluence of the Yukon and Klondike rivers, an entire city had appeared almost overnight. A "boomtown in the bog," Dawson was a sprawling community of canvas tents and false-front saloons, where millionaire miners in mud-caked boots jostled their way through sodden streets past Mississippi gamblers and Belgian good-time girls.

As more and more people swarmed in, the Native population was forced to retreat downriver. Their fishing camp at the mouth of the Klondike would become part of Dawson's notorious "Lousetown" red-light district. For the Han people of the Klondike, the gold rush was devastating.

By 1899, Dawson was the largest city west of Winnipeg and north of San Francisco—larger than Seattle, larger than Vancouver. Out here, in the far-flung reaches of the sub-Arctic, Dawson City was hailed as a "Paris of the North," a heady swirl of brothels, gambling dens, and raucous, boot-stomping dance halls. Canada may never have had a Wild West, but it certainly had a Wild North.

The latest fashions could be seen on the streets of Dawson, and the city boasted all the newest technological marvels—telephones, electric lights, motion-picture cinemas—at a time when many cities to the south still did not. And if the city's elegant false fronts hid rough-hewn log cabins, so be it. It was a false-front sort of town.

The very streets glittered with gold. The muck and mud of the alleyways, and even the sawdust on the barroom floors, actually *sparkled.* The sawdust itself was regularly "panned" for gold at the end of the night. In fact, gold soon lost its meaning; it was, after all, one of the most common commodities around. When a lovestruck suitor held up a restaurant to steal chocolates for his dance-hall sweetheart, he discovered—to his dismay—that although the gold was in the till, the chocolates were locked in a safe. He fled.

Inspired by tales of gold dust and foolhardy treks, I decided to take one of my own, dragging my family to the Klondike along one of the original "Trails of '98." Not by snowshoe or dogsleds, but by plane, train, boat, and automobile. Setting out to retrace the White Pass Route from Skagway, Alaska, to Dawson City in the Yukon, our party of intrepid argonauts included: one (1) Japanese woman unaccustomed to such travails, growing up as she did in the semi-tropics; one (1) wordsmith of the non-versifying sort whose most physically demanding task on any given day involved pressing ALT-CTR-DEL when his computer has locked up whilst playing an especially taxing round of Minesweeper. And their two (2) stalwart offspring: Alex, who, by his own calculations, was "five and three-quarters," and his younger brother Alister, who, though only a little over a year in age, was nonetheless capable of producing twice his body weight in poop daily. I leave it to you to decide which band of stampeders had a more difficult task ahead of them ...

We began our quest for Klondike gold in Skagway, once the haunt of card sharks and con men, where thousands of hapless stampeders were unloaded in '98 in a jumbled mess of chaos and confusion. Amid the lawless arena that was Skagway, miners were often waylaid and separated from their money before ever reaching the trail to the White Pass. Skagway today is a scenic town composed entirely of souvenir shops. Float planes come in on pontoons, looking like little girls wearing their mother's shoes, and eagles turn lazy, lethal circles in the sky, crying *weep, weep, weep.*

When we arrived in Skagway the cruise ships had docked and the shops were swamped with tourists waving fistfuls of money at the locals. Which is to say, not much had changed.

We didn't need to walk single-file through a notch in the mountains, however. (For one thing, getting our kids to walk single-file under normal circumstance is a challenge on par with herding ducks.) Even better, we crossed the White Pass by rail, along narrow-gauge tracks laid after the initial gold rush settled down. The White Pass & Yukon Route Rail, completed in 1900 to move supplies in, and ore out, now runs summer excursions to the summit instead. It's one of the steepest rail grades in the world, and the views are as heady as they are expansive.

It's like scaling clouds. The train wends its way alongside shearing cliffs and then leaps across chasms on heart-stopping trestles, past veil-like waterfalls and above forests so thick they appear cross-hatched. We plunged in and out of mountainsides, through tunnels blasted in granite, and when we emerged we saw—still visible like a memory, like a scar—the original Trail of '98. The path that so many followed into the Yukon.

We chugged past Dead Horse Gulch—where three thousand pack animals, overloaded and treated cruelly, tumbled to their death, the stench and the bloated carcasses described as a scene "out of Dante"— and then, finally into alpine air, we reached the top.

Canada.

Here, right at the summit, the North West Mounted Police once blocked the way. When you crossed over from Alaska to Yukon, from the U.S. to the Dominion of Canada, British-style law and order replaced the freewheeling anarchy of Alaska. If it was a stampede, it was nonetheless an *orderly* stampede. The NWMP, among them the legendary Sam Steele, slapped tough restrictions onto the long line of stampeders making their way into Canadian territory. The Mounties collected a toll, confiscated handguns, made sure everyone entering the Yukon brought with them a year's worth of supplies: a full ton of food and equipment, per person, that had to be dragged up the pass in relays. (A ton of supplies, you say? A mere ton? We had at least that much in diapers alone.)

Having crossed into Canada, the stampeders converged on the frozen shores of Lake Bennett. These were the headwaters of the Yukon River system, and a frenzy of boat-building took place. A race against spring. When the ice broke a flotilla set off, more than seven thousand craft in all: log rafts and listing boats, handmade and jerry-rigged, sweeping along on the Yukon, heading for Dawson.

The gravest dangers still lay ahead. At Miles Canyon, the river suddenly narrowed and sheer basalt cliffs, thirty metres high, created a crashing rush of water. It became a shooting gallery of hazards—hidden sandbars, sudden boulders, bone-crushing log-jams—and it only got worse. Having made it through the canyon, the flotilla faced a series of whitewater rapids that spewed up like the manes on wild stallions. It was an image that would give both the rapids and the town that developed beyond them their name: White Horse.

No, we did not shoot the rapids with two small children in tow, if only because the White Horse Rapids no longer exist. They were drowned in 1957, when a dam was built, the same year the town's name was contracted to Whitehorse.

The Yukon River has been tamed, and a tour boat, the MV *Schwatka*, took us upriver through Miles Canyon instead, chugging along waters where more than a hundred vessels once went down and a dozen men drowned in the first few weeks of the stampede.

At one time the Yukon River was a major supply line, but with the highways and daily flights of today, it's all but deserted. A wide, murky flow, a pewter-grey expanse of water, it snakes its way below us on our bumpy flight north from Whitehorse.

At Dawson, the silty waters of the Yukon meet the clear-running Klondike. And gold—or rather, the *pursuit* of gold—was evident from the moment we landed. We drove into town in a rented SUV, churning up loose gravel as we passed the caterpillar-like maze of rubbled tailings. Over the years the entire Klondike Valley has been recontoured and reworked by thousands of restless workers: first by freelance miners, then by large earth-chewing dredges, and now back to independent miners, still restlessly working the ground, sifting it for gold.

Dawson today is home to about two thousand permanent residents, and though small-scale mining still continues on the creeks, its main industry is "mining tourists" in the same way that the city once mined the miners.

It's a remarkable town: the muddy streets and wooden sidewalks, the false fronts and tin roofs, the buildings that lean drunkenly, riding upheavals in the permafrost. The dogs that lope by, big barrel-chested mutts soaked in mud, and the purple-sheened ravens—trickster creators of Native mythology—that croak out their tuneless welcomes as they eye you like pickpockets sussing out a crowd.

From the elegant Commissioner's Mansion to the ramshackle Westminster Hotel with its patchwork of adjoining rooms, from the S.S. *Keno* sternwheeler docked at the pier to the paint-peeling abandoned bank beside it (the very bank where a poet by the name of Service once worked as a teller), Dawson is still Dawson. I'd expected to find a ghost town, wistful and lonely—and there are ghosts aplenty in Dawson—but there is no sense of wistful nostalgia here. Only the celebration of a glorious and unprecedented moment in human history, when an Arctic gold rush created a city unlike any other.

Among the businesses and the derelict buildings, along the river-banks and the roadsides, there are bursts of colour. Fireweed, in full bloom. Spires of flowers forming pink and magenta stalks. The first plants to grow after a wildfire, fireweed, like the ravens that loiter along the telephone wires, are a territorial emblem. A sign of reclamation and regrowth, fireweed flowers are also—suitably enough—entirely edible.

When the wildfire of the gold rush swept through the Klondike, the Han people were caught in the conflagration. Chief Isaac, leader of the Klondike Han, could see what was coming and in a remarkable moment of foresight sent a delegation of singers and dancers across the border to the Native community at Eagle, Alaska, to teach them their Han songs and dances. They asked the people at Eagle to "keep" these for them, to preserve them until the Klondike Han were able to come back for them. At one point there were only five fluent speakers of Han left. But in the last few years the songs and dances have indeed been returned, intact, from Alaska, and the language and culture of the Klondike Han is being revived, slowly, stubbornly. Fireweed, taking root.

Dawson itself is a fireweed town, reclaimed, reinvented. At Diamond Tooth Gertie's Gambling Casino, girls dance the can-can amid a froth of ruffled skirts. And though there's little evidence that the can-can was ever danced in Dawson, Diamond Tooth Gertie was real enough. There really was a Klondike Kate as well. Two of them in fact, the title being in dispute even now.

Skookum Jim, Silent Sam, Swiftwater Bill, the Rag-Time Kid, the Lucky Swede, Lime-Juice Lil: the Klondike Gold Rush was an arena of nicknames and tall-striding characters. And Dawson City today remains an eclectic mix of cosmopolitan culture and backwoods charm. For the most part, one *chooses* Dawson. It takes a conscious act of will to settle here. And among those who chose this life is a laidback young man from East Germany named Holgar.

"Call me Holly," he said, smiling from under a broad-rimmed floppy hat as we climbed aboard. It's a nickname not quite up to Yukon par with "Silent Sam" or "Skookum Jim," so I introduced myself as "Wandering Willy." He didn't blink.

Holly owns a Belgian workhorse named Clyde and a wagon he built by hand. He runs his "Slow Rush Tours" in a suitably ambling manner, with Clyde plodding along, up and down the anecdote-rich streets of Dawson, along the Yukon River and up past Robert Service's cabin.

Holly crossed the Chilkoot Trail by foot in 1998, on the hundredth anniversary of the first rush, and he never looked back. "Germany is good," he said. "But this is where I belong."

"You're a lucky man," I said. "You found what you were looking for; a lot of people never do."

He replied, with an easy grin, "A lot of people never look."

On our last night we found gold, though it wasn't really gold, and it wasn't really night. It was that soft dusk that passes for night up here, the dusk of an Arctic summer, when the world doesn't so much darken as dim. A time of day when the land itself seems to be emitting light.

As Alister slept nuzzled in his car seat, we made a farewell drive out to Bonanza Creek, where his older brother and I walked down to where the Bonanza meets El Dorado.

"Right here," I said, standing beside shallow waters trickling over rocks. "Right here is where it all started."

Alex suddenly pointed. "Look!" And before I could stop him he went splashing into the waters of Bonanza, ankle-deep, to pull up a rock the size of his fist. "Gold!" he said. And I saw in that moment how the madness begins, because it wasn't gold; it was just a yellowing piece of granite, stained by peaty water.

But what if it wasn't ...

I whispered to him, "You know, they never found the motherlode. Some say it's up in the valley somewhere, waiting to be discovered."

His eyes glowed.

Ghosts
of a Nation

There is a general rule in travel writing that goes like this: *If someone draws you a map to a ghost train, take it.* It's up there with "Never play cards with a guy named Doc" and "Never eat at a place called Mom's."

When you drive into St. Louis, Saskatchewan, two things stand out: one is the sign proclaiming the village on the banks of the South Saskatchewan River to be HOME OF THE NHL PLAYER #47 RICHARD PILON (who, interestingly enough, ended his career playing for the St. Louis Blues); the other is the massive iron girders of the town's bridge, six truss frames lined up like a child's Meccano set construction. So massive is this span, and so heavy its brooding presence, that at first sight St. Louis seems less a community than a bridge with a town attached.

There is more to St. Louis than its bridge, though, and the surname of its NHL star provides a clue. This is a Métis settlement, established in the 1880s by families who arrived in creaking Red River carts— the Canadian equivalent of the covered wagon. First the Boyers and Bouchers, then later the Legares, de Laviolettes, Ouellettes, and Pilons. Of mixed Cree and French Canadian heritage, the Métis had been migrating west, into the Saskatchewan River Valley, since the 1860s. The CNR bridge wasn't built until 1914, though, with two "wings" slapped on later for cars. With traffic splitting, going in one direction on one wing and another direction on the other, it's a strange bridge to cross—and rickety as well. As a rail link, however, the bridge today serves no practical purpose. The rail line is long gone, the tracks pulled up and the rail bed overgrown. The trains don't run through St. Louis anymore. It's like the opening line of a Gordon Lightfoot song.

"Ah, but they do run." The lady at the local hotel/hardware store was adamant about this. (If you're asked, "What type of town is St. Louis, Saskatchewan?" the answer is, "The type of town where the hardware store is located inside the hotel.")

I wasn't sure I'd heard her correctly. "The train?" I asked.

"That's right. Out where the old tracks used to be, a few miles from town." The Ghost Train of St. Louis, manned by an undead crew, is stoking the fires still, it would seem. "You can see the lights most nights," she said. "Hundreds of people have, even our mayor. Starts off as a yellowish glow, then turns red. Comes right toward you … then suddenly disappears."

She drew me a map and off I went, across the "ghost bridge of St. Louis" and then down and around on the highway. I came to a gravel road, steered in, and followed it until I came to another, smaller road. I followed that one till I reached a rusted gate barring the way. Beyond the barrier, the old rail bed—the tracks long since pulled up—forms a narrow, raised lane through the bushes.

I rolled my rent-a-car to a stop, turned off the headlights.

Dusk was settling as imperceptibly as dust, and the night air was cool and light, almost sweet tasting. Posted on the barrier, a warning read with ominous illiteracy: NO TRESSPASSIG.

Burnt offerings. Rutted tracks. Scattered bottles, broken glass. Bonfire pits that look like the scorched marks of a mortar attack. A trysting spot for local teenagers, from the looks of it—scratched initials, angry accusatory graffiti, an unravelled condom—but there were no gangly mobs of hormonally inflamed youth prowling the woods that night. I waited, and the moon rose. Or a part of it anyway. A thin sliver of steel.

A glimmer of light appeared at the end of the lane, but I couldn't tell if it was the ghost train's or simply distant flickerings from the highway. Light diffraction, maybe, expanding through gaps in the trees. The change to red might simply be brake lights going the other way. The abandoned rail bed naturally points toward St. Louis, so perhaps I was just seeing the headlights of cars passing over the bridge, bouncing off the atmosphere somehow.

Ah, but there's no fun in that. And as anyone in St. Louis will tell you, "So-and-so's grandmother saw the light back when there were no cars!"

It's an eerie effect nonetheless, and, reports of clanging bells and lonely whistles aside, eerily silent as well. The lights grew engorged, seemed to hover, and then—*vanished,* only to be replaced by new lights, pale flashes and ember reds. A chill, not wholly related to temperature, ran a fingernail down my back and I decided to leave because it obviously wasn't a Ghost Train I was seeing. Unless it was.

I headed back to town as a procession of pickup trucks filed by, on their way, presumably, to catch a nightly glimpse of a phantom …

I had come to the low rolling hills of the central Saskatchewan parklands in pursuit of ghosts, historical and otherwise. I'd come to retrace the battles of 1885, when Métis resistance broke into armed rebellion.

Urged onward by Louis Riel, the self-proclaimed "Prophet of the New World," the Métis under Gabriel Dumont had engaged Canadian forces in a series of skirmishes, pitting British-style regimentation against the frontier tactics of the buffalo hunt.

Dumont, a hunter turned ferryman, was already a legendary figure. He spoke five Native languages as well as French (but not a lick of English), and had battled the Sioux in his youth. It was said he could "call the buffalo." But the buffalo were gone, the Cree and the Blackfoot were being forced onto reserves, and the steel spear of the railway was even now pushing its way into the North-West.

Louis Riel had led an armed resistance years earlier at Red River, which in turn had led to the creation of the province of Manitoba, making Riel a "Father of Confederation," albeit one with a price on his head.

Riel had fled south into Montana, but he was called back by his would-be angel protector, Gabriel. When demands for language protection and land rights fell silent, loudly ignored by John A. Macdonald and the federal government in Ottawa, the Métis prepared for war.

The North-West Rebellion of 1885 has been portrayed both as a source of Western alienation and as a clash of cultures. It has also been dismissed as little more than a misguided religious crusade. French vs. English. Native vs. white. West vs. East. Prophet vs. infidels. It was all of these things and more. It began as a protest movement over land rights, grew into an act of political defiance, and eventually became a matter of cultural survival. And as Riel grew increasingly delusional, it finally took on the characteristics of a messianic religious movement, with Riel proclaiming a New Jerusalem on the Plains. The Métis, he decided, were the Chosen People, and he would be their "infallible pontiff." God was on their side; how could they lose?

Louis Riel declared a provisional government in the Métis village of Batoche. Soon afterwards, at nearby Duck Lake, his men clashed with a contingent of North West Mounted Police, who, under heavy gunfire, were forced to retreat, leaving their dead where they lay in the snow. The Métis lost men at Duck Lake as well, including Dumont's brother Isidor, and Dumont himself came within an inch of death when a bullet creased his scalp, spurting blood down his face. And Riel? Riel emerged unscathed—even though he rode about on horseback the entire time, unarmed and exposed to enemy fire, waving a large crucifix as he urged his men onward. *"Fire! In the name of the Son and the Holy Ghost! Fire!"* It was the Métis' first victory of the rebellion; it would also be their last.

In the end, it was the railway that defeated the Métis, with one national dream overriding another. The North-West was no longer a remote hinterland, and within ten days of the initial shots

Major-General Frederick Middleton, head of a hastily organized Canadian Field Force, was unloading thousands of armed men at Fort Qu'Appelle, just a few hundred kilometres south of Batoche.

The Métis had urged the Cree and Blackfoot to join them in their battle, but for the most part the First Nations remained stubbornly neutral throughout the conflict. The violence that did erupt farther west wasn't part of a coordinated Native uprising, but rather the result of simmering anger and starvation conditions. Cree warriors within Big Bear's camp, led by the war chief Wandering Spirit, attacked unarmed settlers at Frog Lake, killing nine, including two priests, even as Big Bear tried to stop the massacre. Wandering Spirit's followers then surrounded Fort Pitt as the police fled downriver in a leaky scow, abandoning the civilians. Not the noblest moment in NWMP history.

At Battleford, meanwhile, Poundmaker's band of Cree and Assiniboine had looted homes and torched buildings while the settlers took refuge inside a police post. In response, Middleton sent one column of over three hundred men in pursuit of Big Bear, and another column to Battleford to lift the siege. At Cut Knife Hill, Poundmaker's small band of fifty warriors met and routed the Canadian forces under Colonel Otter. Had Poundmaker not stopped his men from pursuing their panicked, fleeing foe, Cut Knife Hill could have easily gone down as our Little Big Horn, with Otter cast as Canada's Custer.

The Cree and Assiniboine victory at Cut Knife Hill, and the earlier massacre at Frog Lake, were undercard fights to the main event, however. The real battle for control of the North-West would occur at Batoche.

Middleton marched his third column north—and straight into an ambush. In a wooded coulee near Fish Creek, Gabriel Dumont staged a surprise attack on the Canadians. Instead of following a standard military approach, Dumont took the *low* ground, a very effective tactic in the rolling hills of the parkland. Middleton's men were silhouetted against the sky as they came over the lip of the coulee. It was, as Dumont said, "like shooting buffalo."

The Métis fought Middleton's men to a standstill at Fish Creek. In all, they would clash with Canadian police and military three times—at Duck Lake, Fish Creek, and finally, Batoche—and their record would stand at a win, a tie, and a loss. But given the way that the Battle of Fish Creek unnerved Middleton while bolstering the morale of the Métis, it might be more accurate to move Fish Creek over to the "win" side of the equation. Not that it matters. In any war, the only battle that counts is the last one, and the Canadians won that.

Horses, grazing in a meadow. Backlit by sunlight as though outlined in gold ...

I was staying at Jack Pine Stables, north of Duck Lake, at a lodge run by Lawrence Mullis and his wife, Darlene. Lawrence, a gregarious man with quick sense of humour, is the great-great grandson of Patrice Fleury, who fought at Batoche alongside Gabriel Dumont. Like his wife, Lawrence has an unabashed love for horses. Together, they run trail rides out of their lodge.

"We have all kinds of horses," Lawrence said with a grin. "We have skinny horses for skinny people. Fat horses for fat people. Shy horses for shy people. Spooky horses for spooky people. And for people who've never ridden a horse, we have horses that have never been ridden."

The trails had been churned into loam as soft as talcum powder, and footpaths wandered through juniper and hazelnut, past the Jack pines that give the property its name and into thick stands of black-dabbed poplar. There were even prairie lilies in blood-red bloom set against a field of faded green, looking every bit like provincial flags.

I began at Duck Lake.

The town, with its wide streets and modest homes, has been turned into an open-air art gallery. Historical murals depicting Dumont and Riel, Big Bear and Poundmaker, adorn the curling rink and various storefronts, several now boarded up. It's a town that had seen better days and, murals aside, reminded me of my own hometown in northern Alberta. The same Cree accents—low, almost furtive, lacking the sound of *sh* so that words like *shy* become "sigh"—and the same dusty demeanour.

Duck Lake is a Cree-French-Métis town. So, naturally, the local cuisine is Chinese. I went in—it reminded me of my hometown as well, where the joke was "There's only one café, and you're better off eating at the other one"—and I pulled up a chair. It was a friendly enough place. (Ever notice how, when you go into a Chinese café in a small town in the prairies, the family is always sitting around a big table eating heaping trays of delicious items that are never on the menu? No chicken balls with packets of radioactively orange plum sauce for them. They eat real food.) At the Duck Lake café I broke my steadfast rule of "Never order coffee at a Chinese café"— I needed the boost and the coffee that slowly trickled out of the pot into my cup was only a week or so old, which is to say, fresh by prairie Chinese café standards—and I asked around for directions to the battle site.

"Not in town," I was told by one table.

"On the Rez," said someone else.

That would be the Beardy Indian Reserve, just north of Duck Lake, where I eventually found the battle site. There was very little to mark it as the spot where the first volley of the North-West Rebellion was fired, though. Just a cairn, really, in poor repair. Some poplars in a grove. A gopher-hole-and-packed-dirt parking lot.

I was pacing it out, trying to sort out where the two sides would have lined up and where the initial skirmish might have occurred, when a pickup truck drove in. It was one of the men from the reserve.

"You look lost," he said.

"Not lost," I replied. "Confused."

He tried his best to help, pointing out where he thought the police officers might have stood and where the Métis might have taken cover, but it wasn't his battle and it wasn't his history; the Cree on Beardy didn't take part in the rebellion. "They should do something with this," he said, looking across the battlefield. *They* being the government.

They being the Métis. The land might be Cree, but the battle was not.

Back at Jack Pine Stables, I told Lawrence about my somewhat forlorn trip to the Duck Lake battle site.

"We had this one guy," said Lawrence, "from England. Nice guy, but I think he was expecting to see Indians decked out in headdresses when he got here. He kept asking me if it was possible to 'enter' the reserve. If he needed to pass through a checkpoint or something. I almost told him 'Yeah, you have to pay a $50 fee to enter,' and I was gonna send him down to the band office to try to buy a travel permit to allow him on Indian land, just for a joke. But I didn't. I drove him through the reserve instead. Not much to see, really. Just people's houses." There was a pause. "I had the feeling he was disappointed."

Fort Carleton on the northern branch of the river has been reconstructed; it was burned to the ground by accident as panicked NWMP officers fled to Prince Albert after their defeat at Duck Lake. This fort was once a focal point of the famed Carleton Trail, a trade and transportation corridor first blazed by Métis hunters and Hudson's Bay Company traders. It was like a Roman road to the interior, running across the plains and woodlands from Fort Garry at present-day Winnipeg all the way to Fort Edmonton. Trappers and itinerant tradesmen, hunters and horsemen, explorers and homesteaders, Mounties, surveyors, and footsore priests—they all followed the trail west.

Fort Carleton was also where the Cree chiefs gathered to sign Treaty Six. The buffalo hunt had collapsed and their people faced starvation, but not all of them submitted to the terms laid out by the government. One chief who refused to sign rode away with his followers in search of better hunting grounds. His name was Big Bear.

As the main artery for trade, and a funnel for law and settlement, the Carleton Trail was the original Trans-Canada Highway. Today, little remains. Those sections used as local routes survive, but the rest has become an overgrown ghost trail. Like the buffalo trade that fuelled it, the Carleton Trail is gone.

Ghost trails, ghost herds, ghost trains. And at Fish Creek, a ghost church.

An impressive structure, first built at Fish Creek after the 1885 rebellion, it has now been abandoned as well, its grounds overrun with weeds, its looming square steeple standing stark against the Western sky.

Not far from this church is the coulee where Dumont's men clashed with the Canadians. As I stood on the edge, watching the wind move toward me, stirring dry grass and poplar leaves, a fragment of poetry surfaced in my memory like the message in a Magic Eight Ball. It was a haiku by the Japanese poet Basho, written at the site of what was once a samurai battle:

Tall grass, all that remains of warrior dreams.

From Fish Creek, I zigged and zagged my way north along access roads, heading toward Batoche.

I grew up in a gravel-road town, in that mythical land Beyond the End of the Pavement, where every car and pickup truck travelled with its own personal cumulus plume of dust; you could spot oncoming traffic miles away, coming at you like an approaching army. I'd learned to drive on gravel, so the back roads of Saskatchewan shouldn't have worried me, but, as it turns out, driving on gravel is the un-bicycle of motor skills. I was in a panic most of the way—not enough to slow down, of course—but enough to worry as I banked from one sliding skid to another.

These are the parklands as well, not the tabletop prairies you get farther south, so the road will dip suddenly—usually at the precise moment another vehicle appears, flinging dings of pebbles at you and throwing a cloud of dust over everything. This is a landscape that doesn't rise up, but drops away, something Dumont had used to his advantage.

But even here the sky is Saskatchewan big, and the slightest rise gives you a view across the crest of hills, all the way to the edge of forever. Coulees and poplar stands. Farmlands looking like dusty blankets. Tractors churning up dry clouds of their own. "We're growing stubble this year," one farmer had said back at Duck Lake, voice full of rue. A sign informed me that the fire hazard was HIGH.

A Métis flag was flying above a rodeo grandstand: the sideways eight of an infinity sign set against a backdrop of blue. And beyond— and above—were the swirling oil paints of Catholic clouds, the type that Jesus is always depicted ascending into or descending from.

Batoche, provisional capital of the North-West and Riel's designated "New Jerusalem," wasn't a remote hinterland isolated from the world. Quite the opposite. Batoche was a key ferry crossing on the Carleton Trail, a crossroads where the East–West route met the South–North.

It was where the Métis would make their last stand. Gabriel Dumont had argued in favour of continued guerrilla warfare, with quick hit-and-run assaults. Strike hard, then melt away into the grasslands. But Riel had insisted that they dig in at Batoche.

Gabriel Dumont built a series of rifle pits with interconnecting trenches, chest-deep with rear access, so that the Métis could run from one pit to the next, falling back or moving forward as need be. These defenceworks would keep casualties to a minimum, but would also cast the Métis in a purely defensive position, fighting simply to hold the Canadians back ... until God intervened.

The heart of the Batoche settlement was near the river. It once boasted a blacksmith's shop, a general store, a tavern, and even a billiard hall. Today, only crumbling foundations remain: cellars and stone ruins amid dry grass.

A wooded lane, once part of the Carleton Trail, leads to what had been Dumont's ferry crossing, and I followed it down to the clay banks at water's edge. I crouched down, reached out, let the cold water of the South Saskatchewan run between my fingers.

The Battle of Batoche lasted four days and left some two dozen men dead. The fighting was farther up the hill, and I walked up the long slope through tawny grass, past rows of trees that had once marked the narrow strips of Métis farms. The sun was now low across the whiskheads and a wind was moving through the grass in finger-print whorls.

Here are the tangled bushes that now mark the rifle pits the Métis fired from. Here, the rise of land where Dumont took note of the wind's direction and then lit the grass on fire, his men advancing toward enemy lines behind a wall of smoke and flame. Here, the picturesque church and rectory, bullet holes still visible. And here, finally, the earthwork of the Canadian defences. It was from this position that the Canadians pushed forward on the final day, past the church and down the hill, capturing Batoche and leaving corpses in their wake. The Métis had run out of ammunition by that point and were firing rocks and melted buttons. God never did intervene.

The dreams of a nation died at Batoche. Overrun, the Métis scattered. Gabriel Dumont lost track of Riel in the confusion: the avenging angel and the prophet of the grasslands—separated by turmoil, by distance, by diverging destinies. Separated by the length of a rope.

Louis Riel surrendered, was put on trial and duly hanged. Dumont escaped across the border into the U.S., where he would later join Buffalo Bill's Wild West Show, a sharpshooter on horseback, "Hero of the Half-Breed Rebellion" dressed in buckskin, shooting glass balls from the air.

Dumont would return to Saskatchewan under a general amnesty. He was buried at Batoche beneath a giant immovable boulder. Big Bear and Poundmaker were sent to prison, and eight Cree warriors, including Wandering Spirit, were sentenced to death. They climbed the gallows steps and dropped into emptiness. It was the largest mass execution in Canadian history.

The Métis rifle pits at Batoche are marked now by tufts of brambles with red berries clustered among the thorns. I crawled into one of the pits and peered out to where the Canadians would have appeared, riflemen moving forward through smoke of their own. They must have looked like ghosts.

Back again at Jack Pine Stables, Lawrence greeted me with warm bannock and strong coffee. "How was Batoche?" he joked. "Still there?"

"Still there."

"I'll put you in the tepee," he said as he lugged out a wolf skin for me to sleep under. "This'll keep you warm. There's a Great Horned Owl lives nearby. You'll probably hear her."

And so I did. Low flappings in the night, a shadow threading its way through branches. That endless question, never answered, as coyotes yelp and scuttle about playing tag and telling jokes.

It had been a long time since I'd been inside a tepee, and I'd forgotten how calming it is to sleep inside a circle. Nestled under fur at the bottom of a canvas cone. Looking up at the narrowing funnel of stars above. The canvas sides moving on a night breeze—slow inhalations, long exhalations. I slept deeply, a dreamless slumber untroubled by ghosts.

Outside a wind was moving through the trees, over buffalo trails and battlefields, out to Batoche and beyond—across the rolling grasslands of warrior dreams.

Love and Loss
in Old Quebec

We move through life trailing former selves behind us like images in a multiple-exposure photograph. Or at least, that's the way it feels sometimes.

It's early autumn and I'm chasing former selves down the narrow streets of Quebec City, and every corner, every angle, offers a snapshot—a photograph of someone I used to be.

This is me, in sepia, huddled in the unswept depths of the Nostradamus Café in the city's Latin Quarter, scribbling down deep and abiding *pensées,* mostly in the form of Very Bad Poetry. There I am, below a street lamp. And there I am, disappearing down an alleyway ...

I first came to Vieux-Québec at the worldly age of nineteen. I followed a girl (as you do). We'd met as volunteers at a work camp in the B.C. interior, and our paths had contrived to cross at several points, braiding back and forth till they met here, in the Old City.

It was raining when I arrived, and she met me on the water-washed boardwalk of Dufferin Terrace. She was from Montreal, but had settled in Lévis, on the other side of the St. Lawrence River, across from the Old City.

"*Là-bas!*" she said, pointing across the rain-misted river. "That's where we are going, us." I would have followed her anywhere, would have followed her off a cliff. Which is what I did, in a way.

The ferry plunged through the storm and we emerged on that far shore. Looking back, the skyline of Quebec City was a ruined water-colour. It still is.

Beyond a few warehouses and various shops near the port, Lévis is very much a clifftop town; we faced a near-vertical ascent on clattering stairs that scaled the heights in a series of flanking manoeuvres.

We may have been ensconced in Lévis, but we spent our evenings in Old Quebec. It was how I imagined Paris would be, and years later, when I finally did make it to France, I remember feeling vaguely disappointed that Paris failed to live up to the compact charm and almost heroic strollability of Old Quebec.

And so the summer went. We'd squander our nights in the jazz clubs of the city and then run to make the last ferry across, and when we reached the other side she would bound up the stairs ahead of me, to the top of the cliffs. Quebec is a city of stairs—with twenty-nine outdoor public staircases, it has more than any other city on the continent—but Lévis was nearly as bad. The stairs of Lévis are a true test of character. They seemed to grow longer with every climb, and I never once made it all the way to the top without being forced to stop, hands-on-side, gulping air, as she slipped away up the next flight, and the next. In my memory I am falling behind still, trying to catch up, never quite making it. I will always be nineteen in Lévis.

As the summer evenings cooled and autumn crept in on cat's feet, I came to realize that I was out of my depth, linguistically and certainly romantically. Like a clumsy country cousin from the backwoods, I was immune to both jazz and the nuances of *la langue d'amour* ("Jazz is different from blues ... how again?") and I constantly found myself stumbling headlong over French syntax. Along the way, I perfected a new gender, neither *le* nor *la*, neither masculine nor feminine, but rather a blend of the two. A glottal *luh* sound, swallowed at the back of one's throat, when properly executed it should sound as though you were about to say something, but suddenly changed your mind. It's not unlike the noise one makes just prior to a retch, and several times the people I spoke with edged away, expecting the worse. *"Oo-aye luh, luh, luh bibliothèque?"* (The situation has hardly improved. On my last visit to Quebec, after a stint in South America and several years in Japan, I ended up speaking a bizarre hybrid of languages: *"Sumimasen, una cerveza s'il vous plaît."* I have limited space on my hard drive, it would seem, and each language I struggled with seemed to erase—or at least confuse—the previous ones.)

The summer ended and so did we. She shot me down at close range, left me for dead at the Nostradamus Café. (You would think, what with Nostradamus' reputation for precognition, that I would have had some inkling of what was about to happen, but *noooo*.) I was sandbagged and the Great Seer was no help.

And now, when I come upon that jazz-bar café on Rue Couillard, even now after all these years, I am instantly hurled back in time, into the stunned silence of that awful moment. Years later, a producer at CBC Radio would confide in me that his Québécoise girlfriend had dumped him at the very same café. "It must be where they bring their Anglo boyfriends when they want to break up," he said somewhat wistfully.

From that clifftop room in Lévis, I moved across the river to the Old City itself and into a bunk bed at Auberge de la Paix, "the Peace Hostel," with its hidden courtyard and benches draped with bandanaed backpackers plotting their next move. As ill luck would have it, the hostel itself was next door to the Nostradamus Café. A daily reminder, that. I took to averting my gaze as I passed.

Interestingly enough, it was on Rue Couillard, in a blond-brick building just down the street from the Peace Hostel and the Café of Poor Prophecy, that the composer Calixa Lavallée wrote the music for "O Canada" back in 1880. I discovered this from a historic marker out front that I'd spotted, my eyes averted from the other side. Our duelling national anthem, mumbled with varying degrees of conviction in both official languages, was born right here. "O Canada" may have begun as a staunch French Canadian anthem, written in honour of St. Jean Baptiste Day, but like the maple leaf and the word "Canadian" itself, it has since been co-opted by English Canadians and applied to the country as a whole.

O to hell with Lavallée. Who cares about "O Canada" when you are young and mortally wounded? I staggered down the narrow alleyways of Old Quebec, collar up, cigarette smouldering, trying my best to look like James Dean. I lingered in coffee shops. I basted in self-pity, marinated in my sorrows, writing the sort of profoundly bad poetry only heartbroken nineteen-year-olds can conjure up from the existential depths of their angst-wrung souls. (Every poem I wrote seemed to begin "Alone, I wander the streets ..." and end just short of exclaiming, "Woe is me!")

I should probably take this opportunity, some twenty-four years after the fact, to apologize to the hapless couple from Massachusetts who made the mistake of sitting next to me at Le Casse-Crêpe Breton and asking, "So, how are you doing?" It was a question they would regret.

In my defence, the imagery of French and English Canada has long had male/female overtones. Even Hugh MacLennan's description of Canada as a land of "two solitudes" is lifted from the poet Rainer Maria Rilke, who wrote about "a love that consists in this, that two solitudes protect and touch and greet each other." (To which my nineteen-year-old self says, *"Ha!"*)

The cultural two-step of English/French, either/or, has faded in the face of multicultural realignments and brute demographics, but this central duality remains a fact of life in Canada. We live in a house divided, a Mighty Duplex of the North, with separate entrances and parallel views. And it started right here, in *la vieille capitale.*

The beauty of Quebec City is the beauty of stone. It's the beauty of garrisons and watchtowers, of vantage points and armed citadels. It's the only walled city remaining in North America, a closed circle.

The city welcomes you with a kiss on the cheek, if not the lips. The open-air gallery of the Rue du Trésor, crowded with tourists and quick-draw artists selling homespun watercolours and assembly-line etchings of the city skyline. (They range in quality from tacky all the way to kitsch.) The breakneck stairs that tumble down to the Lower Town, the endless cafés and outdoor patios, the carriages that clatter by on cobblestone, the spiced-earth aroma of horse manure. And a fleeting glimpse of one's younger self, slipping down an alleyway, disappearing into a courtyard.

Quebec City wasn't built with romance in mind, but war. The upper city, after all, was situated high above the St. Lawrence not because it afforded better views and prettier sunsets, but with military tactics in mind.

There are really two cities, stacked atop each other. The Upper, with its walls and panoramic sweep, and the Lower, with its ferry docks and warehouses and narrow lanes, the corners curved to allow horse carriages to turn. Between these two cities, in a break between the buildings: a glimpse of black cliff-face walls. Vertical bedrock, it's one of the prime reasons the city was built here where the St. Lawrence narrows. A trade route to the interior with built-in defensive heights, it was the perfect site for the capital of New France.

Epic, yet intimate, Quebec City is summed up best, not by the glorious faux-castle of the Chateau Frontenac hotel, with its turrets and spires, but in something much smaller: a single cannonball. Walk west along Rue Saint-Louis and you will come to Rue du Corps-de-Garde. And in the roots of a tree you will find an iron ball embedded, a souvenir of battles past. In Quebec, it is said, even the very trees are wounded.

September 13, 1759. The British forces of General Wolfe have scaled the cliffs under cover of darkness and have massed behind the Upper City, on the Plains of Abraham. Ensconced behind the walls, the French general Montcalm at first refuses to take the reports seriously. "We do not have to imagine the enemy has wings," he sniffs.

But the British don't need wings, only pluck. That, and a general with a death wish, desperate for glory. A foolhardy ploy, climbing the cliffs, but it works. Montcalm, in a moment of rash decision wholly out of keeping with his usually cautious approach, decides to forsake the protective circle of the walls and sends his men forward in a mad rush, French and Canadiens tripping over each other as they charge.

Across from them, the British have formed a thin red line, two men deep. Native allies of the French have begun sniping from the cover of the woods. Bagpipes are playing. Bodies begin to fall. And then ... when the French and Canadiens are just thirty paces away, the British raise their muskets, and on Wolfe's command, they fire.

The Battle of the Plains of Abraham took only fifteen minutes, yet it changed the direction of Canadian history forever. Wolfe died on the battlefield, Montcalm a few hours later inside a convent hospital—his final words those of gratitude that he would never live to see the English inside the city. What he would make of the convoys of anglophone tour buses pulling up daily within the walls is hard to say. (Something along the lines of *"Merde!"* I imagine.)

Still, Quebec wasn't so much conquered as it was abandoned. The French troops fled the city with an unseemly haste, falling back to Montreal where they would regroup and counterattack the following spring. Under the leadership of General Lévis, they came within a heartbeat of recapturing the capital, but when British supply ships arrived, it was all over.

The Fall of New France is the Lamentations of Quebec nationalism. Author Lyse Champagne has described the Conquest as "the Big Bang" of Canadian history, "hurling fragments of the past into the orbit of the future." And she's right.

Even Quebec's melancholy motto, *Je me souviens,* is a testament to the power of the past. In theory, Confederation, a century later, was a fresh start, a new arrangement, in which Quebec negotiated its entry into Canada with protective guarantees for its language, religion, and education. But it is the Conquest, *la conquête,* not Confederation, that burns sharpest in our national memory.

The effect of the Conquest on Quebec society has been examined in relentless, obsessive detail. Less commented upon is the way it has been used—in often unstated but implicit ways—by English

Canadians. Whenever yet another weary unity crisis rears up, the sentiment is always there, just below the surface. "Didn't we beat them on the Plains of Abraham?"

Well, no. We didn't beat anyone, because "we" didn't exist. English Canada hadn't been invented yet, and the only Canadians on the Plains of Abraham that day spoke French.

Beside the Chateau Frontenac stands a monument unique in the world, one that honours enemies, mortal foes, both the victor and the vanquished, in the same structure. The name WOLFE is emblazoned on one side, MONTCALM on the other. Nor is this some recent, politically sensitive gesture. This monument was raised in 1827, with a Latin inscription that reads: *Courage granted them both a common death, history a common fame, posterity a common monument.*

I don't remember this monument at nineteen, but it looms large today. When I stop by, two different groups have gathered below it. On one side is an English-speaking tour group, on the other a circle of French-speaking elementary students, sitting on the grass, chins in hands. Position yourself between the two, and you will hear the respective spiels of the tour guide and the teacher overlapping and, essentially, cancelling each other out. Do this experiment yourself: on a busy day, situate yourself in front of the Montcalm and Wolfe monument and wait.

Snippets of the English tour (direct quotes these): "The French general said 'I'm better than that' and out he goes, through the gates … A monumental mistake … Wolfe, of course, had surprised everyone by climbing the cliffs …" On the francophone side, meanwhile, when you hear the name "Montcalm" you hear *"courage"* and *"sacrifice"* and a reference to Montcalm's own assessment of his rival following the Englishman's campaign of destruction through the habitant farmlands of the St. Lawrence: *"Monsieur Wolfe est cruel."*

Our dual history is played out, not in stereo, but in duelling mono. It's not that we have two contradictory histories, it's that we have two *incomplete* histories, neither of which is entirely correct—nor entirely wrong. Montcalm did blunder. He was a fool to come out. And Wolfe *was* cruel.

In the small park behind the monument: leaves on the grass, curling into papyrus. The first hint of autumn.

Walk the walls of the Old City and the French defences blend into the British, with the walls of Quebec leading toward the British defenceworks of the Citadel. A sunken star-formation of barriers and moatlike corridors, hidden below eye level, it was built to defend against an American threat.

Beyond the Citadel, the silver sheen of the St. Lawrence. Tankers are on the move. You can hear metallic clangs all the way up here from the river below.

The Plains of Abraham. The very name sounds biblical, evoking as it does images of a child to be sacrificed and a god appeased. But the name actually refers to a farmer who once owned land on the heights in the 1600s, and the Plains themselves are anything but. Undulating earthworks amid forested groves, they have become the city's communal living room, a place for families and picnics, for romping dogs and droopy-headed lovers. I walk across rolling waves of green, the hollows and curves giving the park the feel of a battlefield grown over. Of craters covered with mossy grass. Of objects under a blanket.

Past a Martello tower, set like a chess-piece castle atop a hillock of grass, I follow a nature trail that disappears into leafy green. A forest of maple and birch, of American elm and smaller, shrublike hawthorns. The autumn wildflowers are looking like pressed petals falling from the pages of a book.

Many of the plants growing here aren't native, but rather crossed the ocean as seeds and spores caught in the robes of missionaries or the hems of sailors. Even the ubiquitous dandelion—that sun-splotch of yellow which turns so easily into cotton-tufted blow—isn't native to Canada. It came from Europe. And the comfrey herb, once cultivated by Europeans for its medicinal qualities, has long since escaped the confines of the garden and now grows wild, its roots spreading outward, then upward, continually spawning new plants and new roots.

I emerge from the comfrey and hawthorn back onto the Plains, and realize that at some point I crossed the lines of battle and am now behind British lines.

After the grassland eulogy of Batoche, I know how the past lingers, how landscapes can hum like an anvil long after a hammer has hit. In this Kingdom of Lost Causes, defeats are often, as they say in Quebec, "as glorious as victories." Batoche and the Plains of Abraham: two very different battles, in two very different regions, separated by a hundred years of history. But both evoking that same sense of beauty and loss.

I've come to Quebec City on the anniversary of the original battle to try to map out the memory of what happened here. Using a detailed battle plan and a modern street map, I'm trying to project the past onto the present, creating a palimpsest of sorts, and I pace it out, starting at the monument to General Wolfe. This marks the spot where the thin, anemic young Englishman is believed to have died. Whenever tensions arise, this is usually the first monument they blow up. It sits, sword and helmet, in the middle of a small traffic circle, just past the Musée du Québec.

From the Wolfe monument, if you walk north along the tree-flanked avenue you will reach Grande Allée. Turn right on Grande Allée, and you come to Avenue Cartier, with its row of croissant shops and small cafés. This is where the British soldiers stood, that thin red line, muskets levelled like pikes. If you look down Cartier, past the sushi bars and gelato stands, you are looking directly across the British front lines.

Back onto Grande Allée, hurrying now—ahead of the volley. This is where the bullets would have been flying, where clouds of acrid smoke would have rolled across the dead and dying.

Gunpowder and glory. The taste of blood on the tongue. Cries of the wounded. Running now, up Grande Allée, past a church to Avenue de Salaberry, and you have crossed over to the French side. Here at Salaberry is where the great surge forward would have faltered, where the French advance was broken.

You are picking your way through corpses now. A boutique hotel on the corner of Avenue Galipeault would have been right in the thick of the battle, and in this gap between Cartier and Galipeault lies one of the chasms of Canadian history, that central fault line upon which this country was built.

Early evening. The day has bled away. Kids are practising skateboard moves on cobblestone lanes (no small feat, that) as couples flutter past, trailing laughter in their wake.

A woman heads home, weighed down with groceries. She tries to blow a loose strand of hair from her eyes, fails, and gives me a weary half-smile as she passes.

Taxis sweep up and down the side streets, and an undershirted man sits on a fire escape, reading a newspaper by window light. In the alley below, backpackers intoxicated on youth and evening air cluster past, caught in the search beams of the taxi headlights. Freeze-frame images, there then gone.

Breakneck stairs tumble downward. Rounded corners. Carriages that clatter past under street-lamp mist. It's as though I've wandered into the 1800s by mistake.

I'm not really sure why I'm here, in the Lower Town. Not sure why I'm boarding a ferry to Lévis. Ropes are thrown free and the city slides back. The lights of the Chateau Frontenac form connect-the-dot constellations above, in the Old City.

The low, subliminal throb of the ship engines. A sky the colour of a deep bruise, clouds heavy with rain. Confetti bursts of seagulls scatter upward in the distance, the white of their bellies now a pale shade of blue.

The St. Lawrence is more a presence than a river, a sensation more than a scent. A highway of cold water flowing outward from the continental heartland, reaching for a distant sea. *The River of Canada.* That's what the Europeans first called it.

The other shore comes to meet us and I disembark. Pools of light in an empty parking lot.

I think about my nineteen-year-old self sometimes. I wonder where he went. I wonder what became of him.

I know what became of *me*. Life. Got married, had kids. Mortgaged myself into a house with the usual accessories. I'm not really sure what I hope to find here, or why I'm seeking out the landmarks of my youth. Maybe it's just nostalgia, or simply curiosity. I want to know if I can still find my way there in the dark.

From the Lévis ferry port, I map it out in my head: *Across the parking lot, turn right, past the warehouses, then up the stairs to the top of the cliff. Left down the first lane, right on the next. Third door up, second window from the left.* Perhaps I'm hoping to meet one of my former selves along the way, or maybe catch a glimpse of a girl disappearing around a corner ahead of me, slipping out of sight as I make my way up the stairs.

I stop—more than once, hands on hips, lungs gasping—and when I finally reach the top, on creaking knees and flushed of face, nothing is quite as familiar as I'd hoped. *Is something half-remembered worse than something not remembered at all?* It takes me almost an hour, retracing one side street, then the next, to find it. But I do.

Someone's built an addition onto my memory, that's why I didn't recognize it. The building has almost doubled and the yard is gone. Just a large vinyl-sided box, really. I feel a sense of ownership nonetheless, as though I should be able to stride in and say, "I was here. This is where the bodies fell."

I find the window. That small square of light. And I want to throw a pebble against the pane, see who peeks out from inside. But the ferry back is leaving soon, and I have to go. I've got a cliff to descend and a river to cross.

An Open Letter to Montreal on Behalf of Calgary

When I tally the ledger of my life, taking stock of opportunities squandered and bridges burned, I'm grateful to the gods of happenstance for one particular item: after my failed foray into Old Quebec, I had the good sense to flee—not back home to Alberta, but to Montreal, where I spent a summer working with a conservation-trail crew just north of the city. I contrived to spend as much time in Montreal as my work schedule and sparse funds would allow. I was part of a contingent of volunteers, mostly from outside Quebec, a cultural immersion of sorts in which, as one of my colleagues put it, "I learned just enough French to not get laid."

In Montreal, you will often find yourself in need of a scarf for shoulder-flinging, sitting, as you do, over espressos and folded newspapers, thinking in aphorisms and wishing you still smoked. In Quebec City, one dodges horse apples that occasionally tumble from the leather-diapered carriage drays. In Montreal, you dodge Montreal. Jaywalking is an art, yielding is considered a sign of weakness, and lane markings are merely suggestions. I remember Montreal, especially at night, as a giant, hashish-fuelled pinball machine, all razzle-dazzle and ricochet.

My brother Sean, Alberta-born and backwoods raised, just as I was, has been in Montreal for more than twenty years. A talented composer, his work has taken him deep into the francophone music scene. And though he floats between languages with an enviable ease, he is still not "of the island," and never will be. "Basically, I'm an allophone whose first language is English," he says with a (slightly rueful) smile.

Sean occasionally stumbles over words in his first language, groping through French for the correct term in English. And like many Anglo Montrealers he uses the verb "pass" far, far too much. ("We'll pass by a dépanneur on the way home and pick up some wine." That sort of thing.) Neither fish nor fowl, but a bit of both, he fits in well with the city.

I enjoy Montreal and I'm always happy to find an excuse to stop by. So when the Montreal-based magazine *Maisonneuve* was compiling a special "Canada Issue" and asked me to write something on Calgary, I countered with "Why not Calgary—in relation to Montreal?" Having previously penned open letters to women on behalf of men, and to Americans on behalf of Canadians, it seemed a natural way to go.

Ironically, of all the things I've written over the years, this is the one that got the angriest response. No points for guessing from which city most of the angry emails came. Hint: It wasn't Montreal and it wasn't Calgary.

Dear Montreal,

Calgary here. I'm writing today because I have a problem. No, it's not my rugged good looks. Or my square-shouldered Western sensibilities. And no, it's not that my wallet is weighted down with so much money I can hardly get a decent mosey going. No. The problem is pie, and the allotment thereof.

A certain author (oh, let's call him "Will") has been criticized for pointing out the simple fact that Canada has no main city, no central metropolis. No equivalent of London or Paris. No Tokyo, no Buenos Aires. No single centre that dominates the country. "Well," comes the challenge, inevitably from Toronto, "what about Toronto?"

Well, what about it? The author in question lived in Toronto for many years. It's a fine city, but that doesn't change a thing. First off, we're dealing with a nation that is roughly 25 percent francophone.

So right out of the gate, with Toronto you're only talking about *English* Canada, not the whole country. More importantly, London, Paris, Tokyo, and Buenos Aires, et cetera, are national capitals. Toronto is not.

"Ah! But what about English-language media? Isn't that centred in Toronto?" Um, no. The vast majority of Canadians (sadly, but undeniably) still prefer to plug into American pop culture than into anything produced in Toronto. Canada's two national English-language papers and various nightly news broadcasts may originate there, but Peter Mansbridge and *The Globe and Mail* do not a Paris make.

"That we're even having this debate proves my very point!" cries our stalwart author. In Britain and France no one doubts the overwhelming importance of London or Paris. Not for a second.

In Canada, Ottawa may be where our MPs congregate, but—and this is why I'm writing you today, *cher Montréal*—political clout is still centred primarily in two cities: Montreal and Calgary. These two cities, for better or worse, are the ones setting our national agenda. There is a "Calgary school of thought" (on the hard-hearted right) and a Montreal one (on the muddle-headed left). The first is ascendant, the other older and more entrenched, but both seek to dictate the terms of debate. How to divide the pie then?

At this stage, many readers will no doubt be pulling their hair out by the clumpful over Calgary's growing influence and *this neo-con hell we're living through!*™. And, with Monsieur Harper now rounding up kittens at gunpoint and sending them to Iraq, it will only be a matter of time before we have, right here at home, soldiers! With guns! In our streets! (Or rather, this being the Canadian military we're talking about, *Soldiers! With a gun! In our streets!*) Yes. A Calgary-fuelled military coup is all but inevitable, but in the meantime—and until that glorious day when jackbooted shock troops in Stetsons scissor-march into Ottawa and across the river into the idyllic innocence of Hull—I'd like to present you with this complimentary fruit basket and two-for-one coupons from Peters' Drive-In (drinks & gratuities not included).

Montreal and Calgary are shaping our national agenda and may be for some time, so we need to come to an understanding. A *rapprochement*, if you will. First, you need to understand that, Iraq-bound kittens aside, we aren't quite the boogeyman you've been led to believe. Calgary is the straw man of Canada's political left.

Know also that as the author of this epistle, I have no particular vested interest in Calgary. My work is not based in Calgary, I did not grow up here, nor do I have family here. My wife and I came to Calgary seven years ago, and for the same reasons many people do: the clean air, the opportunities, the sheer and unyielding optimism. It was refreshing. After all these years, people still come West to reinvent themselves. Case in point: Toronto's own Stephen Harper. And what a cuddle-bunny he turned out to be!

True, Calgary does have a large proportion of American expats, but it's only around 6 percent of the population—and most of them are Democrats. *Our* Americans voted for Al Gore, which is to say they're left-leaning (by American standards anyway). The influence of Calgary's "Al Gore Democrats" has been greatly exaggerated, mainly by people looking for a way to justify their own biases against the city. "Calgary is just so … so *American*," they say, voices dropping on that last pornographic term.

I can assure you that Calgary is very much a Canadian city. And proudly so. Contrary to popular opinion, the Liberal Party of Canada does not hold a monopoly on what constitutes "Canadian values."

Want to know Calgary's real secret? All that "working man," "grassroots," "squinting into the horizon with sun-creased eyes" stuff? Pure bunk. Calgary is not in any way a working man's town. We don't *build* anything. We have no equivalent of Vancouver's docks or Montreal's port. Calgary is a city of CEOs, a city of head offices. There's a reason we don't have a pall of smog hanging over the city— that would require industry.

Edmonton is the real heart of Alberta's oil patch. That city's hockey team is aptly named. The Oilers! With Calgary's team, a better choice would have been something like "the Executives!" or "the CEOs!"

(Though chanting *"Go, Calgary Chief Executive Officers, Go!"* might take some doing.)

Calgary is a hopelessly white-collar town, so if you do come for a visit, please ignore the self-conscious "howdys" and Stampede-induced "yee haws" that grip the city annually. Imagine if once a year Montrealers dressed up like French Canadian voyageurs and donned colourful sashes and carried canoes around and piled stacks of beaver pelts in their bank lobbies and hotel foyers—and then complained that "everyone thinks we're just a bunch of voyageurs!" That's how surreal the Stampede truly is.

Another interesting nugget o' truth for you to chew upon: Calgary, with a population of well over one million, is more ethnically diverse than Montreal. Shocking! But true. Don't believe me? Check StatsCan. Of course, "more multicultural" does not mean "more fashionable," "better dressed," or "more insouciant," and Montreal's status when it comes to nightlife, cuisine, spectacles, new music, and general all-round *joie de vivre*-ness remains unassailed. (Though, I gotta say, in terms of pure fun, St. John's may have you beat.) And anyway, as far as the whole multicultural thing goes, Vancouver and Toronto trump us both on that score. Neither of us can claim to be the most ethnically diverse anything.

What Calgary does have, especially when it comes to problem-solving, is common sense: relentless, unwavering, at times ruthless, common sense.

This is a city of oil-company head offices whose transit system is wind-powered (that is, it runs on electricity generated by wind; they don't have windmills atop the C-Train or anything). Wind-powered transit. Why? Because it makes sense, that's why.

Calgary is also one of the most educated cities in Canada, second only to Ottawa in the number of postgraduate degrees. And despite its public image, it's a green city as well. In a point-by-point overview, Montreal's *Maisonneuve* magazine describes Calgary's commitment to green power as "the largest in North America," with targets in place to have the city run on 75 percent green sources within a decade. No other city in Canada—or the continent, for that matter—can match this. We don't dump raw sewage into *our* river.

This is a city where they were preparing to build a new hockey arena, but when they surveyed the city's youth they found that skateboarding was far and away the number one sport, so they tossed out the plans for an arena and built a massive, state-of-the-art skateboarding park instead. (The city then turned around and—this is classic Calgary—immediately launched a crackdown on skateboarders *outside* the park.)

There exists no Gordian knot large enough that Calgarians can't slice through it. This is a city whose official civic motto is simply "Onward." There is a clarity of purpose here that may seem blunt at times, even cold, but which can also be invigorating, like a bracing wind coming in over the mountains. And as anyone who's ever suffered through one of those intensely unfocused, maddening debates that Montreal seems to specialize in, clarity is not necessarily a bad thing, just as endless dithering is not necessarily a virtue. (Remember Junior Martin? Exactly.)

In Montreal, the issues are always so messy. There's always yet another esoteric and only tangentially related aspect of an argument to be considered, always more angles to mull over, more nuance to be layered on (with a trowel, if need be). In Montreal, nothing ever seems to get resolved and every statement is inevitably followed with a "Yes, *but* …"

Here in Calgary, you're more likely to encounter a "So?" than a "Yes, but." And that is the crux of these two opposing views. In Calgary, you get simple answers to complex questions. In Montreal, you get complex answers to simple problems. Neither approach is inherently superior; it depends entirely on what is being discussed.

The undeclared tug-of-war between Montreal and Calgary is only going to intensify.

So. Here's what I suggest. Let's not fight. Let's work together. Let's divvy things up, based not on ideology, but temperament. You be the heart, we'll be the head. You can be from Venus, we'll be from Mars.

When there's a problem that calls for hard-nosed logic—the sort of problem that can be solved with a calculator, say—we'll take over. When long nights over coffee and cigarettes are called for, the field is yours.

Rather than slugging it out, let us embrace. Let's make it not a boxing match, but a dance. A tango, perhaps, with its smouldering subtext and competing dance steps. A battle of wills set to music.

Consider this an invitation. The hand is extended. Will you join the dance?

Avec best wishes,

xoxo Guillaume

Big in Toronto

Some people have skeletons in their closets. I have a shiny blue jumpsuit.

Blame it on Moses, but I once worked as a professional space cadet, dressed in full Buck Rogers garb and spouting techno-babble at Tour of the Universe, "the world's first large-scale simulator ride," an attraction so fantastic it could only have sprung from the fertile (dare I say fecund) imagination of Moses Znaimer Himself. It's the part I usually omit on my résumé: *"Was employed as one of Moses Znaimer's space cadets."* My only defence in taking such a job is that I was a student at the time, which is to say, I plead poverty.

If you visited the CN Tower between 1986 and 1987, you may have run into me—unless I had my space helmet on with the visor down (the better to nap with). Tour of the Universe was set in a Toronto spaceport in the year 2019, complete with customs clearance, space inoculations, boarding passes, security checks, and long, unexplained delays.

Passengers would descend in a special "time machine" (i.e., elevator) into the "very depths of the earth itself!" (i.e., the basement) where they would be "entertained" by out-of-work "actors" (out-of-work actors: are there any other kind?) before boarding a Shuttlecraft to the outer moons of Jupiter, where they'd inevitably hit an asteroid (same damn asteroid every time) and be forced to return to Earth.

The journey itself was excellent; Znaimer and company had purchased a pair of authentic NASA flight simulators that rumbled with every asteroid bump. Alas, the rest of the attraction, the part involving people in costumes, had a strained "Let's all pretend we're in the future and having fun" desperation about it.

I worked in Customs for a while, and then Security, and was later bumped to Medical, where I was soon reassigned after parents complained that the shrieks of pain I emitted when demonstrating the laser inoculations were scaring the children. I eventually ended up in the Spaceport Lobby—the worst assignment possible—where my signature "bit" was convincing entire groups to chant *"Will deserves a raise!"* loud enough for the administrators upstairs to hear.

The "captain" of our Jupiter-bound flight was actually just a video loop of a man in flight uniform who would appear now and then to address the passengers. He was called, ahem, "Captain Moses." *Hello, my name is David Moses and I'll be your captain today. Please buckle up your seatbelts and we'll be on our way.* Same damn video every time. Same damn actor, same damn script too.

Boredom is the mother of creativity, and I decided to have some fun with Captain Moses. When the tour groups were about to board the Shuttlecraft, I would go on the PA system and announce: "Ladies and gentlemen, your pilot today will be Captain Anderson, one of our finest ... Hold on." I would then pretend to listen to a message from my headphone. "What? *Captain Moses?* They're not going to let that guy fly again, are they? After what happened last time! Look, the man was clearly drunk, we're just lucky he didn't hit an asteroid and kill everyone on board!" And then, to the crowd: "Not to worry, your captain will be Anderson. I assure you, Captain Moses is a menace to space travel and will most definitely NOT be your pilot today."

And then later, when Captain Moses appeared on the video screen, there'd be a moment of stunned silence followed by laughter (albeit nervous laughter). I think I got fired at some point.

Being a professional space cadet was the strangest job I've ever had—that goes without saying—but not just because of the uniforms. (And what is it with the future's fondness for jumpsuits? Is the Glorious World of Tomorrow really going to be one extended ABBA reunion?) No, the strangest thing about Tour of the Universe was that although I worked at the CN Tower, I was stuck in the basement.

The whole point of the CN Tower is its height. The soaring views and architectural vertigo, the windows dabbed with nose smears, the sense of freedom: I was far removed from it all, which is a shame because the CN Tower is ripe with superlatives. *The Guinness Book of World Records* recognized it as the world's tallest free-standing structure, but that's only the start. The CN Tower also boasts the world's highest bar, the world's highest public observation deck, the world's highest revolving restaurant, as well as the world's highest graffiti, courtesy of local schoolchildren who were invited to paint their names on the final crowning piece, which was then heli-lifted to the top of the tower when it was completed in 1976. The CN Tower even has the "world's highest wine cellar," which is surely an oxymoron of some sort.

The oddest fact about the CN Tower? It's hollow. I discovered this firsthand in my film-student days when I made a documentary about a charity stair climb. The film crew and I (i.e., me and Dale) took an elevator to the top and then went down a few flights of stairs to get footage of people staggering up toward the finish line. ("Keep it up! You're halfway there!" Dale yelled cruelly to the runners as they passed.)

In between shouting encouraging messages to participants, we noticed a small stairwell service door that had been left unlocked. When we peered inside, we saw a metal catwalk, several service lines snaking past, and below that … darkness. It was the tower turned inside out, a straight plunge into nothingness, the Elevator Shaft of Infinity.

It was, in the words of my crew, "The perfect place to dump a body."

Stranger still, the CN Tower *sways*. As much as two metres from its centre in a high wind, which only underlines what an incredible engineering feat the structure truly is. A few years ago, the American Society of Civil Engineers (ASCE) included the CN Tower on its list of "Seven Wonders of the Modern World," alongside the Panama Canal, the Golden Gate Bridge, the dykes and land reclamations of Holland, and the England-to-France Chunnel.

"Today's modern wonders are more than simply awe inspiring," declared the ASCE. "They are functional, operational masterpieces that have revolutionized civil engineering and benefited humanity. They are a tribute to the universal human desire to triumph over the impossible."

And you thought the CN Tower was just a really big antenna.

No, it is an embodiment of universal human desire. And what did they build right beside it, right next to this towering erection? An oval dome that opens and closes depending on the weather (i.e., its mood). These two enormous structures, these totems to fertility, loom very large indeed. Freud would have had a field day with Toronto's skyline.

Now, something as spectacular and superlative as Toronto's tower naturally inspires equally spectacular and superlative descriptions, what I like to call "hot dogs to the moon." You know the type of thing: statistical comparisons that are so bizarre, so utterly removed from reality, that you can't even begin to visualize what they mean, let alone find them useful. *"The Acme Wiener Factory produces enough hot dogs every five weeks to stretch to the moon and back two and a half times."*

The CN Tower is rife with these "hot dogs to the moon" type numbers, many of which seem to involve (a) elephants and (b) football fields. I'm not sure who decided that football fields and elephants would henceforth be the standard unit of measurement for Really Big Stuff, but the tradition has continued at the CN Tower. Some examples, gleaned from CN Tower literature:

Fact: The CN Tower took more than three years to complete and is the height of 5½ football fields stacked end on end.

Fact: The CN Tower weighs 117,910 metric tonnes, which is the equivalent of 23,214 large elephants. (I'll give you a moment to picture that.)

Fact: If you piled all the hot dogs consumed at the CN Tower cafeteria in a single day on top of each other it would be incredibly disgusting.

I had a friend named Josie who worked as an elevator operator at the tower, and it almost ruined her. Statistics such as those listed above tend to stick in your brain like a neural virus, burrowing through grey matter and gnawing at the synapses.

Years later, she can still reel off CN Tower data in much the same fashion as an ex–Hare Krishna trying to escape a mantra. (CN Tower guides really ought to be "de-programmed" after working the elevator circuit.) The last I heard from Josie, she was a radio host north of Montreal. I imagine that in moments of weakness, even while on air, she finds herself starting to slip into the spiel: *"We are now ascending at a rate of five and a half large elephants per hot dog."*

There are only a handful of numbers that we share as a nation: 24 Sussex Drive. '72 Summit. War of 1812. Group of Seven. Two-four of Molsons. Ten-pack of Timbits.

I would like to add another: 1816. This is the height, in feet, of the CN Tower: the largest free-standing whatchamacallit in the world, and as such, the epitome of Stunt Architecture. Hockey players and beer aside, the CN Tower is one of the very few areas where Canadians can really lord it over the Americans, which is why this figure is given in feet and not in those tricky base-ten metric numbers that our neighbours to the south are having such a hard time figuring out. (To impress the rest of the world, the number is 553—metres, not feet.)

Please note: I said "free-standing structure," and not "tower." The truth is, and even now I am loath to admit it, there *are* towers taller than the CN. The Americans have TV towers that are higher, but they cheated; they used wires.

But if you say "free-standing structure" fast enough and with just the right amount of breezy confidence, it still sounds impressive. Don Harron said the CN Tower was built "to teach Canadian men humility," but I say, no. It is an ode to Canadian *virility*, not a lesson in modesty. (*See:* "SkyDome, proximity to" above.)

Case in point: At Tour of the Universe, the spaceport and launching pad were supposedly 1816 feet beneath the surface: as far below as the tower rose high. The Shuttlecraft was then "blasted into outer space" from inside the shaft of the tower itself—engines throbbing, floor shaking, lights flashing, speed increasing, faster and faster and faster and faster until ... you suddenly burst out from the top and soared toward the heavens in a euphoric dreamland of zero gravity. *Ahhhh.*

Who says Toronto isn't sexy? I mean, other than everybody.

Which is why it came as such a disappointment when I took my family to the CN Tower only to discover that Moses Znaimer's "jaunt to Jupiter" had long since gone. The World of Tomorrow had been packed up and put away, the future had been shut down. *Tour of the Universe, 1985–1992, R.I.P.*

So I took my wife and then-toddler son up the tower's turbo-charged elevators instead, a heady rush of acceleration that hurtles you to the observation deck in fifty-eight seconds flat. When we arrived at the main level, people were standing in mid-air. This was the tower's famous glass floor, which allows you to walk out at cloud levels and look straight down. It has a breathtaking, dizzying effect.

Things not to do when you have a sleeping child strapped on your back and your wife is afraid of heights: Walk out onto the glass floor at the CN Tower and say, "C'mon honey, it's fine."

She was waving frantically from the sidelines. "You have our child on your back!"

"But it's perfectly safe," I said. Then I jumped up and down a couple of times just to, you know, demonstrate how safe it was. "See?" I said brightly. "We didn't fall through."

Things not to do when you're standing on a glass floor more than a thousand feet in the air with your child strapped to your back and a spouse who is yelling at you to come back: Jump up and down.

When my repeated hoppings failed to reassure her, I started quoting statistics. "Look, right here in the pamphlet, 'The Glass Floor is strong enough to withstand the weight of fourteen large hippos!' Fourteen hippos, honey. *Fourteen!*" But it was no use, and the panic in her eyes and the boiling of her blood eventually forced me to abandon my gravity-defying, mid-air frolic.

It was only then that I noticed the view.

We tend to fixate on the tower itself and forget about the panorama it offers: a fish-eye look at the city, with Lake Ontario laid out like a great swath of fabric, the arc of the shoreline, the curve of the Earth, and there, in the distance, a faint rise of mist: Niagara. You feel as though, if the light is right and you squint your eyes just so, you might even see the Rocky Mountains themselves. Perhaps that's why the CN Tower is such a Canadian icon: in a country as big as ours, it takes a tower this tall just to get a decent view.

The Kingdom of Anne

It was a time of innocence that never was. A time of small rebellions and summer lanes, when having rust-red hair was the greatest trauma a girl had to face, and life's crises resolved themselves with a storybook certainty …

Rolling hills and country churchyards, wind-washed beaches and sandstone cliffs. Red earth at sunset—that warm shade of vermilion, somewhere between rust and blood. If Prince Edward Island didn't exist, we'd have had to invent it. And in a way, we did.

Maritime writer Harry Bruce calls it "the Seductive Myth of the Perfect Island." Part fiction, part fact, part wish fulfillment, PEI at times seems less a province than a pastiche, a patchwork of pastoral idylls sewed together in a warm and comforting quilt.

I arrived in PEI after living in Japan. I knew what an enduring and inexplicable allure Anne of Green Gables held for most Japanese women (my wife being one of the few exceptions I ever met). So, we moved to the Island in the hope that I might be able to fob myself off as a sort of freelance "Japan expert."

My wife, eminently more employable, quickly landed a job with CP Hotels. Inspired by her example, I decided to focus on the world of travel and tourism as well. Avonlea Tours, a local company, was looking for someone who was fluent in Japanese and had a background in travel management. Lacking either qualification, I decided to apply.

At that time, the Japanese government had a series of standardized tests they used to evaluate Japanese language ability. Level One represented the fluency required to work as an interpreter or translator. Level Two included the ability to discuss detailed economic proposals. Level Three was less advanced, but with a solid basis in *kanji* characters and the intricacies of Japanese grammar. Level Four, the bottom rung, also known as "barroom Japanese," required conversational abilities only, along with two hundred or so common kanji characters.

I had a Level Four. Which is to say, you can plop me down anywhere in Japan and I can find a hotel, book a room, order a meal, chat up the locals. I could bluff my way through the basics, but I certainly couldn't discuss complex business arrangements. So, when asked about my second-language proficiency during my interview with the PEI tour company, I leaned in, lowered my voice, and said, "Sir, I don't mean to brag, but there are only four levels of Japanese fluency, and"—I paused here for full dramatic effect—"I have reached *the fourth level.*"

It wasn't exactly a lie, you understand. It was more a fortnight-in-purgatory, don't-do-it-again sort of thing. But hey, it worked. I was hired on, given a snappy job title and a modest expense account, and off I went.

Fortunately, my work would primarily involve selling Anne of Green Gables tours to the Japanese, which was about as difficult as selling a glass of water to someone whose hair is on fire. Unfortunately, one of my very first duties was to welcome a VIP tour from the Japan Travel Bureau. These were big shots. *Corporate* big shots. I greeted the JTB contingent at the airport while my unilingual Canadian boss, Roger, looked on. The Japanese were dressed in severe blue suits and had suitably severe expressions on their faces.

Taking a deep breath, heart aflutter, I gave what was perhaps the most heartfelt speech of my life: "*Yokoso Prince Edward Island e!* (Welcome to Prince Edward Island!) *Sumimasen, demo watashi wa*

Nihongo pera pera ja nai (I'm sorry, but I can't really speak Japanese very well). *Demo, shacho wa shirimasen* (But my boss—I pointed to Roger at this point—doesn't know). *Barasanai de kudasai* (Please don't tell him)."

There was a moment of dead silence ... and then the blue suits broke into laughter and applause. Roger beamed, confused but happy. As the VIPs filed past us into the waiting minivan, one of the head honchos took Roger aside and said, with a gesture in my direction, "His Japanese. Very good."

When Roger asked me in a whispered aside why they'd been laughing, I said, "I opened with a joke. You know, to break the ice."

The best thing about my work in PEI? It provided me with a ready alibi whenever I wanted to play hooky, and I spent many a leisurely hour driving down the Island's back roads, exploring hidden coves and far-flung villages—all in the name of "research." I would draw up elaborately ambitious proposals for possible tours to PEI's lesser-known attractions, which I duly submitted and which were just as duly ignored. "We were thinking more about something involving Anne of Green Gables ..."

When you get beyond the tourist beat, PEI rewards you handsomely. Old barns and fishing piers seem to have been arranged on purely aesthetic principles. Shorelines curve toward distant light-houses. There is a mood that overtakes you, one of exhilarated calm—if such a thing is possible.

In a nation defined by the space it takes up, this little island, so perfectly self-contained, is something of an anomaly. The entire population is just 136,000. (In comparison, there are more than twenty cities in the rest of Canada that have populations larger than that. Saskatoon alone has more people than the province of Prince Edward Island.)

In a Maritime region, PEI is an island of farmers. In an urban nation, PEI remains resolutely rural. Vancouver Island is larger than PEI, so is Cape Breton. Both of these islands have populations bigger than PEI, and both were once self-governing colonies too, and yet neither of them became provinces.

So why PEI? By what right did such a tiny, underpopulated place claim full provincehood where Vancouver Island and Cape Breton did not?

The answer: stubbornness. Pure and simple. Cape Breton and Vancouver Island allowed their colonial status to be withdrawn. PEI refused. The roots of Island autonomy date back to 1769 when the British broke it off from Nova Scotia, making it a distinct colony complete with its own governor and an overly elaborate constitution. At that time, the Island's population was less than three hundred, almost none of whom were of British descent. Prince Edward himself—Duke of Kent, father of Queen Victoria, and the very man for whom the island colony was named—argued that the Island was too small to justify its independent colonial status and urged that it be re-annexed to Nova Scotia.

Prince Edward's advice—namesake or not—was roundly ignored. PEI would become an experiment, a playground of would-be colonizers, a pet project of British dandies looking to build their own personal Edens in the New World. PEI was a fiefdom created by royal fiat. Unique among the colonies of British North America, it was owned entirely by absentee landlords.

Just how arbitrary this process was is illustrated by the manner in which the property was divvied up. The Island was surveyed into lots, and the lots were put in a hat and drawn, lottery-style, for patrons back in Britain. These absentee landlords were then required to ship in tenant farmers to break the land. Most never bothered.

Comment is often made about the effects of the seigneurial system on New France, and by extension Quebec, but in many ways the PEI version of feudalism was much worse. At least the seigneurial lords of New France for the most part lived on or near the property they were granted, and the French habitants who worked the land had at least a chance of someday owning it. Not on the Island. The landlords of PEI were an ocean away. It was the ultimate hobby farm. Bit of a lark that, owning an estate in the colonies.

The hardscrabble farmers who tilled the red soils of PEI—the

Scots and Irish and Acadians—were little more than serfs, mere tenants on someone else's land, as were their children and their children's children. And yet, they persevered with a dedication worthy of ownership, transforming the Island into an agricultural oasis in a salt-water sea. They called it the Garden of the Gulf. The Million Acre Farm.

It was ever thus. Jacques Cartier called it "the fairest land 'tis possible to see." And the Mi'kmaq referred to it as *Abegweit*, romantically translated as "Cradled on the Waves." ("Low along the water" is probably more accurate.) No matter. In PEI the romantic version of events always takes precedence. It began with a romantic vision, and some would argue it has remained a prisoner of that vision ever since.

The reality of life in an already anachronistic feudal system was much harsher. But out of this a distinct Island character emerged, one stemming from a shared sense of physical and political isolation. As historians David Weale and Harry Baglole note, "Year in and year out, generation after generation, this singular geographic situation dictated both a sense of unity and separateness, of inclusion and exclusion."

It took a century and a half of protests and petitions to finally wrest control of the Island away from its proprietors. The settlers denounced their status as "vassals" and "slaves," and at times the situation grew explosive. Rent collectors were harried into hiding, armed troops from Halifax had to be brought in to maintain order. It was a long, hard-fought battle, and the last absentee proprietor did not relinquish the last parcel of land until 1895, more than forty years *after* the French Canadian seigneurial system had been abolished. And by that time the Island was already a province. Which is to say, PEI entered Confederation as an anomaly, not only in size but in system. A fiefdom disguised as a province.

And though it likes to promote itself as "the Cradle of Confederation," the Island was dragged kicking and scratching into Canada. The original Confederation Conference took place in PEI not because the Islanders were especially keen on the proposal for colonial union, but because it was the only way the other delegates could be sure that the Islanders would bother showing up. As it was, PEI rejected the offer. It wasn't until 1873, when a disastrous railway venture—as crooked in its route as it was in its financing—had driven the colony to near bankruptcy, that the Islanders finally, begrudgingly, agreed to join Canada. When the Proclamation of Union was read in Charlottetown the audience consisted of a grand total of three—count 'em, three!—passersby, none of whom seemed particularly impressed.

What unites Islanders today is an image they have of themselves as a distinct breed of people and the knowledge that they've staked a claim on Paradise. "There are only two kinds of people," I was often told. "Those who are from the Island, and those who *wish* they were from the Island."

PEI exists both at the centre of the universe and outside the flow of time. And in PEI there are only two geographic locations: "on the island" and "off island." Could be Moncton, could be Peru; it doesn't matter. It's all "off island." And if you don't have the good grace to be born here, you are permanently considered a "come from away," an outsider. Your mother may have given birth on the ferry over, but you'd still not be fully "of the Island."

I used to write a column for the Charlottetown paper, and I noticed something odd about the style sheet we were using. The term "Islander" was capitalized, but "come-from-away" was not. Shouldn't it be, I asked the editor, "John Smith, a Come-from-away, and Sally Jones, an Islander, were wed today"? He just smiled tightly, said nothing. The style sheet stood, as did its strange but subtle form of capitalizational discrimination.

No one helped shape the Myth of the Perfect Isle more than Lucy Maud Montgomery.

I was born, praise to the gods, in Prince Edward Island,
that colourful little land of ruby and emerald and sapphire.
Compassed by an inviolate sea, it floats on the waves of the
blue Gulf, a green seclusion and haunt of peace.

Montgomery grew up in the village of Cavendish, picturesque even by PEI standards, and in 1895 she jotted down an idea for a short story: "Elderly couple apply to orphan asylum for a boy. By mistake a girl is sent them."

The story turned into a novel, and the novel languished for many years before being published at long last in 1908. *Anne of Green Gables,* the story of a plucky red-haired orphan, made Montgomery an instant international celebrity, the J.K. Rowling of her day.

No one was more surprised about this than she was. "I can't believe," she wrote in her journal, "that such a simple little tale, written in and of a simple PEI farming settlement, with a juvenile audience in view, can really have scored somewhere out in the busy world."

It wasn't just young girls who read it. Northern trappers and British royalty, missionaries in China, monks on distant monasteries, ranchers in Australia—the letters and cards poured in, praising the book and begging for a sequel. The author obliged. *Anne of Avonlea* came out the following year and was another instant hit.

Montgomery penned six more instalments in the Anne series, as well as more than a dozen other novels, a collection of poetry, a serialized autobiography, and some five hundred short stories. Mark Twain was an early fan, describing *Anne of Green Gables* as "the sweetest creation of child life yet written." Twain, no slouch when it came to creating endearing childhood characters (Tom Sawyer, Huck Finn, et al.), considered the character of Anne Shirley to be "the most moving and delightful child since the immortal Alice."

The story of Anne has since been published in more than forty languages and still has a devoted following around the world. Translated into Japanese as *Akage no Anne* ("Red-Haired Anne"), it went on to sell more than a million copies in Japan and has inspired numerous stage productions over there, along with an animated series, fan clubs, festivals, even cookbooks and art galleries, all dedicated to Anne. When the "Canada World" theme park opened in northern Japan, the exhibits consisted solely of Anne of Green Gables. The park not only painstakingly recreated the buildings and locations referred to in Montgomery's books but also hired a cast of characters, led by a red-haired Anne herself, to mingle with the crowds. They even brought in truckloads of red sand to simulate PEI's soil. The second-largest nation on earth was thus reduced to its smallest province.

"Canada World" is now a public park, but the allure of Anne among the Japanese is as strong as ever. It has been likened, with tongue only slightly in cheek, to a religion, one complete with a Holy Book (*Anne of Green Gables*), a Founder (L.M. Montgomery), a Saint (Anne Herself), a Shrine (the house in Cavendish that served as the inspiration for Green Gables), and of course, a Holy Pilgrimage: the journey to Prince Edward Island itself, culminating at the gravesite of L.M. Montgomery. I wasn't selling package tours, I was selling a rite of passage.

Montgomery's book helped ruin the very thing it celebrated: PEI's quiet seclusion. Sixty years ago, and long before the Japanese arrived, Montgomery was already complaining that "Cavendish is being overrun and exploited by mobs of tourists and my harmless neighbours have their lives simply worried out of them by carloads of 'foreigners' who want to see some of Anne's haunts." Note: this being PEI, the term 'foreigner' could refer to anyone from off island, whether they be from Hungary or Halifax. (The fact that the character of Anne herself was born "off island," in Nova Scotia no less, is something the good people of PEI have never quite reconciled.)

Today, it's only gotten worse. More than 700,000 tourists arrive each year. Germans, Yankees, Poles, and those bloody insufferable Upper Canadians with their monocles and waxed moustaches—they all come to worship at the altar of Anne, to see for themselves where little Anne Shirley grew up. *Anne of Green Gables* is the story of an island as much as a girl: the two are inseparable, and the border between fiction and reality often becomes blurred. Avonlea is really Cavendish, Green Gables is a combination of locales, and the Babbling Brook, Lovers Lane, the Haunted Wood, they can be visited even today.

The real became mingled with the imaginary, and no one seemed to know exactly where one ended and the other began, least of all the author:

When I am asked if Anne herself is a "real person" I always say "no" with an odd reluctance and an uncomfortable feeling of not telling the truth. For she is and always has been, from the moment I first thought of her, so real to me that I feel I am doing violence to something when I deny her an existence anywhere save in Dreamland.

When they visit Montgomery's grave, or even the Green Gables house, Japanese visitors sometimes become overwhelmed by emotion, their eyes welling, voices trembling.

If Anne is the fictional made real, then Prince Edward Island is the real transformed into myth. A dream of innocence packaged for popular consumption.

Here's something you won't find in travel brochures: the true scent of PEI? It's not salt or sea, or lobsters simmering in a pot. It's the smell of squashed skunk. Skunks themselves aren't native to PEI; they were introduced by an ambitious though somewhat naive would-be furrier who thought their luxurious fur would be ideal for women's fashion. The fur was thick and luxurious, true. But it was also still skunk. And no woman, no matter how soft the pelt she was offered, was willing to "wear" skunk. The business failed spectacularly. Unable to bring himself to kill his charges, the owner turned them loose instead. On an island without natural enemies (save cars, which hit them with a pungent predictability), skunks have flourished. Many a night in Charlottetown, my wife and I would be awakened by their odour wafting through open windows.

And never mind the long winters when the entire province seems to shut down and the tea shoppe signs creak on cold winds.

"No other province," writes Harry Bruce, "is so tortured by the gap between a beautiful dream and a homely reality. More than all other Canadians, Islanders allow a fairy tale to dominate politics and distort visions of their homeland destiny."

Lucy Maud Montgomery married a local Presbyterian minister and left the Island. She would later move to Toronto with her spouse and two sons. Her husband was not well at this point. He suffered from mental illness, and Maud became more and more troubled, both in her private life and with the world around her. World War I. The Depression. The rise of fascism. It became harder and harder to reconcile the beautiful dream with the harsh reality, and in 1938 she suffered a nervous breakdown. She eventually slipped into a deep depression, and on April 24, 1942, Lucy Maud Montgomery died of a drug overdose in an apparent suicide. Beside her bed, a note:

> May God forgive me and I hope everyone else will forgive
> me even if they cannot understand. My position is too awful
> to endure and nobody realizes it. What an end to a life in
> which I tried always to do my best ...

It is forever summer in PEI.

The tour-bus convoys roll in and the Anne impersonators pose for photographs with Green Gables in the background. Here, the tour guide tells us, is where Lucy Maud Montgomery was born. Here is where she wrote the book. Here is where she lived. Here is where she lies.

And here—here is the windswept coast where Anne would have run when she was young. When we were young. Here are the fields and the forests, the country lanes and the flowers, growing free. Here the ocean, rolling blue. Here the innocence, regained.

A Kiss in the Dark: The Unintentional Beauty of Covered Bridges

The floodwaters had been rising all day. The road was submerged and the Bayard Bridge was listing badly to one side. Slowly at first, and then with a groan, it collapsed and was washed away. After seventy-seven years and generations of horse and buggies, cars and kisses, it was gone.

Crowds had gathered to watch the sad finale. Once a local landmark, the covered bridge in Welsford, New Brunswick, was now just a jumble of lumber set adrift in a muddy river.

I was lost in poignant thoughts—of life and death, the transient nature of beauty, time and tide, that sort of thing—when a woman turned and said, "Well, we needed a new bridge anyway."

I was taken aback at first, but she was right. The Bayard Bridge hadn't been built for painters and poets to swoon over; it was a practical, workaday structure whose time had passed. Even its flood-water, slow-motion death on this rain-swollen day in March was appropriate. It had served its purpose, and now it was gone.

The beauty of New Brunswick is not one of grandeur. It's not the soaring heights of the Rocky Mountains or the turrets and ramparts of Old Quebec. It's a hidden, almost neglected beauty, one best captured in the faded wood of her covered bridges. These bridges are New

Brunswick's unofficial symbol: anachronistic structures falling into sway-backed disarray, planks loose, the sides a silvery grey.

Covered bridges were first introduced to the Maritimes by Loyalist refugees fleeing the American Revolution in the 1780s. And much like New Brunswick itself, the plank-wall exteriors hide a complex interior structure: a latticework of crossbeams and trusses, with interlocking triangular patterns that prefigure those of the geodesic dome.

The design spread inland as far as Quebec, though Ontario never really took to them. Of the seven covered bridges that were built in Ontario during that era, only one is still standing: the West Montrose Bridge near Waterloo. (All others in Ontario are modern recreations.) None survived in Nova Scotia, and Western Canada and Newfoundland never had any to begin with. But in New Brunswick, with its abundant forests and small communities with numerous creeks and rivers that need crossing, hundreds of covered bridges were built.

New Brunswick today has the highest concentration of such bridges anywhere in the world. Quebec is a close second, but in Quebec the bridges have often been painted and re-sided, and most are well-maintained. They lack that distinct New Brunswick charm that only benign neglect can give. Like old barns and train trestles, like prairie grain elevators and lonely lighthouses, these bridges weren't built to be beautiful; they became beautiful. The Japanese call it *wabi-sabi:* "the imperfect, the humble, the impermanent, the everyday made sublime." Unintentional beauty.

Nor were the bridges covered for aesthetic reasons; it was a matter of basic economics. Sun and rain quickly rotted exposed beams, and the early settlers were constantly having to mend and replace bridges. An uncovered bridge would last ten years, a covered one would last for seventy—or more. There are covered bridges in New Brunswick built in the late 1800s that are still standing, while not a single uncovered one from that time has survived.

Summer and spring were the hardest seasons. Winter was not. Contrary to popular belief, the bridges weren't covered to protect them from snow. In fact, because horses pulled sleighs in the winter, snow had to be shovelled *into* covered bridges.

In spring, horses often balk at rushing water, so they found the enclosed bridges comforting. The bridge builders—taking note of this—made the entrances more and more barnlike in design. Which is how they often appear: as barns perched atop rivers.

Another danger (perceived if not real) was the vibrations caused by horse hooves and wagon wheels. Pseudo-scientific superstition had it that a fast-moving team could create a standing wave that would shake the sturdiest bridge into a pile of rubble. So a bill was passed in the New Brunswick legislature of 1845 dictating that "no Horse or other Beast, or Carriage of any kind, shall be taken over the said Bridge at a pace faster than a walk on pain of forfeiture of twenty shillings." This included covered bridges, and it had an unforeseen, but fortuitous, side effect. At least, for gentlemen who were accompanying young ladies, as it forced them to slow their horses down and spend what was often an inordinate amount of time within the dimly lit structures. With the darkness providing a ready alibi, the structures became known as "kissing bridges."

The amount of kissing varied according to the length of the bridge. Hartland, New Brunswick, is home to the world's longest covered bridge, built at the turn of the last century. At 391 metres long, it was considered scandalous to many of the town's respectable, clean-minded citizens of that time, who could well imagine, in vivid detail, the lewd things their less-restrained brethren might be tempted to perform in its extended privacy. A petition was circulated to prevent the bridge from being covered, with a local preacher thundering on the subject, issuing grave warnings that the bridge would turn into a veritable "ram pasture."

"In many cases," wrote one prominent citizen, "where a bridge situated near a village has been covered, it has proved very objectionable on account of rough characters who frequent it at night, frightening women and children and making a regular nuisance of it."

Handed over to the government, the petition declared that

covering the bridge "would seriously jeopardize the morals of the young people of Hartland."

The bridge was covered anyway. As one official dryly noted, "If the morals of the young people are so badly bent that it only requires a covered bridge to break them completely, there is little we, as the government, can do."

Covered bridges could also be eerie—especially at night. Not a few were haunted. All were deemed magical. If you closed your eyes and made a wish when you entered, your wish would come true when you left. "Kissing bridges" and "wishing bridges" (as well as, one supposes, "wishing to kiss" bridges), they were—are—steeped in romance and folklore.

At times, it's hard to remember that these modest grey structures were built for purely practical reasons. If the builders had had access to chemically treated wood or cheap concrete, they most certainly would have used them instead—and they certainly wouldn't have gone through all the trouble of covering them. By 1919, the citizens of Hartland were hoping their bridge would be replaced with a fine concrete structure, which would "look much better."

In New Brunswick, wood was always plentiful while quarried stone was not, so the bridges were made of wood. In many cases, building a covered bridge was actually cheaper than using landfill, which is why one often comes across great, lumbering structures perched over tiny gullies with the smallest trickle of a creek below.

The bridges are the constant; it's the landscape that changes. This is part of their appeal: the instant familiarity. With covered bridges, context is everything. The structures look more or less the same: elongated barns, unpainted wood, an almost austere lack of ornamentation. You might find one painted vermilion now and then, but for the most part it's their location that distinguishes them. They span tidal flats, cross ravines and marshland creeks, and hop small gullies and clear-running streams that empty into salt-water bays.

The early roads tended to follow rivers, so when covered bridges were built they were often forced to make a sharp turn, crossing the water at right angles. This wasn't a problem for plodding horses, but with the advent of automobiles the design created dangerous blind corners. Covered bridges were built high, to allow for hay wagons, but they were also notoriously narrow. Many couldn't support heavy motorized vehicles, and several collapsed. Along major highways, where rerouting was considered too expensive, the Department of Highways simply knocked down the covered bridges and replaced them with modern structures. And those that weren't replaced were often taken away by log jams or with the spring ice at breakup. Several were ransacked for firewood. More than one was burned to the water by arsonists.

The oldest bridge still standing was built in 1870. Most were built in the early 1900s. In 1950, New Brunswick had 307 covered bridges. Today, there are only 62 still standing.

Many of New Brunswick's bridges have fallen into disrepair, but a few have been restored and are being preserved primarily as tourist attractions. The irony is sweet. They're becoming exactly what they were never meant to be: impractically preserved objects of sentimentality. The original builders would be nonplussed.

But it is, of course, their very lack of pretension that gives covered bridges their appeal. When the authors of *The Real Guide: Canada* write with a sniff of condescension that there is "nothing graceful or aesthetically satisfying about [the Hartland Covered Bridge], it is just long," they're missing the point. In covered bridges we're not looking for grace or contrived aesthetics. We are looking instead for a piece of ourselves, a part of the past, as textured as unpainted wood and weathered with age.

Nothing matches the sudden intake of breath you get when you drive through the forests of New Brunswick, or along the seacoast or over a hill and into a village, and you suddenly come upon a covered bridge, unexpected and understated. You gear down, bring your car to a crawl, and enter a tunnel of wood, light shimmering through the planks like an old movie.

Inside the pooled darkness, the flickering light creates a zoetrope effect, a landscape in motion, and when you hit a certain speed—usually around twenty kilometres an hour—something happens. The bridge ... *dissolves.* It becomes a ghost image that you can look straight through.

They glow, these sway-backed bridges, silvery grey, perched over canyon and creek. They glow, they breathe.

There is romance in the old girls yet.

Magnetic Hills
and Backwards Falls

I know it may sound crazy, but I think the Bay of Fundy is trying to kill me.

This has been going on for some time now. Personally, I trace it back to a kitchen party I attended in St. Andrews. In the Maritimes, any party worthy of the name eventually ends up in the kitchen. Were the Oscars ever to be held in New Brunswick, I have no doubt the Hollywood glitterati would find themselves crammed into a kitchen somewhere, saying "'Scuse me" every time someone opened the fridge to get a beer.

I was at one such soirée, wedged up against the sink, when I mentioned, just in passing—seeing as how St. Andrews was in a small bay off Fundy—something I found rather interesting. Namely, that the tides in Fundy may not be the highest in the world after all. There were higher tides in northern Quebec, or so I'd heard.

Well, you'd have thought I'd peed on their rug. I was quickly shouted down and threatened with various forms of physical violence, some quite anatomically improbable, to say the least, and—even worse—banishment from the kitchen.

I began to fear for my life soon after that, for I had clearly angered the Gods of Fundy.

Our first son was born on the Bay of Fundy. Not literally, of course. He was born in Saint John, but still. You'd think his coming into this world along that coast would have placated the wraiths of the Bay, but no. We were driving back to St. Andrews with our newborn swaddled in his baby seat, following the Fundy highway when—suddenly—the air liquefied. Fog turned into rain, and the rain to sleet, and the sleet to a blizzard-like squall, with snow and ice pellets in equal parts strafing the road. The temperature plummeted, the slush froze, and visibility was soon reduced to near zero. I peered through flailing wipers as I gripped the wheel with a grim resolve.

"At least there isn't a large semi behind us," I said to my spouse.

At which point I checked the rear-view mirror, and *voilà!* Right on cue: an eighteen-wheeler from Hell. It came roaring right up my (already clenched) tailpipe, with horns blaring, as my wife went mute with fear. Our newborn slept the sleep of the innocent as we were more or less pushed along by the rig behind us. Snow and fog continued to swirl, and I thought to myself, *Fundy is trying to kill us.*

Flash-forward to the following spring, with skies now sunny and Fundy a deceptively calm shade of blue. A local handyman had invited me to go "fishing" in his "boat." Turns out, the word "fishing" in the regional dialect this fellow spoke actually meant "drinking," just as "boat" actually meant "wooden contraption held afloat in defiance of all known laws of buoyancy."

Off we went in his rowboat onto Passamaquoddy Bay, only to get caught in the grip of a slow but powerful current. It was Fundy, pulling at us, and we rowed and rowed and rowed and rowed and rowed—without moving an inch. We eventually gave up, and as we drifted away from an already distant shore, my travel companion stretched out and said, "We'll wait her out." And when would the tide shift? A shrug. "Ten hours. Maybe twelve. Too bad I didn't think to bring some poles, we could'a fished while we were waiting."

We weren't sucked out to sea, but we did waste an entire afternoon surviving on nothing but beer and beer. Which is to say, by New

Brunswick standards, the fishing expedition had been a resounding success.

Life began in tidal pools, in the wobble of the moon and the movement of water rolling back and forth. Tidal flats, neither wholly sea nor completely land, represent a liquid bond between the two.

Fundy is a watery wedge separating the provinces of New Brunswick and Nova Scotia, and the bay's ineluctable brute strength is everywhere in evidence. To see this firsthand, you need only make the trek to the high-spanning observation deck above the limestone cliffs at the mouth of the Saint John River. Twice a day, in a struggle between the river's outflowing current and the tide's incoming force, the Saint John River is forced back on itself. Its tumbling rapids—they aren't really "falls," except in the mind of local tourist boards—are slowly submerged and then eventually reversed. It takes a couple of hours for this tide vs. river drama to be played out, which gives you lots of time to enjoy the vista of pulp mills nearby and the enchanting odour that drifts across from them.

You may be asking yourself, out loud so as to justify the use of quotation marks, "What kind of tide would be capable of such a feat? What sort of tide could stop a river in its tracks and roll back a waterfall?" Why, only the mightiest tides in the world, of course. A surging 100 *billion* tons of sea water churns into the Bay of Fundy with every tide, lifting ships from where they lie stranded on the sand and putting the spin back on Old Sow, the largest tidal whirlpool in the western hemisphere.

Consider this: the magnitude of water that surges into Fundy every twelve and a half hours nearly equals the total daily flow of all the rivers in the world *combined.* That's a lot of hot dogs. At peak tide, Fundy can rise as high as a four-storey building.

Why is Fundy so freakishly high? Three reasons. First, shape. The fjord-like bay acts as a funnel that forces the water up onto itself as it pushes in. Second, depth. The Bay of Fundy grows shallow evenly, leaving few side pockets or sudden drops to be filled with the influx of water, so, once again, the sea has nowhere to go but up. Finally, length. Fundy is exceptionally long—almost three hundred kilometres in total—and because of this, the tide is never able to catch its breath. As the ebb tide tries to roll out of the bay it runs into the next, incoming high tide, which then carries the ebb tide back in with it, creating a double-wave phenomenon known as resonance. The bad news? Resonance is never permanent. Over time, as the sea levels shift and the shape of the bay gradually changes, the incoming and outgoing swells will fall out of phase, and the high tides of Fundy will come to an end.

Mi'kmaq legends ascribe the high tides of Fundy to the mythical giant Glooscap, sloshing about taking a bath, while a whale set the water moving back and forth with its tail. It's a remarkably accurate description of how the tides work. The Atlantic Ocean is essentially one extended wave that rocks back and forth with the pull of the moon and the sun. In Fundy, this wave rocks just that much higher and that much harder. The result is something in which people on either side of the bay, in New Brunswick and Nova Scotia alike, have invested a certain misplaced proprietorial pride.

Joseph Howe, opponent of Confederation and Nova Scotia patriot, caught this feeling perfectly. "Boys," he said, "brag of your country. When I'm abroad, I brag of everything that Nova Scotia is, has, or can produce; and when they beat me at everything else, I turn around on them and say 'How high does your tide rise?'"

With so much pride-by-proxy at stake, it's no wonder that the heirs of Howe bristle at any suggestion that their tides might not be quite as brag-worthy as they seem. The Inuit village of Aupaluk in northern Quebec has challenged Fundy's claim, arguing that Ungava Bay has higher tides. (According to official government records, Fundy's highest tide is 16 metres to Ungava's 15.9, which seems dubious, if not downright suspicious. How exact can any tidal measurement honestly be?)

The main difference between Ungava and Fundy is that Fundy has millions of dollars in tourism revenue riding on its title to the "world's highest tides," whereas Ungava has mainly seals and a few icebergs riding on its claim. And you should never underestimate the power of tourism councils when it comes to fudging certain unpleasant facts.

Exhibit A: the muddy Petitcodiac River that slides sluggishly into Moncton, New Brunswick. The Petitcodiac is home to a phenomenon called "the tidal bore." Twice a day, the incoming tide from Fundy forces the river Petitcodiac to a standstill and then sends a mighty wall of water rushing forward in one, single wave. Well, not exactly a "wall," perhaps. More of a ripple, really. A majestic, muddy ripple.

The look of stunned disappointment on the people who have gathered to witness this is something you don't soon forget. I spoke with a family from Vermont, who had studied tidal charts and plotted mileage with military precision so that they could arrive at exactly that climactic moment. Their teenage son ruefully dubbed the phenomenon "the Total Bore."

In fairness, a lot depends on the time of year and the phase of the moon. Why, I once saw a bore that was almost a foot high! *A foot high, I tells ya!* The seabirds that were feeding there didn't even bother leaving; they just bobbed along with it as it passed under them. A breathtaking scene, to be sure.

Nor is the aptly named tidal bore the only zany, topsy-turvy, pushme-pullme attraction in the area. To Saint John's Reversing Falls, you can add the dry-land equivalent: Moncton's Magnetic Hill.

Drive your car to the bottom of the hill, put it in neutral, and you will slowly roll backwards *uphill.*

Magnetic Hill is one of the Maritimes' biggest attractions, and the tourists arrive in convoys. Families in station wagons, New Agers in VW vans searching for mystical experiences—they show up by the thousands every year. The attraction is almost … well, magnetic. It kind of seems to, you know, *pull* visitors in, which is spooky if you think about it.

Magnetic Hill began as an urban legend that turned out to be true. (Though in this case, *rural* legend is probably more accurate.) Tales were whispered of a parson who'd stopped his automobile on a quiet lane outside of Moncton and got out to stretch his legs only to have his vehicle roll uphill, as though possessed, with the parson himself forced to sprint after it and leap inside to wrest control back from whatever ungodly forces were at play.

The search for the Devil's Hill was launched in 1933, during the graveyard shift at the Saint John *Telegraph-Journal.* It was a quiet night in the newsroom, and three young reporters decided to pile into a Ford roadster and head for Moncton to find the legendary spot. They arrived in the early morning hours and, using a brilliant strategy, began randomly trying different hills along every dirt road and country trail within a ten-mile radius. Incredibly, it worked.

At one hill, the car did indeed roll uphill. They'd discovered Magnetic Hill. They also immediately recognized the reason for the phenomenon. It was an impressive, but simple, optical illusion. The road *seemed* to dip and then go up, but in fact it didn't. The landscape around it was tilted, and the downhill dip that looked as though it then curved uphill was actually just a slightly less steep downward slope. As the reporters were quick to note, a small stream beside the road was also running "uphill."

And so, at the very moment of its discovery, Magnetic Hill was recognized as an illusion. And yet visitors just as quickly ascribed other-worldly factors at play. Years later, Stuart Trueman, one of the original trio who'd discovered the Hill, noted how "most visitors would much rather find a way to justify the magnetism theme. One Torontonian comes back every year and claims the electrical currents help his arthritis. A Californian insists he can sense the magnetism in his bones and has to use conscious force to focus his eyes. He knowingly asks: 'Where do you keep the magnets?' Another American insists that he can feel the nails being drawn out of his shoes ..."

The author of *We Are Not Alone,* meanwhile, ascribes the phenom-enon to "anti-gravity." Another paranormal researcher describes Magnetic Hill as a "portal to another dimension." And the tourist centre encourages this sort of thing with a giant magnet at the crest of the hill. Much like Niagara Falls, the hill itself is just the hook, with the site boasting a wide swath of attractions: a water park and wave pool, gift shops and a miniature railway, an outdoor extravaganza stage, and even a zoo featuring such local Moncton fauna as zebras and gibbons. The Pope Himself even showed up in 1985. No record as to whether His Holiness tried the Kamikaze Run at the Magic Mountain Water Park.

Other such "secret portals" exist, but they're not as well promoted as Moncton's. Ontario has its own Magnetic Hill near the village of Darce in the Ottawa Valley. So does Montreal, apparently, along Chemin de la Côte-des-Neiges, though I'll be damned if *I* could find it. Scotland, meanwhile, has its "Electric Brae," where a similar effect was attributed to the then modern marvel of electricity (as opposed to magnetism).

Having visited both Magnetic Hill *and* Electric Brae, you'd think I'd be something of an expert, but unfortunately I was travelling with my girlfriend's father at the time, a Scotsman who drove straight through Electric Brae without slowing down, let alone stopping. The conversation went something like this:

Me, checking my guidebook: Isn't this Electric Brae? Where cars roll uphill?

Father of then girlfriend: Aye.

Me: Wow. That sounds really interesting.

Father: Aye, it is.

And on he drove. True story. No lie.

Though I never technically *stopped* at Electric Brae, I can say that of the two, Magnetic Hill had more tourists.

Farther up from Moncton, at the very end of the Bay of Fundy, at that narrow isthmus that prevents Nova Scotia from being an island, the tides end not in a roar but a whisper.

Here are the grassy meadows and salt marshes of Tantramar, reclaimed centuries before by Acadian settlers who accomplished a singularly impressive feat: they held back the tide. As early as the 1670s, the Acadians were building elaborate dyke-work sluices that drained off the water and transformed the headlands of Fundy into "the world's largest hay field." Even today, Tantramar remains a land of marshy meadows and grassy idylls.

Between the meadows of Tantramar and the mighty bore of Moncton is a landscape of stone pillars that are exposed at low tide: the Hopewell Rocks. Tree-topped islands, "flowerpots" as they are known, these rocks have been contoured by countless currents.

The Hopewell Rocks exist only in the moment in between, in that Sisyphus-like pause before the tide rolls back and the landscape is again submerged. The tides of Fundy pull innumerable pranks—pushing down waterfalls, changing the course of rivers, toying with rowboats, pulling the water out from under large ships like a table-cloth parlour trick—but nowhere are the effects as incongruous or as impressive as they are at Hopewell Cape.

My wife and I visited Hopewell at low tide and walked out onto the silty-soft seafloor of Fundy. Wandering among the towering flowerpot rocks, feeling like a Lilliputian in Gulliver's garden, I stopped to pose for a photograph at the base of a notably tall formation.

"Here," I said. "I'll just lean against this large boulder that appears to have fallen from the sky."

There was a long pause.

I looked up, directly above my head, two storeys high, and saw where the slab of stone had once been. "Or maybe not."

My wife remembers the moment fondly, in particular the way I held my hands over my head as I ran. *That'll stop a boulder!*

Some landscapes are meant to be admired from a distance. Especially when they're trying to kill you.

Naked Girls
in New Brunswick

For sound journalistic reasons, I decided to visit a strip club in Saint John, New Brunswick. My interest—and I must stress this right at the start—was strictly sociological.

Now, I consider myself a rough-and-tumble kind of guy. The type of fellow who knows his way around the seedier side of things, the type of man who—when his wife is out of town—isn't afraid to venture into the darker porno bins of life. I've backpacked in Bali, hitchhiked across Japan. Was even robbed at knife point in Amsterdam by two guys who grabbed me from behind and then sauntered off—chuckling—with my wallet. (Over the years the story has been fleshed out a little more, though, and usually ends with me fending off my attackers whilst armed only with a jagged beer bottle and my own indomitable will.) So I figured I was ready for whatever Saint John threw at me, sociologically speaking.

Chez Cherie was the first strip club to open in the city, an event that sparked an uproar among Saint John's more upstanding citizens. Packs of placard-carrying protesters blocked the club's private entrance and tried to shame customers from entering, actually shouting the words "Shame, shame!" Headlines of the font size usually reserved for D-Day landings kept the public breathlessly up to date on this burning issue, and parsons and politicians denounced the opening of Chez Cherie with a passion worthier of a better cause, which only heightened the forbidden allure of it.

I was surprised that a strip club was considered news at all. Seemed like Saint John would be rife with them. It's a salt-water town, blue-collar and raw-knuckled. A "drink your whisky and punch your landlord" type of town. The matrons manning the barricades, and the public hissy fits over Chez Cherie, were, I suspected, a ruse. A sly way of drawing attention to the titillating possibilities behind those doors.

Surely, I reasoned, the strippers of Saint John would be a breed apart: tough, jaded women who smoked and chewed gum at the same time, who spit on the floor and kicked back shot glasses of cheap rum, snarling, "Whatchya lookin' at?" when your gaze lingered too long. Chez Cherie, I was sure, would be the sort of place you'd see Popeye and Bluto duking it out.

So. As a precaution against the type of brawling and bottle-breaking that was sure to occur, I asked a friend to come along as backup. I'll call him "Bruce" because that's his name (although he spells it without the quotation marks). Hard to believe, but he'd never been to a strip club before. Nor was he your typical tattooed, cigar-chewin' Maritimer either. Quite the contrary. A graduate of the New Brunswick College of Craft and Design, Bruce was an artistic young man well-attuned to the sensitive post-feminist mores of our age. You could tell this by the way he responded. "Strippers? Sure! When do you want to go? Let me grab my jacket."

So off we went.

Narrow stairs led to a dingy barroom ...

The decor was definitely of the Popeye and Bluto variety—lots of rickety chairs and unemptied ashtrays (this was back before smoking laws kicked in)—but the atmosphere was not. Everyone was oddly subdued. Almost embarrassed. There were no fisticuffs, no hoots. Not a single holler.

Bruce and I sat with our backs to the wall and ordered Moosehead draft, straight up. It set us back $3.50 each, which isn't bad.

Establishments like these usually gouge you every chance they get. But not Chez Cherie. There hadn't even been a cover charge.

How did they make any money?

Up on stage, a listless strobe light was giving everyone a headache as a portable smoke machine coughed up throat-abrasive fumes that drifted across the bar, making eyes water and waitresses wheeze. This was to create an erotic atmosphere.

"Gentlemen," said the disembodied voice of the DJ. "Put your hands together for the lovely and exotic Jasmine, who comes to us all the way from Germany."

Germany? Imported talent, in this dive? Jasmine appeared through the smoke, a skinny girl with big hair and a wide snaggle-toothed smile. She didn't look very Teutonic, but she was very keen and she launched right into her dance without waiting for the music to start—or even catch up. The Lovely and Exotic Miss Jasmine had several dance moves which she performed by rote. Any connection between said moves and the actual beat of the music was purely coincidental, but no matter. What she lacked in skill she made up for in sheer enthusiasm.

Jasmine finally turned, centre stage, and slid free of her dress to reveal—I sat back, absolutely agog at the sight—pasties. Pasties and a G-string. And not even artistic pasties, no silk tassels or gold glitter, just two crossed pieces of masking tape on each breast.

Her three-song repertoire over, she bounded off the stage.

"Gentlemen, coming up next, the lovely Miss Amber."

I knew that Maritimers were often behind the times, but really. Pasties?? Suddenly, $3.50 seemed like an awful lot for a beer.

The Lovely Miss Amber, meanwhile, was finishing her own set of moves, most of which were obviously cribbed from Jasmine's repertoire, and the low voice of the DJ told us to "stay put" because coming up next was "the Lovely Miss Starr, followed by the always exotic Angel, and the naughty but nice Miss Candy Kane."

Bruce leaned over to me and said, "Somehow, I suspect those are not their real names."

"Stage names," I said knowledgeably. "And there's always at least one named Bambi. I think there's some kind of rule." Sure enough, the next girl up was none other than the lovely *and* exotic Miss Bambi.

As the exotic Miss Bambi prepared to wow us, Jasmine from Germany appeared, dressed in a frilly black French maid skirt. She sat down at our table. "Hiya," she said.

Handshakes all around.

"So, you're from Germany?" I said.

"Yup, from Berne."

"You mean Berlin," I said. "Berne is in Switzerland."

"Oh yeah, Berlin. That's what I meant to say."

"So you speak German?" I asked.

"Depends," she said. "Do you?"

"Not a word," I said.

"In that case, I'm like, fluent."

Bruce was eyeing her with suspicion. "You have a definite New Brunswick accent," he said.

She shrugged happily. "Berne. Berlin. Whatever. So you guys want more drinks? I'm supposed to talk you into having more drinks."

"Sure," I said, and she waved the waitress over.

After the next round had been delivered, I leaned in and asked, "What's the deal with the pasties? I thought this was a strip club. The sign outside says Naked Girls. We aren't here for the ambience. This is my friend's first time in a strip club, and we were expecting something a little more, well, current. I mean, what's next? You going to bring out a vaudeville comedian?"

"I can take my clothes off if you want," she said. "Including the pasties. But we have to go upstairs for that. In New Brunswick, you can't have alcoholic beverages when you're with a naked girl. It's against the law."

Against the law? If it weren't for alcoholic beverages most men would never *see* a naked girl.

"Upstairs is like a separate club," she explained. "Youse can get a private dance up there—so long as you leave your beer down here."

"Ah, I see." It was all coming clear now. "And how much is it for one of these so-called private dances?" I braced myself for the sting.

"Seven dollars," she said.

I wasn't sure I'd heard her correctly. "Seventeen? Seventy?"

"Seven," she said. "Or, if you want the VIP suite, that's, like, two dollars more."

"What the hell," I said, feeling suddenly magnanimous. "Give us the VIP treatment."

"Sounds good," she said. "Who's first?"

Rock beats scissors, so up I went, leaving Bruce to guard our drinks. The second floor at Chez Cherie was even seedier than the one below, and the "private room" turned out to be a plyboard partition furnished with a couple of mismatched chairs and a rug with cigarette holes burned through it. The "VIP suite," meanwhile, was exactly the same but with a couch. A second-hand couch at that, and one that had clearly been rescued from a dumpster at some point. Overseeing this entire cavalcade of excitement was a scruffy-looking bouncer, profoundly bored, who sat across from us.

"You'll need a loonie for the jukebox," said Jasmine. "Sorry."

As noted, these places try to squeeze as much cash out of you as possible, so I wasn't angry. In fact, I was quite charmed by it. There was something disarming, almost sweet, about a strip club trying to stiff you for a loonie. Only in Canada, I thought. Only in New Brunswick. Out here, even the dark underside of society was hopelessly affable.

"You go ahead and make yourself comfortable," said Jasmine. "I gotta go use the flush." Flush is a distinctly Maritime term, originally used to distinguish indoor toilets from outdoor, but now used for washrooms in general. I don't imagine a lot of young women in Berne, Germany, use that term. Obviously, this was a lass who picked up on the local vernacular quickly.

I sat there, humming to myself and looking about at the cheesy photos that had been taped up on the walls. There were fashion ads and centrefolds of airbrushed beauties who were, apparently, not scheduled to perform tonight. From the other side of the partition I could hear the girls in what must have been their dressing room.

"Look," said one of them. "I'm not accusing anybody. But if you want to borrow my mascara, you gotta ask, okay?"

Jasmine returned from the flush soon after and asked, suddenly, "Do you speak French?" Not an unusual question, this being New Brunswick, where 30 percent of the population is Acadian.

"Why?"

"Well," she said. "We have French songs and we have English songs. I can dance to either."

I chose French, just for that extra bit of sizzle. She put my loonie in the jukebox, and sure enough, everything came off—and rather quickly. When she pirouetted, there was a pink ring around her bum from the toilet seat, which tended to diminish the mood. The song ended and she began to get dressed.

"That's it?" I said. "One song?"

"Sorry," she said. "But that's the rule. One song per customer."

I sighed and paid her the $9 VIP rate, along with a generous $1 tip.

"Thanks!" She was a wonderfully sweet girl. Even if she was from Berlin.

Downstairs, Bruce couldn't wait to leave.

"Don't you want the VIP treatment? They have bubble baths and champagne up there. It's like something out of the Playboy mansion."

"No," he said. "I want to get out of here. This place is giving me the creeps."

I shrugged. "The girls don't seem unhappy. It beats trying to get by on EI or minimum wage."

"Not the girls," he said. "The customers."

But it was the same in any club, from Montreal to Manhattan. The majority of the regular patrons at any strip club are middle-aged men who sit, eyes on stage, barely breathing. The lusty cries of "Take it off!" exist primarily in Hollywood scripts—and at Chippendale dance clubs, where it's the women doing the hooting. The men who go to strip clubs are generally passive. They run a tab, then shuffle off home. If you turn your gaze from the stage to the audience—when you see it from a stripper's point of view—it is very sad indeed. The only people being exploited at most strip clubs are the men.

Later that night, as Bruce and I were trudging through the wet Atlantic night, we passed a sub shop. Jasmine was there, and she waved us in.

"Hiya," she said.

"Um, hello," said Bruce.

She smiled at me. "You're the one who wanted receipts for everything."

"That was for Revenue Canada," I said quickly, more for Bruce's benefit than hers. "You know, research. Expenses. It's all deductible."

"Sure," she said. "Y'don't need to explain. Listen, I gotta go. My break's almost over, but come back to the club any time, okay? It's Ricardo, right?"

"That's right," I mumbled. "Ricardo."

"Ricardo?" said Bruce as we walked away. *"Ricardo??"*

"Come on," I pleaded. "I can't go around using my real name in a place like that, can I?"

Sandstone City

It's the most postmodern street corner, in the most postmodern city, in the most postmodern country in the world:

1st Street and 10th Avenue SW, in downtown Calgary.

Head south under the rail tracks and behind the Palliser Hotel, and there on the corner you'll find Buzzard's Cookshack & Waterin' Hole, a country-style eatery straight out of a B-movie western with a sign out front that all but "yee-haws" its message at you. Buzzard's is "an authentic cowboy restaurant" offering genuine "cowboy cuisine."

Cracked leather saddles are draped over rough-hewn wooden fence posts outside. Superfluous wagon wheels line the entrance, branding irons and cattle skulls adorn the walls. It would almost feel authentic, in a kitschy sort of way, were it not for the fact that, directly above this "cookhouse & waterin' hole," vehicles are parked seven storeys high. At the corner of 1st and 10th, a concrete downtown parkade and a good ol' fashioned country cookhouse inhabit the same space like a Zen koan. *When is a parkade not a parkade? When it is also a cowboy saloon.*

Calgary is a self-invented city, and as such it is postmodern by default as much as design. The eclectic mix of traditions, the confusion of folklore and fake-lore, the blurred borders between historical realities and invented pasts: Calgary is both a glistening city of commerce and a Western Canadian theme park.

It's two cities, superimposed on top of each other. When viewed from a distance, the skyline shimmers like a mirage with the Rocky Mountains themselves as a backdrop. This version of Calgary has a certain clean, geometric beauty. It is the beauty of tinted glass, of right angles. Of steel. Up close and on foot, however, Calgary is another city altogether. In the downtown walkabout, sandstone creates a veneer of history, with the office towers and convention centres rising behind the storefronts of an older town.

Calgary's original nickname wasn't "Cowtown." It was called the Sandstone City, a reference that dates back to the 1880s and a style that lives on even now in the Old City Hall and the Lougheed Mansion and numerous churches. This blond stone, quarried from the banks of the Bow River, has largely been replaced with glass and steel, but the texture of Calgary remains that of sandstone: abrasive, yet soft. Gritty, yet malleable and prone to erosion.

When it came time to leave St. Andrews, my wife and I considered our options. She wanted to move to Vancouver, I wanted to go to Halifax. We split the difference and chose Calgary. It was meant to be a stopgap measure, a temporary move until one or the other of us capitulated, but then we began our slow discovery of the city.

The village-within-a-village that is Kensington. The hilltop lookout of Marda Loop. The slightly frayed charms of Inglewood and the hard-luck pride of Victoria Park. The cafés of 4th Street and the drunken college kids on 17th Avenue. The handsome Warehouse District and the echoing "market" at Eau Claire. In Calgary, the neighbourhoods are folded into the city like blueberries in a pancake breakfast (to use the proper Calgary-centric image). The city seems all dough and flapjack at first, but poke about and you'll find those hidden bursts of flavour.

Calgary is a city you learn to love, not one you fall head over heels for. And once you get past the SOBs in their SUVs, and the endless gauntlet of construction sites you have to run every day, you realize that it's still a very livable place, even with the constant hue and cry of construction cranes battling for dominance above skeletal skyscrapers that are constantly being torn down and rebuilt. Calgary does not go out of its way to win your affection. The longer you stay, though, the harder it is to leave. It's a slow shift in perception, but the day eventually comes when you no longer view the city as a way station en route to somewhere else, but as a place you can almost imagine calling home.

I'll admit, it took me a long time to warm to Calgary. (The feeling was probably mutual.) Coming here after living in the Maritimes, I was surprised by how busy everyone seemed to be, always hurrying about, talking on cellphones. It was as though the entire city was late for a meeting.

"It's a no-nonsense town," a friend explained. "That's part of its appeal. You want laidback, you should've stayed in the Maritimes."

I agree. In a country where so many of us try to crowd into the mushy middle, Calgary stands as a stark exception. In Calgary you're encouraged to Think Big. To dream big. From ranchers to oilmen, from cowboys to capitalists, it's one of the most testosterone-driven cities I've ever been in. This is not a place for the half-hearted, and it can be unforgiving at times.

But if you can stay on the horse for eight seconds, you might just win it all ...

I am tramping through the underbrush with historian Harry M. Sanders, author of several books, including a walking guide to Calgary's Union Cemetery. Today we're looking for a different sort of headstone.

Harry goes crashing into the brambles and thorn bushes, until— "There it is," he says. The fragments of a fallen chimney: red bricks and mortar. "And over here"—he shows me a section of sandstone wall—"this would have been the garden."

We're exploring the ruins of one man's dream. Dubbed "Lindsay's Folly," it's the remnant of a grand mansion now overrun with weeds.

Neville James Lindsay was a doctor who arrived on the first passenger train into Calgary in 1883.

"Which is like coming over on the *Mayflower*," says Harry.

Dr. Lindsay would later trek north to strike it rich in the Klondike, and when he returned he decided to build himself a proper manor. He purchased Calgary's original Presbyterian church and had it destroyed. Then he dismantled the sandstone blocks and brought them here to a wooded escarpment above the Elbow River.

The history of Calgary has always been one of boom and bust, and in Lindsay's case, the boom went bust at the worst possible moment. His house was abandoned just a few months after construction began, and there it lies, looted for most of its sandstone, the proud arch long gone, with little more than a retaining wall and crumbling foundation left behind: an Ozymandias arrangement in the hidden hills of Calgary, as much a parable as a historic site.

"An early example of the dangers of doctors investing in real estate," says Harry.

Calgary is a city of venture capital, a city that thrives on risk. The downside of this is that economics tends to trump everything. It's a city where the bottom line is king.

In my little neighbourhood there was an agreeably eccentric collection of small shops: a Russian restaurant named The Kremlin, a flower shop in a hand-painted cottage, a combination Greek restaurant with a spectacularly tacky painting of the Venus de Milo on one side and a family-run burger shop on the other, which advertised itself as "Calgary's second most favourite burger spot!" It served everything from ostrich to buffalo between hamburger buns, with the tagline "We cook our meat at higher than required temperatures to ensure that NO BACTERIA SURVIVES!" (Canny marketing, that. I know that whenever I bite into a burger I want assurances that any bacteria I'm ingesting are thoroughly dead.) Now, none of these shops were architecturally significant in the least, but collectively they added to the ambling, take-a-stroll atmosphere of my street.

And yet, this entire block—from the Kremlin to the Venus de Milo—was bulldozed to the ground to be replaced by a shiny condo-and-chain-store complex of the type with which Calgary is already glutted. A huge excavation was dug, foundations were laid, rebar was inserted, and then … a boom went bust. Seven years later that gaping eyesore is still there. The flower shop and ostrich burgers are not.

Or consider Penny Lane. Red-brick warehouses filled with boutique shops and small offices, Penny Lane was one of the few nooks in downtown Calgary that still had any real sense of interior character. Penny Lane added something tangible to the city, but the interlocking buildings themselves weren't deemed "historically signifi-cant" (a very slippery designation in Calgary, where "heritage status" seems to count for very little). So Penny Lane is gone as well, replaced by yet another tall building. And it's not as though Calgary needs another tall building.

When I found out they were going to tear down my beloved Penny Lane, I got so angry I went home and started to pack. "I can't live in a place that values character so little," I told my wife. "We're moving back East." She nodded and said nothing, knowing full well it was all bluff and bluster. The moment passed, true enough, but the sense of loss lingers still.

Our hillside archaeology completed, Harry and I are at Buzzard's Cookshack having a beer. Pick any building, at random, and Harry can tell you a fascinating story about it. If you could vacuum his brain, you'd come up with a twenty-four-volume encyclopedia of the city. Once, while we were walking down 17th Avenue, we passed the Magic Room Beauty Shop and Harry said, offhand and casually as can be, "Did I ever tell you about the double murder-suicide that happened in that building back in 1912?"

When I suggested we go to Buzzard's for a drink, I asked Harry if he knew the place. "Sure," he said. "It's home to an annual Testicle Festival."

A what?

"Prairie oysters—there's a big cook-up at Buzzard's once a year. I think the slogan is 'Go On, Have a Ball.'"

At Buzzard's, incongruities abound. Skewered Thai shrimp and pan-fired scrotum of young bull appear on the same menu, and amid the cowboy clutter and Western bric-a-brac, a television is playing *Star Trek* with the volume muted. Spaceships leap soundlessly into hyperspace as the restaurant's tinny music system plays a relentless Eurotrash techno-pop beat. It's a perfect mishmash of time frames and cultural touchstones, so eclectic it makes your head hurt.

We are drinking Irish beer in a cowboy café, with those seven storeys of parking stacked above us, and I'm speaking wistfully about the loss of Penny Lane and the small shops on 4th Street.

As a historian, Harry is naturally sympathetic. He's given entire lectures about "vanishing Calgary," detailing the transformation of historical buildings into historical parking lots. At times, Calgary seems less like a city than it does an architectural Etch A Sketch.

But Harry the Historian is philosophical about this as well. "People come West to remake themselves. They leave whoever they were behind and they become someone else. Calgary does that too. Every generation or so, it reinvents itself."

Perhaps this is why I find Calgary such a compelling place in spite of everything: it embodies the promise of something more. It offers the chance to rebuild your identity, to turn church stones into manors. Bust into boom. It may pander to a tourist-concocted image of itself as a Cowtown caricature, but Calgary does not live in the past. Or even the present, really. It exists in future tense. A city that is always *becoming*.

Postmodern in the best sense of the word, Calgary embodies the belief that all things are possible, that the past doesn't have to dictate the terms of the present, that you can pick and choose the components of who you are, can mix and match, can cut and paste.

It's a city that rewards initiative and scorns indecision. It is the New World made manifest. Part saloon, and part inner-city parkade.

"To Calgary," I say, raising a glass.

Wawa to Black Diamond: A Cross-Canada Tour of Big-Assed Objects by the Side of the Road

My father was a connoisseur of roadside kitsch, and whenever I visited him in Manitoba we inevitably ended up driving for hours across open prairie to some Large Object by the Side of the Highway.

"It's folk art," he liked to say. "On a Canadian scale."

Not all of it was silly. I remember, vividly, the sight of a towering white horse by the Trans-Canada west of Winnipeg. It was dark by the time we arrived, and the horse was lit up like a spectre in the night, which was apt. The White Horse honours a Plains legend of star-crossed lovers, a desperate flight, and a ghostly steed.

"History becomes myth, and myth becomes a roadside attraction," my dad would say. "Now, wasn't that worth the drive?"

On a later visit we drove south, to the town of Boissevain to see their Giant Turtle, and on another, north to Glenboro to see their Giant Camel. There was often a playful logic to these attractions. The Boissevain Turtle commemorated the town's "turtle derby" and the Glenboro Camel (named "Sara" as in Sahara, get it?) was a reference to nearby sand dunes.

"Statues of statesmen and generals, monarchs and prime ministers, who needs 'em!" Fayther had absolute disdain for these European-bred affectations. "Those are top-down approaches to history; greatness

Ms. Claybelt, New Liskeard, Ontario

Jumbo the Elephant, St. Thomas, Ontario

Giant Potato, O'Leary, PEI

World's Largest Atlantic Salmon, Campbellton, New Brunswick

World's Largest Axe, Nackawic, New Brunswick

Happy Rock, Gladstone, Manitoba

World's Largest Turtle, Turtleford, Saskatchewan

The Big Nickel at Dynamic Earth, a Science North Attraction

World's Largest Lobster, Shediac, New Brunswick

descending from on high. But giant objects by the side of the road? That's democracy."

Monuments erected by common folk, for common folk, they are at once knowingly ironic and guilelessly sincere.

My father had a weakness for bad puns as well (the town of Minnedosa, he insisted, was "named in honour of a minor Italian venereal disease"), and a few years before he died, we made the trek to Gladstone to see its newly unveiled mascot, a fifteen-foot fibreglass character named Happy Rock. (The measurements of Big Objects are invariably given in feet, rather than metres, and I have followed suit.)

As we stood in front of the Happy Rock, my dad said, "Get it?" But of course I didn't.

Fayther sighed. "Glad*stone*, Happy *Rock*. Now, if only we could've made it to Gimli," he said. "Big Scandinavian community up there. They have a giant Viking. Your grandmother was Norwegian; you should make the effort."

As with Gladstone's Happy Rock, Canada's roadside attractions are often elaborate sight gags, and some of them are downright clever. In Elm Creek, Manitoba, the town's water tank has been transformed into the World's Largest Fire Hydrant—and there are plans afoot to paint a giant dog beside it. Seriously.

Visual puns abound. In Alberta, the town of Pincher Creek has a giant pair of pincers; the town of Castor has a giant beaver (making it a *bilingual* visual roadside pun); and the town of Black Diamond has, naturally, a giant black diamond (though the paint was peeling and the aluminum had a couple of dents in it when I went by).

In Saskatchewan, the town of Turtleford has a Really Large Turtle, naturally, and Moose Jaw has a giant cement moose (though an actual Jaw of Moose would've been cooler). Indian Head has a sculpture of, well, you can probably guess. And Dildo, Newfoundland, meanwhile has a giant ... whale.

A few years ago, on Vancouver Island, I jumped off a Nanaimo-bound train in Duncan because the conductor happened to mention that the town was home to the World's Largest Hockey Stick. How can you not go to see something like that? Even better, it came with—are you ready for it?—the World's Largest Hockey Puck. The two are lit up at night in the sort of glittering outline usually reserved for parliament buildings or a diva's dressing room mirror.

The Almighty Hockey Stick of Duncan rises like a ceremonial sword above the town's rec centre, but throughout the downtown area a veritable forest of totem poles has also been erected. The giant hockey stick pales in comparison to the artistry of these poles, and yet the two aren't as different as you might think. Totem poles, after all, are as Canadian an icon as any hockey gear. And raising a giant stick to appease the gods of shinny is in itself a totemistic act. Surely it's no coincidence that the vast majority of Large Roadside Attractions are animal effigies? Kenora's Husky the Muskie and the Wawa Goose are but two examples. Enormous ducks, leaping trout, spawning salmon, mighty buffalo, and manys the giant moose—the highways of Canada are teeming with wildlife totems.

Large objects may have a definite tongue-in-cheek cachet, but there's a surprising amount of local pride invested in them as well. Fashion editor Denise Wild of *Flare* magazine hails from Vermilion, Alberta, an area rich in Really Big Stuff. "It was great," she says. "There's the Giant Ukrainian Easter Egg in Vegreville, the Giant Perogy-on-a-Fork in Glendon, and over in St. Paul, the world's only UFO landing pad."

A UFO landing pad?

Why not? From outer space, Canada must look like one big suburban lawn, cluttered with giant pink flamingos and other such oversized ornaments. High ideals of democratic folk art and totemistic effigies aside, Canada's roadside attractions are the national equivalent of garden gnomes. Really big garden gnomes. (Memo to any communities still without a large object of their own: the World's Biggest Garden Gnome remains up for grabs.) Even better, there's a Giant Kolbasa Sausage in Mundare, Alberta, so if you swing by the Giant Perogy and Giant Egg, you can make a meal of it.

And what would our visitors from outer space make of the

massive coins that are scattered like spare change across this Great Land of Ours? In Ontario alone, we have a Giant Loonie in Echo Bay and a Giant Toonie in Campbellford, not to mention the iconic Big Nickel of Sudbury. (That's a Giant Latte right there.) Plus, we have the Gigantic Penny of Salmo, B.C., and the World's Largest Gold Coin in Virginiatown, Ontario. So many coins, in fact, that we even have doubles; there's *another* Giant Loonie in Churchbridge, Saskatchewan, and *another* Giant Nickel in Boiestown, New Brunswick.

As my unsuspecting wife soon found out, I inherited my father's strange fascination with roadside kitsch, and when we moved from Japan to New Brunswick one of the first things we did was drive up to Nackawic to see the World's Largest Axe.

This was followed by a trip east to Shediac, "Lobster Capital of The World!," where the love of big objects crosses cultural and linguistic boundaries. The Acadians of Shediac have built themselves the World's Largest Lobster. It's a very realistic looking crustacean, weighing in at fifty tonnes, with a statue of an unsuspecting fishermen about to be caught in its claws. My young bride was impressed, I could tell.

"Canadians are … interesting," she said.

On a later journey through northern New Brunswick, we made a detour to the village of Plaster Rock where fiddlehead ferns are part of the local cuisine. A chainsaw sculpture has been erected in their honour, along with a sign that reads WORLD'S LARGEST FIDDLE-HEADS! (Now, I'm going to go out on a limb here and say that not only is this the world's *largest* monument to edible ferns, it's also the world's *only* monument to edible ferns.)

"No dulse?" Terumi asked.

She was referring to another New Brunswick dish, a dark seaweed considered a delicacy by some, a practical joke by others. Much like prairie oysters and 7-Eleven hot dogs, dulse is a food that's consumed almost entirely on a dare. As are ferns, I imagine.

"Dulse?" I said. "Not to worry. I'm sure someone, somewhere is working on it." (Note to Maritimers: the title of World's Largest Dulse is also up for grabs.)

After New Brunswick, Terumi and I moved to Prince Edward Island and I made a special point of driving us out to the village of O'Leary to visit the PEI Potato Museum.

"So," I joked to the woman at the entrance, "when are you putting up a giant potato?"

She seemed startled by my comment, and once she'd regained her composure, she lowered her voice and said, "Who told you? It's supposed to be a secret. We haven't announced it yet."

Turns out I'd stumbled onto a Major Journalistic Scoop. Sure enough, not long after, it was revealed that O'Leary would be funding the construction of a Giant Spud. And there it stands today, proudly rising up fourteen feet high and looking just like—well, like a fourteen-foot-high potato. (Note to purists: the potato depicted is a Russet Burbank. It is not some generic "potato." In PEI they take these things seriously.)

Having children didn't slow down our cross-Canada quest for Large Objects. Quite the opposite. On the highway from Edmonton to Regina, I endeared myself to our three-year-old son, Alex, by stopping at every single roadside attraction we passed, from the World's Largest Tomahawk in Cut Knife (a symbol of "friendship" according to the local tourist board) to the World's Largest Coffee Pot in Davidson (which is decorated with murals and is tilted toward what I'm assuming is the World's Largest Coffee Cup).

Saskatchewan's many roadside oddities helped break up what was a very long trip, and Alex relished every pit stop. Especially Kenaston, which boasted the Giant Snowman, an eighteen-foot fibreglass chap in a top hat and earmuffs plopped down in front of the town's grain elevators. Alex loved it. Why a snowman? To promote Kenaston's claim to being "The Blizzard Capital of Saskatchewan," of course.

Given that these objects are meant to be tourist draws, you have to wonder about some of the choices. Komarno, Manitoba, for example, promotes itself as "The Mosquito Capital of Canada" with a gigantic, evil-looking mosquito that has a fifteen-foot wingspan. It turns in the wind like a weathervane. (*Komarno* being the Ukrainian word for mosquito, this too qualifies as a bilingual roadside pun.) In the community of Inwood, meanwhile, a creepy reptilian statue celebrates the fact that the town is apparently crawling with snakes. *"Gosh honey, I just can't decide. For our vacation this year, do you want blizzards or snakes or mosquitoes? It all sounds so good!"*

But the oddest, by far, is the Giant Horse Ankle Bone in the town of Macklin, Saskatchewan. Macklin, you see, hosts the World Bunnock Championships—*bunnock* being a Russian folk game that involves the throwing of bones. Specifically, horse ankle bones. Which is why a mighty bunnock now rises majestically from the prairie parklands of Macklin, beguiling unsuspecting travellers who slow down with an inevitable *"What the f...?"*

Back in the eighties, I worked as a youth volunteer at a nursing home in St. Thomas, Ontario, and at that time there was talk in the town about building a giant statue of ... an elephant. Not just any elephant, mind you, but Jumbo himself. Jumbo the Elephant was not born in St. Thomas, and Jumbo the Elephant never lived in St. Thomas. Nor did Jumbo ever perform in St. Thomas. But Jumbo was *killed* in St. Thomas, and for that the townsfolk are eternally grateful.

In 1885, the pachyderm star of the P.T. Barnum Circus was being led across rail tracks in the dead of night outside of town when the animal was hit by a train and killed. Its carcass was so big that it had to be carved up and set on fire before it could be disposed of. Here's an actual passage from a St. Thomas souvenir booklet marking this joyous event:

> The burning of the mountain of flesh was described by
> local papers as "the most tremendous roast of the season."
> Six cords of wood were used. Carving juicy slices from the
> bloody flanks, a local youth astonished many by eating
> roast elephant steak ... The hide of Jumbo alone weighed
> over 1,600 pounds and when removed from the beast, was
> transported to Griffin's Pork Factory, where it was pickled ...
> Jumbo's heart weighed 46 pounds.

Oddly enough, when I was living in St. Thomas not everyone was in favour of commemorating the violent death of a beloved circus animal as a point of civic pride. The community had once been a thriving rail hub, so why not honour the railway instead?

As the "rail vs. elephant" debate raged, I sent a letter to the paper suggesting the obvious: that the two sides compromise and build a giant replica of a train *hitting* Jumbo, but no. The elephant faction triumphed, and the statue went ahead as planned. It was unveiled the following year amid a festive Jumbo Days celebration. "*Welcome to St. Thomas, Ontario! Not only did we kill Jumbo, but we skinned his body, cut out his heart, roasted his flesh, and pickled his hide!*"

And that's not even the only elephant statue in Canada!

There's a Giant Mastodon in Stewiacke, Nova Scotia, that looks like Jumbo's rougher, rowdier twin and which was built to mark the discovery of mastodon bones in a nearby quarry. And Kyle, Saskatchewan, has a statue of a woolly mammoth named Wally, which was built to commemorate a similar find.

As luck would have it, after St. Thomas, I ended up in New Liskeard, Ontario, working at the agricultural research college—where my contribution to the scientific field of animal husbandry consisted mainly of shovelling sheep dung, cow patties, pig poop, and horse flops. Oh, the joys of youthful employment.

New Liskeard is in Ontario's clay belt, and when I arrived the township had recently commissioned a Giant Belt Made Entirely Out Of Clay!! Not really, no. Like the good people of St. Thomas, they ignored my canny suggestions and went instead with a huge Holstein cow, twelve feet high. This was to honour the dairy farmers of the clay belt.

Other giant cows roam the Canadian landscape (there's one in La Broquerie, Manitoba, *two* in Sussex, New Brunswick, plus the venerable "Snow Countess" of Woodstock), but what made the New Liskeard cow truly memorable was (a) its name—more specifically its title, and (b) its location.

New Liskeard's Giant Cow Committee, acutely attuned to

modern sensitivities, named the giant bovine statue "Ms. Claybelt." That's right, *Ms.* After all, why should we designate the cow's marital status in our choice of honorific?

Even better, they built the cow at the edge of town, right across from the local McDonald's. Is that sick, or what? Sort of like boiling a giant pot of water next to the Shediac lobster.

During my sojourn in New Liskeard, I once helped deliver a calf that got stuck halfway and had to be pulled out forcibly. I ended up with both my hands up inside, covered in slime, trying to—I'll spare you the details. It was exhausting and messy, and it cured me forever of any illusions I had about the miracle of childbirth. When my own sons were born, I was just grateful no one asked me to roll up my sleeves and take off my wristwatch.

In New Liskeard, with the calf safely out, and having scrubbed the afterbirth from my hands—scrubbed until the skin was raw—my supervisor, partly to make amends, decided to take us out for lunch. To McDonald's. And as I sat there, chewing on my quarter pounder thoughtfully and looking out the window to the statue across the way, I knew I'd never look at Ms. Claybelt in quite the same way again.

Just up the road from New Liskeard, meanwhile, is a massive metal bison that once stood guard outside the Earlton Zoo. In the interests of science, I suggested that the New Liskeard Cow be mated with the Earlton Bison, giving us a Giant Beefalo. Beefalo burgers are delicious.

And for the record: World's Largest Beefalo? Still available.

BATTLE OF THE BIG OBJECTS

With hundreds of giant objects vying for attention along the roadsides of our nation, and with the awe-inspiring prestige that accompanies the title of "world's biggest," it's inevitable that conflicts will arise. In the interest of journalistic integrity, therefore, I've decided to settle five of these competing claims once and for all. (I've rounded to the nearest foot, and have given the measurements in metres as well for maximum accuracy.)

1. World's Largest Snowman: Kenaston, Sask. vs. Beardmore, Ont.

The Kenaston snowman is 18 feet tall (5.5 metres).
The Beardmore snowman is 35 feet tall (10.7 metres).
  Winner: Beardmore.

2. World's Largest Bee: Falher, Alta. vs. Tisdale, Sask.

The town of Falher, self-anointed "Honey Capital of Canada," presents itself as a community "buzzing" with activity (sigh). It has a giant bee that's 23 feet long (7 metres).

  Tisdale, meanwhile, calls itself the "Land of Rape and Honey"—meaning rapeseed, or as it's now known, "canola." It boasts a giant bee that is 18 feet long (5.5 metres).
  Winner: Falher.

3. Canada's Largest Turtle: "Ernie" in Turtleford, Sask. vs. "Tommy" in Boissevain, Man.

Measured tail to nose, Ernie is 28 feet long (8.5 metres).
And Tommy is ... 28 feet long as well (8.5 metres).
  Winner: A tie!

4. World's Largest Muskoka Chair: Gravenhurst, Ont. vs. Varney, Ont.

The Gravenhurst chair is 13 feet tall (4 metres).
The Varney chair is 22 feet tall (6.7 metres).
  Winner: Varney

5. World's Largest Fiddle: Harvey, N.B. vs. Sydney, N.S.
The Harvey fiddle is 14 feet high (4.3 metres).
Cape Breton's Big Ceilidh Fiddle in Sydney is a whopping 52 feet high (16 metres).

Winner: Sydney, hands down ... but the village of Harvey *was* Don Messer's hometown. So points for that.

As the Irvings Turn:

A Maritime Soap Opera

As the Irvings Turn was a weekly radio soap opera I wrote and performed that was distinguished primarily by the fact that it was cancelled during its first episode, while the episode was being broadcast.

This was back in the nineties. I was living in New Brunswick at the time, and a producer at CBC's *Main Street* program in Saint John asked if I would write a weekly ten-minute commentary for their drive-home show. I suggested a weekly comedy segment instead, an ongoing soap opera of sorts, with lots of local references. The result was *As the Irvings Turn*.

The show was produced on a shoestring budget. My friend Steve Stackhouse wrote and performed the theme song, and I came up with the scripts and did all the voices (except for the female characters, who were often played by whichever producer or intern we could cajole into reading for us that day). It was recorded in studio with stock sound effects from the CBC library. (The *SFX: STING* that you see throughout the scripts was this terrific "da-da-DAHH!" musical zinger we found.)

Anyone who's spent time in New Brunswick knows how the entire province—and most of the Maritimes, in fact—can feel like one big company town. I'd often joked that the provincial motto was "Welcome to New Brunswick, a Division of the Irving Corporation." Gas stations, oil refineries, shipyards, newspapers—you name it, the Irving logo was either on it or lurking somewhere in the background.

The patriarch of the family was the late K.C. Irving, who'd passed his business empire to his three sons, nicknamed "Gassy," "Greasy," and "Oily." So I thought, what if there was a fourth Irving? Named "Rusty." Poor—by Irving standards anyway—disowned, and down on his luck, Rusty Irving would travel the byways and back roads of the Maritimes in search of his fortune.

The CBC being one of the few institutions in New Brunswick *not* owned by the Irvings, I figured we were safe. I threw in other family-run companies as well—the McCains and Ganongs and even the Rankins. It was all in good fun, but the complaints started immediately. Calls began coming in while the first episode was being aired, and I was told the decision to cancel it had been made before that first episode ended.

My producer fought hard for me, and the powers that be finally relented and gave us a second chance. But we were clearly on probation. So I quickly rewrote the ending of the next episode to make it a cliff-hanger, with Rusty shot in the chest and listeners wondering how he could possibly survive. That way, when the show was cancelled again—as we knew it would be—we were able to plead our case by saying, "We have to let people know what happened. You can't leave things up in the air like that!" So we got a third episode, but that was all she wrote.

When the people in charge saw the script for the fourth episode (which, not coincidentally perhaps, included a CBC executive being shot in the ass and then dying), they pulled the plug for good, and no amount of cajolery or disingenuous promises to mend our ways could convince the higher-ups at CBC to keep us on the air, even though we'd already sketched out the next three episodes.

When I read these scripts today, I'm surprised at how gentle a satire it is, and I remain puzzled as to why it caused such a stir. I'd expected some grumblings from listeners about how I'd unilaterally moved the McCain's headquarters across the Northumberland Strait to PEI (a more "potato-worthy locale" I thought). But they were fine with that. I was later told it was the ghost of K.C. Irving that had upset people the most. Not the teenage pregnancies or references to environmental damage, but the flippin' ghost. Go figure.

Here then—for the first time ever!—are the complete *As the Irvings Turn* scripts along with the follow-up summaries for the episodes that were never recorded.

Episode One: "Banished!"

SFX: Ominous music. Foghorns. The sound of seagulls.

ANNOUNCER

(solemnly)

We take you now to the Maritimes, where great families are at war. The Irving Empire is under attack from the Potato McCains. The Potato McCains are under siege from the Chocolate Ganongs.

Families are torn asunder. Brother against brother. Father against son. Daughter against cousin. Cousin against nephew. Nephew against—well, you get the idea. It's really, really bad.

The Irving family is Canada's richest dynasty. Shipbuilding. Gas stations. Oil refineries. Newspapers. Power. Wealth. Prestige. The Irvings have it all. Or do they?

This is the continuing saga of a young man named Rusty. Rusty Irving. The unknown Irving. The *poor* Irving. The Irving you never hear about. We join Rusty at Reggie's Diner in downtown Saint John.

SFX: Restaurant chatter in background.

RUSTY

I'm sorry ma'am, I wish I could leave you a tip, but I can't afford to. Y'see ... *(he holds back a sob)* I'm down to my last billion dollars.

WAITRESS

Don't worry, honey. This one's on the house.

THEME SONG

(in pure Miramichi style)

Gather 'round you people, a story I will tell

About a poor young Irving boy, who didn't do so well

He was the family black sheep

And Rusty was his name

With only a billion dollars, he brought his family shame ...

ANNOUNCER

Poor Rusty. With only a few measly Swiss bank accounts and a paltry handful of corporations to his name, he's an embarrassment to the family. The other children made fun of him.

KIDS

Hey, Rusty, what is that? Last year's Cadillac? Har!

ANNOUNCER

His own brothers disowned him.

BROTHER

You call yourself a capitalist? You're not fit to carry the Irving name. You're a disgrace to the family, a disgrace!

ANNOUNCER

And then, one dark and gloomy night, the ghost of K.C. Irving spoke to young Rusty.

SFX: Wind.

RUSTY

Dad? Dad, is that you?

GHOST

Who—are—you?

RUSTY

It's me, Dad. Your son Rusty, dontcha know me?

GHOST
(in a rage)
I have no son named Rusty! Oily and Greasy and Grimy and Slimy, yes—but no son named Rusty. *I banish thee hence from the Irving Empire!*

RUSTY

But—but—

GHOST

If ye seek my approval, you must go out into the world and make a name for yourself. Only then will you be able to hold your head high as an Irving. That is your quest!

SFX: Seagulls. Foghorn.

ANNOUNCER

And so it was that with only the shirt on his back, 400 million

dollars in unmarked bills, and a Platinum American Express
Card, poor Rusty Irving set out to find his fortune.

SFX: Ship horn.

ANNOUNCER

His girlfriend Muffy waved goodbye from the dock.

MUFFY

Don't go, Rusty. Rusty, don't go!

RUSTY

I'm sorry, Muffy. But an Irving's got to do what an Irving's
got to do … A tautology, I know, but still. I must go. It is my
destiny!

ANNOUNCER

Rusty sailed out of Saint John harbour on board the newly
refurbished H.M.S. *Irving Whale.*

RUSTY

Why, this ship is as good as new! I don't know what all those
environmentalists were whining about.

ANNOUNCER

Unfortunately, the *Irving Whale* collided with the Westfield
ferry and sank in the Bay of Fundy, spewing PCBs into the bay
and killing every fish and seagull in a 200-mile radius.

SFX: Monumental crash. Splash.

ANNOUNCER

As Rusty surveyed the damage, tears welled up in his eyes.

RUSTY

Why does everything always happen to me?

CAPTAIN

Arrrr, matey, said the captain in a stereotypical sea captain's voice. Oh … Wait. I'm reading the director's notes. Hang on. Let's try this again. *Arrrrr, matey. Who will be cleanin' up this awful mess then?*

RUSTY

I dunno. Send the bill to the good people of Prince Edward Island. They've always been sports about this sort of thing in the past.

ANNOUNCER

Waiting for low tide, Rusty walked out along the Bay of Fundy.

SFX: Squelching footsteps.

RUSTY

Ah, yes. Fundy at low tide. Did you ever see such beautiful mud in all your life? *(takes a deep breath)* The scent of raw untreated sewage. Can't beat it!

ANNOUNCER

Onward went our hero, ever onward until, at last, he came to …

RUSTY

St. Andrews! St. Andrews-by-the-sea! Beside the bay! Near the island! Down the road! Exciting St. Andrews! A bustling hive of activity!

SFX: Sign creaking. A mournful wind. A distant coyote.

RUSTY
(in stage whisper, and with growing panic)
Wait a second. Somethin' ain't right. The entire town … it's deserted!

SFX: Sting.

RUSTY
There's no sign of life anywhere. It's—it's as though a cloud of poisonous gas has swept through killing everyone and leaving the entire town—

STRANGER
Relax. It's just St. Andrews in the off-season.

RUSTY
Oh.

ANNOUNCER
Seeking to start his life anew, Rusty Irving sought employment at the world-renowned Algonquin Hotel.

WOMAN
I'm sorry, sir. But this is the off-season. We aren't hiring new employees right now.

ANNOUNCER
So Rusty bought the hotel and fired the entire staff. But even that failed to cheer him up. Onward he went, to the border town of St. Stephen. Where cross-border shopping is a way of life! We join Rusty as he returns from a trip to Calais to buy cheap American gas.

SFX: Car motor.

GUARD

Anything to declare?

RUSTY

Um, no, just some ... gasoline.

GUARD

Okay, go on through.

SFX: Loud trucks, one after the other.

ANNOUNCER

And so Rusty drove his convoy of thirty-two tanker trucks
across the border without incident.

RUSTY

Now then, let's see ... *(punches the numbers into a calculator)*
Profit from my smuggling operation—287,000 dollars. Oh,
what's the use. I'll never make my fortune this way. I'm an
Irving, dammit. I was bred for bigger things.

ANNOUNCER

Just then, the ghost of K.C. Irving spoke to young Rusty.

GHOST

Rusty ... Rusty ...

RUSTY

Dad? Is that you?

GHOST

Rusty, you schmuck. Smuggling? Smuggling is for amateurs. There's no money in smuggling. Now, tax evasion—that's where the money is.

RUSTY

(tearfully)

Dad, I'm in trouble. I'm down to my last billion dollars. I—I don't know what to do.

GHOST

Son, go to the Ganong factory. That is where your destiny lies.

RUSTY

(with heavy significance)

Chocolate. Hmmm. Is that where my destiny lies?

GHOST

I just said it was. Weren't you listening?

ANNOUNCER

Join us next week when Rusty makes a shocking discovery that will lead the Maritimes to the brink of war! Sex. Scandal. Potatoes. And lots and lots of gratuitous violence. It's all here on *As the Irvings Turn.*

Episode Two:
"The Chocolate-Covered Potato"

SFX: *A warble of organ music.*

ANNOUNCER

As the Irvings Turn. A continuing drama in the life of Rusty Irving: the unknown Irving. The poor Irving. The Irving you never hear about. Cast out by his family and down to his last billion dollars, Rusty finds himself in St. Stephen, New Brunswick.

It was here at the Ganong Factory in St. Stephen that the world's first chocolate bar was invented. And it is here, to the Ganong manor, that young Rusty now comes.

SFX: *A heavy door knocker echoes eerily.*

RUSTY

Halloooo? Anybody home?

SFX: *Door creaking open.*

CHOCOLATE ECLAIR

Hi! My name is Chocolate Eclair. This is my sister Butter Pecan and my brother Pal-o-Mine. *(together, in a singsong, keener voice)* We're the Ganongs!

RUSTY

Um, I'm here about the ad in the *St. Croix Courier.* About the job in your laboratory? You know, research and development ...

ECLAIR
(still impossibly chirpy)

Any experience with science and stuff?

RUSTY

Well, I did develop extra leaded gasoline. And I invented a waterproof teabag. That was me. And, um ... *(breaks down in sobs)* I'm down to my last billion. You gotta help me out.

ECLAIR
(hesitates, then)

Welcome aboard!

SFX: Bubbling noises. Loud hammering. Blowtorches.

ANNOUNCER

Late into the night Rusty works, bent over laboratory beakers and bubbling, burning Bunsen burners. Until, in the early morning hours—

RUSTY

Eureka! I've done it. An invention that will change the face of the world—forever! I have invented ... the Chocolate-Covered Potato!

SFX: Sting.

> **RUSTY**
> *(taking a bite)*
> Mm-mmm, delicious! It's chocolatey AND potatoey. It's starch, covered in sugar—why, it's the ultimate Maritime cuisine. I'll make a fortune!

> **ANNOUNCER**
> Meanwhile, across the Northumberland Strait in Prince Edward Island, Potato Capital of the World, corporate spies relay the news of Rusty's discovery to the headquarters of ... the McCains!

> **ANGUS McCAIN**
> *(in a really bad Scottish accent)*
> Right then, what's this a'boot a Chocolate-Covered Potato? I won't hear of it, I won't. Tater! Tater, geet in here.

> **TATER McCAIN**
> Yes, Daddy?

> **ANGUS**
> Call in our man in Madawaska.

> **TATER**
> Our man in Madawaska? But father, he's pure evil. A cold-blooded—

> **ANGUS**
> Just do it, laddie. I want the formula for the Chocolate-Covered Potato—and I want Rusty Irving deed!

TATER

Uh, deed?

ANGUS

Deed, dammit. Deed.

TATER

Deed? Like, a deed to a ranch?

ANGUS

Deed! Like not alive. Like the opposite of alive. Deed, as in checked out. Pushin' up wee daisies.

TATER

Ah, dead. You want him dead— But, father, that's murder!

ANGUS

Just do it, y'big girl's blouse!

ANNOUNCER

Later that night, young Tater McCain meets with the lovely Chocolate Eclair outside the Hartland Covered Bridge.

SFX: Wind. Footsteps.

TATER

Chocolate Eclair, is that you?

ECLAIR

Why did you ask me here? You know our families are sworn enemies.

TATER

I know, but we have to avert an all-out war.

SFX: Car passing.

TATER
We can't talk here. Let's go through the bridge.

ANNOUNCER
And so they drove through the Hartland Bridge, the longest covered bridge in the world. They call them kissing bridges, because young men and women would often take a quick peck in the darkness.

At Hartland, however, the bridge is so long that it's not so much a kissing bridge as a "heavy petting and quick foreplay bridge." Young Tater McCain and Chocolate Eclair drove through the bridge.

SFX: Car roar.

ANNOUNCER
Then they drove back.

SFX: Car roar.

ANNOUNCER
And by the third time—

SFX: Car roar.

ANNOUNCER
—Chocolate Eclair was pregnant.

SFX: Sting.

ANNOUNCER

Meanwhile, back at the Ganong laboratory ...

SFX: A fist pounding on a door.

POMME DE TERRE
(in a really bad French accent)

Open da door! Raht now!

RUSTY

What—what is it?

POMME

Prepare to die!

SFX: Sting.

POMME

I ham da man from Madawaska. My name, it is Pomme de Terre, and dis here—she is my girlfren' Poutine.

POUTINE

Poutine, c'est moi!

RUSTY

Sheesh. Those are like the worst French accents ever.

POMME

Nevair mind! Tie him up, Poutine! Tie him up rael good.

RUSTY
(struggling)

What—what are you doing?

                           POMME
I ham going to k- k- How do you say dat?

                           RUSTY
Kiss me?

                           POMME
No, no dat is not it. K- k- k-

                           RUSTY
Cuddle me?

                           POMME
No, no—

                           RUSTY
Caress me?

                           POMME
Yes! I ham going to caress you, slooowly ... Running ma'
fingers over your body till you cannot stand— Wait. No! I ham
not going to caress you. A'ham going to kill you! Take dat! You
rich Irving snob.

SFX: Gunshot.

                           POMME
And dat!

SFX: Gunshot.

                           POMME
And dat!

SFX: Gunshot.

POMME

Et cetera.

SFX: Three gunshots in a row.

ANNOUNCER

Is this the end of Rusty Irving? Can he survive six bullets to the chest? Will this show be cancelled ... again? And what will become of Tater McCain and Chocolate Eclair? Join us next week to find out!

Episode Three:
"Daddy—I'm Pregnant"

SFX: A warble of organ music.

ANNOUNCER

As the Irvings Turn: A Maritime Soap Opera. This is the continuing saga of Rusty Irving. Cast out by his family and down to his last billion dollars, Rusty sought his fortune at the Ganong Chocolate Factory, where, late at night—

RUSTY

Eureka! I've invented the Chocolate-Covered Potato! I'll make a fortune.

ANNOUNCER

But the McCain family has sent a hit man to kill Rusty and steal the formula for the Chocolate-Covered Potato. The assassin, the evil Pomme de Terre, and his girlfriend, Poutine, have just finished firing six bullets into Rusty's chest.

SFX: Gunshots.

POMME

Let's see. "Take one potato, dip in chocolate." Dis is it! Ah have
da formula! And Rusty, he is dead like da doornail. C'mere and
give me a big wet kiss, Poutine.

POUTINE

Oui, oui.

SFX: Lips smacking.

RUSTY

Not so fast!

SFX: Sting.

POMME

Sacre bleu! How is dat possible? Rusty, you are still alive. But I
shot you many times in da heart. Ah! But of course! You are an
Irving. You have no heart.

RUSTY

A common misconception. In fact, I do have a heart, but it's
small and shrivelled and the size of a raisin. And you missed it!

POMME

Oh, yeah. Dat's good. Very good. But you are still tied up
my fren', so let's see what's happen when I put a bullet right
between your eyes!

POUTINE

Wait!

SFX: Sound of long zipper.

POUTINE

I'm not really your girlfriend. My name isn't Poutine. It's me, Muffy!

RUSTY

Muffy! My true love, you've come to rescue me!

POMME

Wait da minute. If you are not Poutine—then the real Poutine, where she is?

ANNOUNCER

We take you live to Confederation Bridge, where Miss Poutine has been tied to the road.

SFX: Truck getting louder and louder. A voice in the background: "Aidez moi! Aidez moi!"

ANNOUNCER

Can Pomme de Terre save his girlfriend Poutine? Will he get there in time? Will he rescue his—

SFX: Truck zooming by, followed by a loud splat.

ANNOUNCER

Nope, guess not.

POMME

Hold on! Stop da show. Dis is too much da violins. I ham an assassin and even for me it is too much da gratuitous violins.

FRANK

Hi there, it's Frank McKenna, remember me?

SFX: Gunshot. Thud.

POMME
Okay, dat one is not gratuitous. But you understand what I ham saying. Dis show has too much violins. What we need is less da violins and more da sex.

ANNOUNCER
We take you now to the Ganong mansion, high on a hill overlooking St. Stephen.

ECLAIR
Hello, Daddy? Daddy Ganong?

DADDY
Yes, my child?

ECLAIR
It's me, Chocolate Eclair. I have—I have something to tell you. Something terrible.

DADDY
Yes?

ECLAIR
Daddy, I'm pregnant.

SFX: Sting.

DADDY
Mm-hmm?

ECLAIR
But Daddy, I'm pregnant.

SFX: Sting.

DADDY
Yes?

ECLAIR
I'm pregnant … *And I'm not married!*

SFX: Sting.

DADDY
(laughing gently in an avuncular fashion)
So what's the problem? Come now child, tell me which strapping young Maritime lad is going to be forced at gunpoint to be my son-in-law. Is it Jimmy Dougall? The one with the limp? Or maybe the Duncan brothers? Tell me, child.

ECLAIR
It's—it's Tater.

SFX: Sting.

ECLAIR
Tater McCain.

DADDY
NOOOOOOooooooooooooooo!!

ANNOUNCER
Meanwhile, back at the Ganong laboratory …

POMME
You have managed to survive dis time, Rusty. But I'll be back my fren', on dat you can count. And now, I will take da

formula for da Chocolate-Covered Potato, I will run across da
room and I will leap through dat window, and den run away.

RUSTY

Why would you tell us that?

POMME

Well, it's radio. You know, it's not a visual medium. So long
suckairs!

*SFX: Footsteps, window breaking, loud thump, followed by
footsteps running into the distance.*

MUFFY

Let him go, Rusty! We're still alive. That's what matters. Come
back with me to beautiful Saint John, where the air is fresh and
clean and everyone loves the Irvings. Come back with me, my
love. I don't care that you're poor. As long as we're together.

RUSTY

I wish I could, Muffy. But I have to seek my fortune elsewhere.
Goodbye Muffy, goodbye.

MUFFY

Don't go, Rusty. Rusty, don't go!

THEME SONG

Gather 'round you people, a story I will tell
Of a poor young Irving boy, who didn't do so well
    He was the family black sheep
    And Rusty was his name
With only a billion dollars, he brought his family shame …

Episode Four: "Busted!" (never broadcast)

ANNOUNCER

As the Irvings Turn: A Maritime Soap Opera. This is the story of Rusty Irving. Cast out by his family and down to his last billion dollars, poor Rusty turns to scratch-and-win lottery tickets as his only chance for survival.

SFX: Scratching.

RUSTY
(reading)
You have just won two million dollars. *Sigh* ...

SFX: Ticket being torn up.

RUSTY
Oh, what's the use of even trying? I never get a break.

REPORTER
Hi there! I'm Mark Mudraker, reporter with the *Telegraph-*

Journal, an Irving-owned bastion of free speech. I was wondering if I could ask you a few questions.

RUSTY

Yeah, yeah, go ahead. Here to taunt me like the others, I suppose. Tying a billion dollars on a string just to pull it away at the last moment, the way my brothers always did.

REPORTER

Wait!! Is that a loonie totally NOT glued to the sidewalk?

RUSTY
(grunting)

Won't ... budge ... Guess the only thing to do is buy the building and the surrounding sidewalk and have the coin physically removed.

REPORTER

Rumour has it you developed a formula for the Chocolate-Covered Potato.

RUSTY

I did. But an evil assassin named Pomme de Terre stole it from me and ran away.

REPORTER

Sure he did. Now then, any plans for revenge? You know, against society as a whole. Random acts of violence, that sort of thing.

RUSTY
(ominously)

Revenge. Hmm. Not a bad idea.

SFX: Sting.

RUSTY

Revenge. I wonder ...

ANNOUNCER

Meanwhile, across the Northumberland Strait, deep inside the secret Potato Hideout of ... the McCains!

TATER

Father, it's me, Tater. Tater McCain.

ANGUS

Och, laddy. I hear tha' wee Rusty Irving is still alive. I wanted him deed.

TATER

I know, father. But our trusted assassin, Pomme de Terre, did get the formula. So maybe an all-out war with the Ganongs isn't necessary. Maybe it's time we made our peace with them, in the interests of—

ANGUS

Never! The Potato McCains and the Chocolate Ganongs are sworn enemies. We are proud potato people, son, never be forgettin' that! It was starch what built this family, starch—not sugar.

TATER

But father, I—I'm in love with a Ganong girl.

SFX: Sting.

TATER

And she—she's having my baby!

ANGUS

NOOOOooooooooooooooo!

SFX: Seagulls.

ANNOUNCER

Back in New Brunswick, these are sad times indeed for
Rusty Irving. Desperate and alone, he sinks to new depths of
depravity. That's right, he finds a job at CBC Radio.

RUSTY

Oh, the shame—the shame of it all.

FRANK

Hi there! Frank McKenna, remember me!

RUSTY

Didn't we kill you last episode?

FRANK

That's right! But I'm back!

SFX: Gunshot. Thud.

RUSTY

Oh, man. The CBC. This is as low as you can get. The one
place not owned by my family. I might as well be selling rags by
the highway.

ANNOUNCER

Just then, the ghost of K.C. Irving appeared.

GHOST

Son, I'm very disappointed in you.

RUSTY

I know Dad, but what can I do? It's the CBC. They're sending me to their Halifax bureau.

GHOST

Halifax? That's a fate worse than death, son.

RUSTY

They want me to do a two-hour documentary on the men who clean the barnacles off the *Bluenose II.*

GHOST

Forget the *Bluenose II.* Sequels always suck. Find the formula for the Chocolate-Covered Potato instead! That is where your destiny lies.

ANNOUNCER

Meanwhile, on the outskirts of Digby, the evil Pomme de Terre is on his way to catch the ferry to PEI.

SFX: The car radio is playing "Walk Like a Man" and Pomme de Terre is singing along, loudly.

SFX: Siren.

POMME

Eh? H'it's da HarCMP. Da jig, she is up.

MOUNTIE

Licence and registration please.

POMME

What is it, officer? Is it da dead body dat I have in de back seat?

MOUNTIE

No.

POMME

Is it da duffle bag full of human skulls beside me?

MOUNTIE

No.

POMME

Da severed human ear which I ham wearing around my neck like a decorative medallion?

MOUNTIE

No.

POMME

Den—what it is?

MOUNTIE

We've had several complaints—almost three in fact. We're arresting you for speaking in a crude French Canadian accent and perpetuating cultural stereotypes.

POMME

Sacre bleu!

SFX: Courtroom chatter.

BAILIFF

Hear ye, hear ye. All rise.

JUDGE

No need for a trial … Pomme de Terre, I sentence you to forty
years hard labour.

POMME

Are you crazy? Have you heard Angus McCain's accent? Dat
one, it make Sandy McTire seem like a sensitive cultural
portrayal of Scotsmen!

JUDGE

Take this man away!

SFX: General commotion.

POMME
(as he's being dragged away)
You haven't heard da last of me!

ANNOUNCER

Meanwhile, young Tater McCain meets with his true love,
Chocolate Eclair.

TATER

I have terrible news. My father has disowned me. He says the
McCains and Ganongs should never mix.

ECLAIR

Daddy Ganong said the same thing. What ever shall we do?

TATER

There is only one thing to do—we'll leap to our deaths from
Grand Falls in a tragic double suicide.

ECLAIR

Um, you go first …

ANNOUNCER

Meanwhile, back in the CBC headquarters, a shot rings out.

SFX: Gunshot. Woman's scream. A police siren.

POLICE OFFICER
(on two-way radio)

All units ASAP to the CBC on the QT, RSVP! I repeat, all units RSVP! A CBC executive has been shot in the head!

DISPATCHER

Didn't the bullet pass harmlessly through his skull?

POLICE OFFICER

It did. But it ricocheted—hit him in the ass.

DISPATCHER
(alarmed)

But—he'll need that to sit on! Is he …

POLICE OFFICER

DOA.

DISPATCHER

My god. Killing a CBC producer. That's a misdemeanour! Do you have a suspect?

POLICE OFFICER

We do … It's one Rusty P. Irving.

SFX: Sting.

DISPATCHER

Bring him in. Dead or alive! Preferably both.

ANNOUNCER

But wait! What's this? Rusty Irving is stuffing a backpack with dynamite and is hitchhiking toward Fredericton? What is going on?

SFX: Traffic passing.

RUSTY

Revenge. Revenge. Revenge.

ANNOUNCER

The ghost of K.C. Irving speaks to young Rusty.

GHOST

Lumpy, Lumpy, my son.

RUSTY

That's Rusty, for cryin' out loud ... Leave me alone.

GHOST

Son, um, what are you doing with all that dynamite?

RUSTY

I'm bitter with society as a whole.

GHOST

So fire some employees, that always cheered me up.

RUSTY

No, I'm going to Fredericton and I'm going to blow up the Parliament Buildings.

SFX: Sting.

RUSTY

And then I'm going to kidnap the premier. The new guy—
not McKenna, but the other guy, the new guy—the one after
McKenna—you know, what's-his-name. I'm going to force him
to address the plight of downtrodden billionaires. Then I'm
gonna dump him in the Miramichi.

I'm going to blow up the *Bluenose II* and Confederation Bridge.
I'm going to turn back the Reversing Falls and demagnetize
Magnetic Hill. I'll—I'll become a masked vigilante, but
without the mask. I'm going to be famous, Pa! Just like you
always wanted!

GHOST

This is not really what I had in mind, son.

RUSTY

Does it bother you that I am about to injure and possibly
maim hundreds of innocent people?

GHOST

No.

RUSTY

That I killed a CBC regional producer?

GHOST

Lord, no.

RUSTY

That I polluted the Bay of Fundy, spewing thousands of tons of
PCB?

GHOST

Heavens no. But son—terrorism? Where's the profit margin?

ANNOUNCER

Will Rusty succeed in assassinating the premier? Not
McKenna, but the other guy, the new guy, what's-his-name.
Will Chocolate Eclair have Tater McCain's love child? Will
Pomme de Terre escape? And will the Irvings finally buy up the
CBC and pull this soap opera off the air, once and for all? Join
us next week—if we make it—on *As the Irvings Turn.*

Summary of the Next Three Episodes (never recorded)

Episode Five: "Wanted: Dead and/or Alive"

On the road to Fredericton, bomb in backpack, Rusty is picked up by the star-crossed lovers Tater McCain and Chocolate Eclair. On hearing their plans to leap to their death from Grand Falls, Rusty talks them out of it. "My brothers drained those falls years ago so they could fish for salmon without getting wet. If you want to do it right, you should jump off Confederation Bridge instead. That would kill you for sure." Thanking him, they drop Rusty off at the Parliament Buildings. "You two crazy kids get to Confederation Bridge ... while it's still there," he says ominously.

Angus McCain, meanwhile, sends a poison potato to Daddy Ganong, who responds by sending McCain an exploding box of chocolates. News reports speak of an escalating war "between the families."

Rusty's dynamite, manufactured by an Irving subsidiary of the Irving Corporation (a division of Irving International, in partnership with Irving Incorporated), fizzles, failing to do any damage. Rusty flees with a dogged Mountie in pursuit, one Corporal Muffy! (Yes, apparently in the time it took for Rusty to get from St. Stephen to Fredericton, she enrolled in police college, graduated, and joined the force. Such is the magic of radio!) Pomme de Terre, meanwhile, sits in his jail cell, muttering about revenge for the death of his beloved Poutine as he crochets a gun out of his chest hairs.

Episode Six: "An Infestation of Rankins"

Humiliated by his failure to blow up Parliament *à la* Guy Fawkes, Rusty now attempts to kidnap the premier. Unfortunately, no one, including the premier's own staff, knows what the premier looks like, and Rusty ends up kidnapping Frank McKenna by mistake, for whom no one is willing to pay a ransom.

Confronted by Constable Muffy, Rusty flees ... to Halifax, where, that very night, the *Bluenose II* is blown to bits by an unknown terrorist group. Rusty is suddenly the prime suspect, even though he was discussing the theory of *a priori* moral knowledge and social reciprocity with Ashley MacIsaac when it happened. On the run, and with Muffy in hot pursuit, Rusty makes his way to "the far ends of the earth, to the most desolate region known to man!" Cape Breton.

Hiding out in the wilds of Cape Breton, Rusty disguises himself as a Rankin to throw off suspicion. Tater and Chocolate Eclair, meanwhile, arrive at Confederation Bridge only to find it is still under construction. Angus McCain and Daddy Ganong, having discovered their offspring's suicide note, rush to the bridge, but there is no sight of Tater or Eclair, and—unified in rage and fearing the worst—they vow mortal revenge on Rusty. "Damn him and his wee chocolate-covered spud!"

Pomme de Terre is watching TV while getting a massage in the prison's spa and aromatherapy clinic when who does he see on the screen but Rusty Irving, performing as one of the Rankins. Vowing mortal revenge, and using a gun carved into the shape of a potato, he escapes.

Episode Seven: "The Maskless Vigilante!"

Pomme de Terre exposes Rusty as a "fake Rankin" in the middle of a snowstorm during the July 1 Canada Day concert. Fleeing across the ice floes of Cape Breton, Rusty stops to rescue a seal hunter from a band of vicious Greenpeace thugs, thus becoming a hero in Newfoundland—but nowhere else.

Tater McCain and Chocolate Eclair now arrive. In a second attempt at committing lovers' suicide, they decide to leap off the highest peak in Cape Breton, thus severely spraining their ankles. At this point, a mysterious stranger befriends the star-crossed lovers and tells them about the struggles of the CBLA (Cape Breton Liberation Army). Rusty, meanwhile, comes up with a plan to retrieve the formula for the chocolate-covered potato from his nemesis Pomme de Terre, "by asking."

Rusty continues his good deeds. In PEI he rescues a bus filled with Japanese tourists, and later that same day fails to rescue a bus filled with American tourists. For this he becomes a hero.

Wanted by the police, yet helping those in need and wreaking justice wherever he goes, Rusty's fame grows. A movie producer sends his assistant to the Maritimes to track down this mysterious "maskless vigilante." And who is his assistant? None other than Muffy herself, Rusty's long lost love! (Yes, yes, we know she was a Mountie in the last episode. But that too is the magic of radio.)

Semi-Political:

A Look Back

It is now time to cast our gaze back to those heady, carefree days we now know as "the nineties," a time when the Liberal Party bestrode the nation like a mighty colossus and the Right Wing wandered the wilderness, bickering and brawling. This is history on the fly. From not hitting Lucien Bouchard with a pie to advice on how to become PM, the following items, rescued from the vault, give us just a glimpse of that madcap era of the late nineties and early noughts.

A Piece of the Pie:
One Writer's Selfless Search
for Fame and Glory

Well, another Premiers' Conference has come and gone and I'm still not famous.

As summer winds down and we prepare ourselves for that oh-so-exciting first day of Parliament, we would do well to recall those action-packed three days in Victoria and remind ourselves of the many and varied proposals that our stalwart provincial premiers presented to the federal government. Namely: "Give us more money." But more importantly, we must reflect upon why I am still not famous.

I was *almost* famous. It happened at the 1997 Premiers' Conference, which was held in the sleepy resort town of St. Andrews, New Brunswick, where I was living at the time.

Canada's premiers were staying at the Algonquin Hotel, ensconced behind closed doors discussing their latest initiatives (namely: "Give us more money"). So I went over to see what all the hoopla was about. I'm a big fan of hoopla. That and brouhahas.

Throngs of journalists clogged the main hall, forming a massive scrum-in-waiting. But the advantage of living in St. Andrews, and having a wife who was taking a travel and tourism course at that very hotel, was that I knew how to thread my way through its rambling hallways and corridors whilst avoiding possible bottlenecks.

I knew, for example, that an innocuous-looking side door actually opened onto a large rotunda that would put me past the security and media zone. I slipped through—and immediately ran into a friend of my wife's, a young man from the community college who was doing his practicum at the Algonquin. He had just wheeled in a tray of blueberry pies for an upcoming luncheon (blueberry pies being something of a St. Andrews specialty) and the two of us were chatting away when the doors on the far side of the foyer suddenly flew open and out came … Frank McKenna.

Frank was the premier of New Brunswick at that time. He looked at us, and said, "This way?"

I nodded, and off he went through the next set of double doors and into a blaze of camera flash and television glare.

"I gotta go," my wife's friend whispered. "I'm gonna get in trouble." So off he went.

The doors opened again and out came the premier of PEI. He looked at me as well. I had, quite by accident, become a guide. As the premiers and their entourages filed out, I dutifully pointed each of them in the right direction. (And let the record show that not one of those cheap bastards offered me a tip.) One by one, the premiers emerged. And one by one, I pointed them to the correct doorway.

Sure enough, Lucien Himself eventually appeared. The separatist bête noir of Canadian Confederation, and I had him in my sights. A voice whispered in my ear: "Do it, Will. You'll be famous."

Mr. Bouchard had stopped to exchange strategic whispers with one of his aides before making the media plunge. I looked at Lucien. And then I looked at the tray of blueberry pies. And then I looked back at Lucien. It would have been so simple. No bodyguards. Just one step forward, a well-placed splat!, and I'd be famous. I would forever be "that guy." The one who pied Lucien Bouchard. At parties, when I introduced myself to people, they would say, "Hey! You're that guy."

It wasn't pre-planned or anything. I just happened to be there, at the right spot at the right moment. I'd never even heard of Les Entartistes at that time, the Montreal-based band of social activists who'd elevated the pie in the face to an act of political protest. Nor was I inspired by copycat crimes. This was well before PEI playwright and actor Evan Brown pushed a plate of whipped cream into Uncle Jean's inviting face. Chrétien had reacted with barely contained glee to an earlier flurry of pie attacks against his political opponents and had even admonished the victims of these attacks to keep their sense of humour about them, saying that a pie in the face should be considered an affirmation of one's status—and I quote—a "prize."

So, naturally, when Evan Brown pied Uncle Jean, the PM laughed it off and shook Evan's hand, saying, "What jest is this! Thank you for such a wonderful prize! Truly it is an honour."

But of course Chrétien did no such thing. He was livid, and Brown ended up being sent to prison for thirty days, where he was quickly attacked by another inmate. (The prison assault on Brown was not done with whipped cream, alas, and four stitches were required to close a gash in his mouth.)

None of that had happened then, so I had no cautionary tales to hold me back.

It was just me and my (admittedly deficient) conscience in a quiet foyer of the Algonquin Hotel, a ready arsenal of pies at hand and Lucien Bouchard just a few feet away.

I hesitated ... and Bouchard was gone. He walked past me, into the waiting media spotlight, unsullied by blueberries and with dignity intact. And you want to bet that if I had hit him with a pie, I would have made sure to twist it on impact so that the blueberry filling would have gone up his nose. But no. The moment passed and I faded back into a well-earned anonymity.

Times have been tough on pie throwers since that fateful day in St. Andrews. The relentlessly humourless Stéphane Dion, the blustering bully-boy Jacques Parizeau, and our own Goodfella PM have all come down hard on pie protesters. The precedent has been set.

The provincial court judge who sentenced Evan Brown stated unequivocally that pushing "a cream pie into someone's face" is nothing short of "an assault."

But note: the judge said nothing about *blueberry* pies. Which means I still have a shot at notoriety when next year's conference rolls around. Monsieur Landry and Mr. Harris ... consider yourself warned!

Preston Came a'Wooing

The political figure I had the most fun with, by far, was Preston Manning. Now that the Conservative Party bestrides the nation like a colossus and the Liberals wander the wilderness, it's worth recalling that there was once a time when the "unite the right" movement was little more than a comedy of errors and it was the Liberals who were deemed the Natural Ruling Party of Canada.

I've since done public events with Preston, and—as we'll see—I've even scored a free lunch from the man, and though our views rarely lined up, I can tell you that he's a very smart and very funny individual. He would have made a fine prime minister. I wouldn't necessarily have voted for him, and he would have needed a strong Quebec lieutenant, ideally someone who could actually speak French, but I certainly respected Preston's integrity, his sense of fair play, his openness. Even if he always was a bit crafty.

I'll start with the first time our paths crossed. (The reference to Jean Charest at the end of this piece is an allusion to a time in Canadian politics when both the Liberals and Conservatives were vying for the affection of the then wildly popular Tory leader. Oh, how the mighty have stumbled!)

Preston Manning is courting me.

It started off innocently enough; he sent me a love letter. I don't often get love letters from the leaders of major political parties, so when one arrived—in an Official House of Commons Envelope with Official Leader of the Opposition Letterhead—I was suitably impressed.

"Dear Will," he began, and I thought, *Wow, we're already on a first-name basis.*

> Dear Will: Over the Christmas season I obtained and read your *Why I Hate Canadians* and thought it was an excellent piece of work ...

Preston lavished me with praise, slathered me in fact. He said I had a "real gift." He said I had "insight." It was enough to make a fella swoon.

But once my bosom had ceased heaving and my light-headed vapours had passed, I realized that it didn't make any sense. Why would Preston Manning want to write me, of all people, a fan letter? In my book I made as much fun of the right wing as anyone else, at one point openly wishing for a meteor that would squash Preston Manning flat. (That's what we need more of in this country: selective meteor strikes.) My politics tends toward the eclectic. I appreciate the common sense behind fiscal conservatives—public money doesn't fall from the sky; there really is no such thing as a free lunch; you can't tax yourself into prosperity, etc. etc.—but at the same time I've always recoiled at the social conservatism that so often sneaks in under fiscal guise.

In the last election, faced with the dismal buffet of choices offered me, I cast my ballot for a Yogic Flyer instead. It was too weird not to; out here in a largely rural New Brunswick riding, the Natural Law Party had fielded a candidate. And I thought to myself, *That's what I want in an MP! Someone who can levitate.*

I didn't think Preston wanted to teach me the secret to karmic enlightenment, so what was he looking for? An apology? No. He wanted something else entirely:

> My purpose ... is to encourage you to write another book
> on an even more hilarious subject. As you may know, there
> is in Ottawa an institution which is a humorist's dream.
> An examination of its occupants and operations offers an
> infinite number of opportunities for ridicule, sarcasm,
> laughter, tears, indeed the whole gamut of human emotions.
> The name of that institution is the Senate of Canada.

That's right, Preston Manning wants me to write a book. And you know the really weird part? It's not a bad idea. In fact, it's a very good idea. The Upper House is ripe for satirical jibes, and a book on Senate follies would probably do quite well.

I remember trying to explain our august Upper House to my wife, a landed immigrant from Japan still unfamiliar with the subtle mechanisms of Canada's federal system.

"Canada is a democracy," I told her proudly. "Except for the Senate. They're appointed. Without public consultation. For life—or until seventy-five, whichever comes first."

"That doesn't sound very democratic," she said.

"It, um, isn't," I said.

I would love to write a book exposing the silliness and scandals that plague our Upper House. As for research, not to worry. Preston's files are bulging with clippings and exposés. Why, he practically offered to put his entire staff at my disposal.

> If this idea intrigues you at all, perhaps you could arrange
> to get to Ottawa to meet a few of the folks who could be
> helpful. Our research department has a lot of background
> which might be useful—not just dry, technical background,
> but information on absentee rates, patronage, etc., as well as
> a fair supply of anecdotes.

A fair supply of anecdotes! What more could an author ask for? Often, when my supply of anecdotes is running low, I despair of its ever being full again. Here was a golden opportunity. I could be full of it for as long as I wanted. All I had to do was travel to Ottawa and schmooze awhile with Preston Manning.

Still, something seemed wrong. I couldn't put my finger on it, but something was askew. Why me? Why would the Reform Party of Canada be interested in a minor pea-shooter such as myself? True, I favour a hard line with the separatists. And as for the recent flag flap— wherein Bloc MPs complained about the overabundance of Canadian flags in Ottawa—I would have gone even further than Preston. I would have made it *mandatory* for MPs to have a Canadian flag on their desk. I would have nailed them into place. I would have forced every Member of Parliament to get a giant maple leaf tattooed across his or her chest. It could be done as part of a hazing ritual for new Members. (Another good idea would be to shave their heads and make them eat raw eggs.)

Maybe that's why Preston has been courting me. Maybe he thinks we're kindred spirits. Maybe he saw a picture of me somewhere and fell hopelessly in love. Who knows? Alas, it's a love affair doomed from the start. Consider the facts: I don't own a cowboy hat. I support gay rights. (What am I saying, *gay* rights. I support human rights. And last time I checked, homosexuals were still considered human beings.) At the same time, I'm all for gun control and at least some form of socialized medicine. Why? Because there's such a thing as negative freedom: the freedom *from* fear, *from* pain, *from* discrimination.

It seems to me the Reform Party, and indeed the right wing in general, has fixated on positive freedoms and ignored negative ones. (The left wing, of course, errs the other way, forgetting that the freedom to succeed includes the freedom to fail, and that it's not the government's job to wrap us in cotton batting and protect us from the sharper corners of life.)

So the mystery remains: why me? The only thing I can think of is that Preston didn't actually read my book. After all, he's a busy man. What I figure happened is he had an assistant prepare one of those Executive Summaries. You know the kind—where *War and Peace* is rendered in point form and the Ten Commandments abridged down to one. ("Don't.") I imagine the summary in my case simply stated:

Title: *Why I Hate Canadians.*
Question: Does he really hate Canadians?
Answer: No.
So the title would be …? Ironic.
Main Points: Separatists, bad. Future of Canada, good.

On reading this, Preston would have exclaimed, "This is the man for me!" and dashed off a love letter, asking me to come to Ottawa and offering me complete access to his files. It's a wonder he didn't end the letter with a little heart and a row of xxx's.

No. That can't be it, either. Preston Manning is a very calculating person. He's always up to something, that guy. I knew I had to tread carefully. I couldn't go running off to Parliament Hill with my arms outstretched and lips puckered.

So I decided to call my agent.

"Should I write a book about the Senate of Canada, filled with brilliant insights, witty anecdotes, and shocking statistics?" I asked.

"Yes!" she said. "But it would involve a lot of research."

"Not a problem," I replied with the jaunty air of someone in the know. "I happen to have a source high up who'll provide me with all the research materials I could ever need, free of charge."

"Really? That's terrific. Who?"

"Preston Manning."

There was a long, icy silence. "Tell me you're kidding," she said. "Tell me this is a joke."

She refused to believe me until I faxed her a copy of Preston's epistle. "He wants me to come to Ottawa," I said. "What do you think?"

"Don't do it!" she screamed. "You realize what he's up to, don't you? That scoundrel is wooing you."

"Wooing me?"

"Don't be seduced by him."

"Seduced?"

I loved it. I loved being wooed, it makes you feel so—sexy.

Unfortunately, I had to say no to Preston.

Although I would have enjoyed taking my wife to Ottawa to show her firsthand how the government does—or doesn't—work, we really couldn't afford to make the trip. And so, for financial reasons, I had to decline.

Truth be told, I was kinda hoping Preston would send me a plane ticket or a bit of cash, maybe a small token of his affection, but no. Preston never called. He never sent flowers. Nothing. The courtship was over, and though I felt used and abandoned, I am wiser for it still.

Because, if nothing else, for one moment—one brief, shining moment—I knew what it felt like to be Jean Charest.

Shootout at
the UA Corral

I've developed a scientific system for categorizing Canadian leadership, something I like to call, with characteristic modesty, "the Bastards & Boneheads breakthrough!™" It's based on the notion that there are only two types of leaders: active, ruthless, successful leaders on the one hand, and Joe Clark on the other. Which is to say, when I make the following statement, "Preston Manning is a real Bastard," I am speaking only in the most highly scientific manner.

Here's where it gets interesting. The coming showdown between Preston Manning and Joe Clark for a unite-the-right "United Alternative" offers a test case of my theory: Bastard vs. Bonehead, cowboy vs. cowboy, stammering diction vs. ditto. Even better, Joe Himself will be running for office in my very riding, Calgary Centre, taking on Reform in their own backyard.

This has led to many "heated debates" and "open discussions" in Wild Rose Country. (For those wishing to decipher the subtleties of the Alberta political lexicon, I offer the following guide: DISCUSSION: Shouting match. DEBATE: Melee. OPEN DISCUSSION: Melee accompanied by fisticuffs. OPEN DEBATE: Melee accompanied by fisticuffs leading to scorched earth, salted fields, and poisoned wells. HEATED DISCUSSION: Tectonic upheaval, usually resulting in the formation of a new political party that is—in defiance of all known laws of Gestalt—decidedly *less* than the sum of its parts. HEATED DEBATE: all of the above, plus angry letters to the editor.)

Calgary Centre is the political equivalent of Tombstone, Arizona, at the time Wyatt Earp and the Clanton brothers were fighting it out, and I tell you, I fear for my life living here. Often, when I'm on my way to Safeway or Second Cup, I'll find myself caught in a crossfire, the scene unfolding in the shimmering heat as tumbleweeds roll by and the *wa-wa-waaaa* theme from *The Good, the Bad and the Ugly* plays in the background. The clink-a-ching of spurs can be heard as the townsfolk run for cover. The music gets louder, *wa wa WAA*. Two gunslingers square off from each other: Preston dressed in black, Joe in beige.

Other characters in this "unite the right" spaghetti western appear, including Ralph, the sozzled barkeep, who staggers out of the saloon and into the middle of the Preston–Joe showdown, takes one look, burps, and says, "This don't involve me" before staggering back inside for another drink.

Then there's Elsie, formerly a can-can girl with a heart of gold, now the local schoolmarm, rapping knuckles and wearing a sour, disapproving frown. "Why on earth are we fightin' here when the Dalton gang down Kew-bek way is threatenin' to blow up the whole dang town with dynamite?" (That's how they talk in westerns; they say things like "dang" and "varmit." True, Elsie Wayne is originally from New Brunswick, but having her say, "Buddy dere is some bad" would lose the cowboyesque flavour of the piece.)

What of the sheriff? What of "tin badge, tin head" Mike Harris? *"Dear Lord, won't someone stop this carnage?"* comes the plea. But Sheriff Mike just shakes his head and thoughtfully spits (not at the same time, of course) and says, "Wish 'ah could, but them boys are feds. Best to let 'em fight it out on their own. Laissez-faire, you know. That's a French word. Means 'cut taxes.' Or edjakashun. Or somethin'."

"Slap leather," says Preston.

"Ahh ah ah, um, ahh, ahhhh," says Joe.

It all happens in a blur. Joe draws his gun and immediately shoots himself in the foot. Preston spins to the left and fires point-blank at his faithful sidekick, Deputy White. "Sorry, Randy. All's fair in laissez-faire."

Chaos erupts and, this being Reform Country, everybody is armed—up to and including the bystanders. Bullets start a'flying. Bodies pile up. Joe manages to blast four slugs into Preston's chest, trying, in vain, to find a heart. But Preston just shakes it off. He's been pronounced dead so many times already he hardly notices anymore. Instead, he returns fire in a blaze of smoke and mirrors, the bullets ricocheting off Joe's head. "Not the head, Preston! Not the head! It's solid bone to the core!"

Finally the shooting stops. The smoke clears. Bodies and party platforms litter the landscape … The town's undertaker appears, grinning in a certain lopsided way as he cheerfully begins measuring the corpses for coffins. "Hey for me, da business it's good, and I tell you, those guys, if dey want to fight, for me it's not da problem."

In the end only one gunslinger will be left standing. Only one will survive. Who will it be? The answer is obvious. In any showdown between a Bonehead and a Bastard, always bet on the Bastard. *Wa-wa-WAA.*

Staying Ahead of the Puck:
My Lunch with Preston

This is probably as good a time as any to acknowledge a certain creative debt I owe to Mr. Manning. When I received the phone call mentioned below, Preston asked me, "So what are you workin' on now?" to which I replied, "A guidebook with my brother Ian, on 'How to Be a Canadian.'" Preston didn't miss a beat. "What," he said, "like Twelve Ways to Say You're Sorry?" It was a funny line, and when I told Ian about it, he said, "You know, that's not a bad idea actually." Ian ended up writing an entire section on the various ways Canadians apologize, which in turn became one of the most popular passages in *How to Be a Canadian*. So ... Preston, if you're reading this, and in lieu of any, you know, royalties or a cut of the sales or anything, Ian and I would like to take this moment to offer you a heartfelt and sincere "Thanks, eh?"

This is where it happened. Right here, in Calgary Centre. This is where the "unite the right" movement sputtered and died, where the Canadian Alliance and the Progressive Conservatives squared off, eyeball to eyeball, nose to nose, mano a mano—to no avail.

Now, I don't mean to cast aspersions or anything, but even though he is my MP, Joe Clark has never once asked me out on a date. Preston Manning has.

I'd been having my usual fun at the expense of earnest, grassroots populist politicians when one such earnest, grassroots populist politician called me up. At home. I don't know how he got my number. He wanted to "clarify" his position and suggested we meet for lunch, his treat. Now, by the title of this article you will already have guessed who it was, and you may very well be asking yourself, "Surely Will wasn't willing to compromise his journalistic integrity for the price of a meal?" And how! "Where are we going?" I asked. "Can I order dessert too?"

You'd think, what with Preston being an Albertan and all, that he'd at least be good for a side of ribs or a slab of steak, but *nooooo*. He suggested we meet instead at the Good Earth Café, a local organic health-food, free-range, fair-trade type of place. Not a steak in sight, bloody or otherwise.

Preston looked trim, fit. His recent health problems were behind him (literally) and he seemed strangely serene and oddly confident. I smelled a coup d'état. Preston had been muscled aside by Stockwell Day, but Stock's credibility had since plummeted quicker than a Sea-Doo PR stunt plunging upstream over Niagara Falls. Was Preston planning a comeback?

I'd always suspected Preston Manning was a closet Trekkie, and here was proof positive. "As senior statesman and former Leader of Her Majesty's Loyal Opposition, you could have had any post you wanted," I said. "Finance Critic. Foreign Affairs. Health. Why on earth did you choose Science and Technology?" The answer he gave was revealing. "I believe in the Gretzky principle," he said. "You don't go where the puck is, you go where the puck is *going* to be."

The human genome project, the uses and abuses of science, the sorry state of Canadian research and development—Preston became genuinely animated when he discussed these. Of course he wanted Science and Technology. Preston Manning is the political equivalent of Bill Nye the Science Guy. At the leadership convention the Canadian Alliance had voted like giddy schoolkids at a high school pep rally. They'd chosen the good-looking jock over the kid with glasses. And now they were paying the price.

Preston Manning, more than any other politician, has set the agenda for our current political debate. Parliamentary reform, debt reduction, deficit management: these are not Liberal issues, these are Preston's.

During lunch, I chided him for being shameless in promoting his son's rock band. I was surprised he hadn't shown up with a box of CDs to sell me. He laughed. "Listen, I'm just trying to get a return on my investment," he said. Fair enough. Having a son in a rock band is as bad as having a kid in hockey camp. The bills add up. But on another level, I couldn't help wondering: what has been the return on Preston's political investment? He took the Reform Party from angry regional fringe to Official Opposition in less than ten years. And when he failed to break through in Ontario, he set out to forge a wider conservative alliance—only to lose it all.

In spite of everything, in spite of such a lousy return on investment, as we finished our meal and got up to leave, Preston seemed unusually upbeat—sort of like a guy trying to keep a secret.

I had a feeling I knew what that secret was. "He's coming back," I told colleagues and friends—anyone who would listen, really— "Preston's plotting a return. It's palpable."

To which my colleagues and friends, in that sensitive way of theirs, laughed in my face. My track record on political predictions has been lamentably poor. During the last election, I publicly declared that not only would Joe Clark lose in Calgary Centre, but he might very well come in third behind the Liberal candidate. Wrong on both counts. I had earlier predicted that Kim Campbell "might surprise us all." She did, though not in the way I'd intended. But this time, I felt it in my bones. I knew it with something approaching absolute certainty. Preston Manning wasn't ragging the puck, he was ahead of it. He was playing the endgame, and Stock's days were numbered.

"Mr. Day is an idol with feet of clay," I said, biblical allusions being particularly apt in this case. "Mark my words, Preston Manning is about to launch a major comeback!"

Ten days later, he stepped aside.

Lessons from Our Founding Scoundrel

Jean Chrétien and John A. Macdonald share the same birthday: January 11. In light of this, I thought I'd offer some advice to our then PM from Shawinigan. After this political primer ran in *Maclean's*, Mr. Chrétien went on to win a third straight majority. I can't help but feel partly responsible.

Break out the gin! Strike up the chorus! January 11 marks the anniversary of John A. Macdonald's birth, and like Canadians everywhere, I'll be raising a toast to the Father of Our Country on this important national holiday. What? You say that January 11 isn't a national holiday? Surely you jest.

John A. Macdonald was the chief architect of Confederation and our founding prime minister. He oversaw the purchase of the North-West, the entry of British Columbia into Canada, and the building of the CPR. How could he not have a holiday in his honour, especially considering that his old nemesis Louis Riel is about to be heralded in the House of Commons as a national hero? Louis Riel led an armed insurrection against the government that caused the deaths of more than two hundred people, including innocent settlers and two unarmed priests. And yet, in the wonky logic of today's Canada, it's Riel who's now the hero of history and not John A.

Which is a shame, because Sir John was a terrific role model, especially when it came to the artful employment of political tactics. In recognition of this, I would like to offer our current PM the following primer.

MACDONALD'S SEVEN KEYS TO SUCCESS

1. The Party Line Über Alles

An earnest Tory senator once told Macdonald, "I will always support you when I think you are right." But Macdonald was not impressed. "Anybody may support me when I am right," he replied. "What I want is someone who will support me when I am wrong."

Moral: Whether it's a golf course in Shawinigan or a promise to abolish the GST, what matters most is not whether your leader is right or wrong, but that you stick with him, no matter what.

2. The Tactical Use of Humour

Onstage during a public debate, Sir John, visibly drunk, turned to one side and vomited. A horrible, awkward pause followed, but John A. just wiped his mouth, smiled, and said, "I'm sorry. I don't know what it is about my opponent, but every time I hear him speak it turns my stomach." The crowd roared.

Moral: When caught in a tricky situation, simply laugh it off. If, for example, students get pepper-sprayed and clubbed on the head, all with your tacit approval, do not accept any culpability. Instead, turn the whole thing into a joke. "For me, the pepper it's what I put on the plate." The Canadian public loves a leader with a sense of humour. You could see protesters wiping tears from their eyes over this, from laughter I'm assuming.

3. Mocking the Opposition

John A.'s longtime foe was George Brown, a man who was both upright and unwavering. Rather than try to grapple for the moral high ground, Macdonald simply acknowledged the obvious, turning his own weaknesses into a point of pride. "The people would rather have John A. drunk than George Brown sober," he proclaimed. And he was right.

Moral: Whether your opponents are separatists, socialists, or gadflies on Sea-Doos, you can't go wrong portraying them as prudish and straitlaced. Especially if they are prudish and straitlaced.

4. Neutering the Competition

Canada's first separatist movement began, not in Quebec, but in Nova Scotia. The movement foundered, however, when the leader of the Nova Scotian separatists, Joseph Howe, was won over by Sir John's considerable charms. A year after arriving in Ottawa, and to the outraged cries of "Traitor!," Joseph Howe crossed the floor to become a high-ranking minister in John A. Macdonald's government.

Moral: Keep your friends close, and your enemies closer. Minister of Finance, say. (*See:* Martin, Paul. Thwarted political aspirations thereof.)

5. Maintaining the Proper Decorum

John A. Macdonald once charged across the floor of the House and attempted to land a haymaker to the head of an honourable member, roaring as he did, "I could lick him quicker than Hell could scorch a feather!"

Moral: Never give an ounce of respect to your foes. A protester gets in your way, throttle 'em! Throttle 'em good!

6. Dealing with Issues of Ethics

During the 1872 election, John A. Macdonald, desperate to save the railway and his career (the two having become inextricably linked), received campaign "donations" in exchange for implied railway contracts. The ensuing scandal led to Macdonald's becoming the first and only prime minister in Canadian history to be forced out of office on charges of unethical behaviour. Undaunted, he was swept back into power five years later, and he ended his days in triumph.

Moral: In Canada, ethics and politics don't mix. So if you're going to have an ethics counsellor, at least make sure he's in your pocket. You don't want an independently appointed do-gooder stirring up trouble. God no!

7. That "Vision" Thing

For all his flaws, John A. Macdonald oversaw the creation of Canada from a patchwork of eastern colonies to a single nation spanning the continent from coast to coast, sea to sea.

Moral: To be a truly great leader, you must have a shining dream of what this country could be. You must have courage and conviction. You must have a grand vision. But don't worry, Jean ... six out of seven ain't bad.

So let's raise a drink to the scoundrel who started it all. Maybe next year, Sir John will finally get a holiday of his own. In the meantime, Happy Louis Riel Day!

Lord Black,
Formerly of Canada

Now, I'll admit, I'm a chatty fellow. It's the Ulster Irish in me. But sometimes it pays off. When Conrad Black was convicted on fraud charges in an American court, an editor at *The New York Times* called me up. He wanted a quote for a piece they were putting together. Specifically, he wanted to know if I thought Conrad Black represented the brash new face of Canadians. We ended up having a long and lively discussion that ranged from voyageurs to Céline Dion to the War of 1812, and by the time we were done he said, "You know what? You should write this." So I did.

Forget the cowboy. The true all-American hero is the confidence man: breezy, self-invented, ambitious, protean.

So too with Canada. Ignore the scarlet-jacketed Mountie of lore. Up here, the *voyageur*—that indomitable, unpretentious, rough-hewn New World figure—is closer to the Canadian heart than any Dudley Do-Right police constable. Never mind that the back-breaking reality of the French Canadian voyageur was far removed from the romanticized image we have of them today; we're dealing with iconography, not facts.

But just as surely as the Puritan stands in thin-lipped contrast to the American confidence man, so too does the Upper Canadian anglophile stand in contrast to the voyageur of old.

Which brings us to Conrad Black, Canada's fallen press baron.

Although from Quebec, and thus historically a Lower Canadian, Black is still Anglo and Upper all the way through. Newly convicted on three counts of fraud and one of obstruction, Black's charges could just as easily have been boiled down to a single word: hubris. This is a man who thought he could bully U.S. prosecutors in the same way he'd bullied his shareholders.

Standing up to Americans is normally the sort of thing that would endear a Canadian to his countrymen. But not in this case. Instead, there is a quiet feeling of glee over Lord Black's comeuppance. Not because he is rich and powerful and in need of ego deflation, though that's a big part of it, I'm sure. And not because he was revealed to be a swindler on a grand scale either. No. There's schadenfreude at work up here primarily because Conrad Black—for reasons only an Upper Canadian Anglo would understand—has publicly renounced his Canadian citizenship.

Why, you ask? An act of protest, perhaps? The seal hunt, say, or the continued existence of Céline Dion? Nope. Conrad Black renounced his citizenship so that he could dress up as a British lord and play out the ultimate Upper Canadian Anglo dream.

Black was forced to choose between being a Canadian press baron or a British poobah. His entry into the British House of Lords had been blocked, you see. Blocked by a French Canadian voyageur, as it were. Prime Minister Jean Chrétien, a tough little scrapper from the boonies, had refused to allow Black's ascent into the higher echelons of über-snootiness.

"Canadian citizens," said Chrétien, "do not accept foreign titles."

Jean Chrétien and Conrad Black are opposites in any category you care to mention: class, language, culture, diction. Conrad Black is from a wealthy Anglo Montreal family. Chrétien is from blue-collar rural Quebec. And their public feud played out along Canada's classic fault lines as a conflict between Upper Canadian pretensions and French Canadian disdain for those very same pretensions.

It ended with Black stomping off in a huff, renouncing his

Canadian citizenship in order to don the musty robes and puffed-up title of Lord Such-and-Such. This did not endear him to Canadians. True, he wasn't burned in effigy over his apostasy or anything, but he did greatly irk a lot of his former fellow citizens. And there is nothing so frighteningly passive-aggressive as a well-irked Canadian.

More than merely irksome, though, on a deeper level Conrad Black represents that most Anglo Canadian of conceits: the blustering royalist, the imperially infatuated capitalist.

Remember the Tories that you Americans hounded out of your country following the War of Independence? In Canada they're known as "Loyalists." They're considered heroes, men and women of principle who sacrificed everything except honour in the face of American mob rule.

The Tories who came north to Canada paid a heavy price for their loyalties. They also established a precedent, one that lingers even now. In Lord Black we see it: the self-inflicted colonialism and reflexive deference to all things British that has marked and marred so much of the Canadian character over the years.

From British lord to convicted felon, Lord Black's swan dive has been breathtaking. Almost heroic.

In Canada, any disagreement with the United States is typically cast in David and Goliath terms, with Canadians as beleaguered underdogs and the Americans as rapacious swindlers. (*See:* softwood lumber, treaties regarding.) Remember Ben Johnson, the fleet-footed sprinter pumped up on steroids? In Canada, *he* was the underdog. At least, until he got caught. And Carl Lewis? He was the American, which, almost by definition, made him the villain of the piece. The War of 1812? Same thing. We were the underdogs. You were the marauders. (I'm told that in American history books you won the War of 1812. Bizarre.)

This whole "Canada as plucky underdog" narrative hasn't been applied in the case of Lord Black vs. the United States, though. Instead, when Canada's national history magazine ran a contest to name The Worst Canadian Ever, the lovable Lord Black, having denounced his country and been convicted of fraud, was one of the top nominees—if only because he reflects so sharply a side of ourselves we often try to deny: the anglophilia, the once-defiant and now-dated Loyalist mindset, the yearning for a colonial world that exists now only in memory.

On the day the verdict was announced an American newspaper editor called me to ask, "Is Conrad Black the future of Canada? Aggressive, unapologetic, imperially ambitious?"

I thought about the ermine robes, the bluster, the House of Lords pretensions. "No," I said. "Not the future. The past."

Boxing Day, Hooray!

Granted, this next piece is not a political essay per se, but it does lead directly from the preceding one on Conrad Black and touches on many of the same issues (up to and including Céline Dion).

Having presented a Canuckistan view of Lord Black's fall from grace, *The New York Times* next asked me to "explain" (their words) the concept of "Boxing Day" to Americans. In much the same way as I penned the *Flare* article on behalf of men, I decided to present it as an open letter to all Americans from Canada. The final article never actually ran—I got paid and everything, but I suspect my extended riff on the name of *The Beaver* magazine may have been off-putting. Those Americans, so easily off-put.

Dear United States of Americans,

Greetings from your neighbour to the North! (I'll wait while you check an atlas.) That's right, Canada! We keep sending down cold fronts and you keep sending up waves of benign indifference, but as the holiday season draws nearer, I'm writing today to ask a favour of you. I'm asking you to please leave an important Canadian touchstone alone.

I refer to Boxing Day, in all its glory.

Boxing Day is the pugilistic annual event wherein stressed-out parents converge on malls the day after Christmas to return the toys that didn't work or else came pre-broken in the package to save time. You think I made this holiday up, don't you America? But no, I assure you, Boxing Day is a bona fide holiday in the Great White North, one dutifully marked on calendars and formally listed in the Canadian Labour Code, even though there are no specific traditions associated with it. It simply *is*. It's the purest of holidays, almost Zenlike in its resolute lack of purpose.

The roots are said to lie in vague recollections of Victorian households "boxing" up gifts after Christmas for their servants, lackeys, forelock-tugging workmen, and other such riff-raff. No one does that anymore, though. Ask Canadians what Boxing Day is and they'll say, "It's a holiday! Yay!" Ask them *why* it's a holiday, or what exactly one does to celebrate it, and you'll receive only blank stares and open-mouthed, maple-scented confusion.

We already share most of the same Yuletide traditions with you Americans: sending cards to people we don't particularly like, spending forced time with drunken uncles, eating wads of stuffing that has been pulled, still warm, out of the arse of a dead fowl. You can at least leave us Boxing Day.

Canada's Thanksgiving falls in October, but is essentially the same (minus the pilgrims; we didn't have pilgrims, we had fur traders). Ditto Halloween with its refreshing honesty: "Give us something good and no one gets hurt." And now that you have a Democrat in the White House and Céline Dion in Vegas, our December 26 holiday is one of the few remaining cultural divides still separating us. We see the same movies, listen to the same music. You can at least leave us Boxing Day.

It's a throwback to our genteel colonial roots. We never had a Revolution, you see, which is why we still bask in the Victorian glory that is Boxing Day.

Indeed, a great deal of English Canadian nationalism turns on the narcissism of small differences, on defining ourselves as Not American. We often announce ourselves in Monty Pythonesque terms as "The People Who Say Zed Instead of Zee!"

An example of how small differences can lead to big misunderstandings: Canada's national history magazine is named *The Beaver.* This, of course, is to honour our stalwart web-toed national hero, the waterlogged rodent who gave his pelt, quite literally, for Canada's sake. The fur trade defined us, after all. In the words of historian Arthur Lower, "Canada is a canoe route." America was a covered-wagon trail.

Which is why I was so puzzled as a teenager when my American cousins came to visit over Christmas and got all excited when they found a box stashed in the attic labelled "Dad's Beaver Magazines."

My cousins hustled me into the bathroom, locked the door, pulled out the first issue, and breathlessly started to flip through the pages, giddy with anticipation. That month's fold-out, I believe, was a portrait of Samuel de Champlain. *"Samuel Champlain founded Quebec City on July 3, 1608. His likes include long walks on the beach and making maps. His dislikes include negative people and the English."* It was history, all history, and you could see the awful crush of disappointment as they rifled through, looking for something, anything. Lucy Maud Montgomery on a half-shell, anything.

Their disappointment only increased when the 26th of December arrived and we announced, "It's Boxing Day today!" They waited for something to happen—party hats, horns, special Boxing Day desserts, games, anything. But that was it. We just said, "It's Boxing Day!" and went back to gnawing on the turkey carcass that would comprise our meals over the next three weeks.

Sadly, retailers in Canada have been trying to hijack the True Meaning of Boxing Day, turning this cherished institution into just another sales event. They've even taken to calling it "Boxing Week!" in the hopes of stretching it out even further. Were American store owners to find out about this, I fear it would destroy the purity of this sacred holiday.

Which is why I am writing you today, on behalf of Canadians everywhere, asking you to leave us the many venerable traditions associated with Boxing Day, whatever those may be.

Sincerely, Will Ferguson
(on behalf of Canadians everywhere)

Why Canada Is NOT
Northern Ireland and
Montreal Is NOT Belfast

A St. Patrick's Day piece I wrote for the *Maclean's* backpage.

Last year, I spent two months hiking across Northern Ireland. I was following the Ulster Way, an 856-kilometre path that exists primarily in the imaginations of local tourist bureaus. A good deal of my time was spent stomping about in the rain, arms flailing wildly as I cursed the quaint lack of signage in Ireland.

I was on one of those ill-advised "ancestral homeland" treks of which we North Americans are so inexplicably fond. My grandfather was a Belfast orphan, and I thought that somehow I'd be able to "reconnect with my past" and "discover my roots" by walking through muddy fields for two and a half months on feet so blistered they began to resemble bubble wrap.

My trip took me through every county and every region— Protestant and Catholic, Orange and Green—but my proudest achievement was this: I think I introduced a new joke to the Irish of Ulster (as the North is traditionally known). Here's how it goes:

An Irishman releases a genie from its bottle and is granted a single wish. But in the spirit of reconciliation, he's informed that whatever he receives, his neighbour will receive double. The Irishman thinks for a moment, then says, "Can you put out one of me eyes?"

The alternative punchline is "Can you beat me half to death?" But however I told it, it was greeted with roaring approval by the people of Ulster, who have a certain affection for their own shortcomings. "Aye, it's true all right," they would say—proudly. I was just surprised they hadn't heard the joke before.

In the wake of the current peace accord, I had—rather naively— assumed that all would be sunshine and smiles in the Land of Ulster. But the tribal allegiances and dark undercurrents were still there, seething just below the surface, bubbling in the cauldron, festering like a wound gone septic, and Ulster remains a land mired in its own past.

"This isn't a country," it was explained to me. "It's a stalemate."

Two solitudes, mutually antagonistic and nursing old grievances. Sounds familiar, no? So why didn't Canada descend into similar sectarian violence? Why didn't we become the Northern Ireland of the New World? Canada was built along equally deep fault lines: French, English; Catholic, Protestant; the conquered and the conquering.

The timeline is also similar, with the October Crisis of 1970 paralleling the Bloody Sunday uprisings of 1972. In both cases, a besieged minority lashed out at the establishment: francophones in Quebec; Catholics in Derry. In both cases, civil rights were suspended and martial law declared.

So why didn't Canada spiral into its own cycle of attack and counter-attack, of atrocity and reprisal? I'd always assumed it was Pierre Trudeau's draconian War Measures Act that did the trick, stopping Quebec's nascent terrorist movement dead in its tracks. But the British took the same approach following Bloody Sunday.

In Northern Ireland, the troops didn't stay for a month; they stayed for thirty years. More than three thousand people died during the Troubles. In Canada, the tally—including bombing victims and political assassinations from the start of Quebec's Quiet Revolution in 1960 through to today—stands at exactly ... seven.

On its own, the War Measures Act resolved nothing. It was a counterpunch, not a TKO. So what did rescue us? A preliminary report by the Royal Commission of Bilingualism and Biculturalism. That's what saved us, not the presence of armed troops in the streets. It was this now-forgotten Royal Commission that led directly to the Official Languages Act of 1969, the terms of which were being implemented even as bombs were going off in Montreal.

Canada's Official Languages Act undercut both the power and the appeal of the FLQ message. It became harder and harder for Quebec radicals to portray themselves as oppressed. In Canada, advocating separatism wasn't outlawed, but violence was. And starting in 1976, the democratically elected Parti Québécois was allowed to bring in a series of language laws that restricted English and promoted French. These very laws, ironically, helped take the wind out of separatist sails. In Canada we bend so as not to break, and today the most hardline extremist in the Quebec National Assembly would be considered a moderate in the sectarian world of Northern Ireland.

Following the Bloody Sunday riots, the British were unrelenting and unflinching. They never wavered, never bent, never buckled—and the result was a guerilla war that spanned more than three decades. Imagine the October Crisis of 1970 lasting thirty years. Imagine the FLQ still wielding a puppet-master influence on the political agenda. Imagine RCMP stations barricaded behind sandbags and razor wire. Imagine police officers being considered "legitimate targets." Imagine.

On St. Patrick's Day, Canadians have much to celebrate. Not the least of which is the fact that we are not the Ulster of North America, that we are not the punchline to particularly pungent joke. Canada, rescued from the brink by a Royal Commission. How very apt.

The Vancouver 2010
Closing Ceremonies

My involvement with the Vancouver Winter Olympics began with an invitation to attend a "VANOC Ceremonies Symposium." Not knowing what a VANOC Ceremonies Symposium was, I accepted …

All the World's a Stage

The VANOC Ceremonies Symposium, as it turned out, was an intimate gathering of a hundred-plus theatrical directors, designers, artists, musicians, playwrights, professors, choreographers, producers, and assorted community leaders from across Canada who were brought to Vancouver in groups of twenty-five for staggered meetings over three days to discuss what we felt should be included in the Opening and Closing Ceremonies of the 2010 Winter Olympics. How Canada should be presented to the world, that sort of thing. Panel discussions, basically. Lots and lots of panel discussions. My eyes had glazed over by the third hour of the first day. By the end of the second day, my buttocks were so numb you could have performed ass surgery on them without the need for anaesthetic. By the end of the third, I needed a stiff drink just to enter the room. Had there been a fourth day, I have no doubt I would have ended up mainlining heroin on East Hastings.

It wasn't the organizers' fault; I just have a low tolerance level for meetings. Jacques Lemay, producer of the Calgary Winter Olympics Ceremonies, was there, along with a host of other luminaries. But the symposium—or rather, symposia—were staged mainly for the benefit of David Atkins, executive producer of the 2010 Ceremonies, and his partner in crime, Ignatius Jones, the Ceremonies' artistic director.

Their company, DAE (David Atkins Enterprises), specialized in staging Really Big Events. DAE was the creative force behind the Sydney Ceremonies, still considered a gold standard, mixing as it did moments of sheer beauty (the lighting of the Sydney flame against a backdrop of falling water) with a goodly dose of humour (the banner that dropped down welcoming the world with a "G'day eh!" and the lawnmower-riding Aussie scattering dancers).

Unfortunately, David and Ignatius were—through no fault of their own—Not Canadian. They were, in fact—and again, through no fault of their own—Australian. True, Canada and Australia do share a certain affinity, both being oversized, underpopulated, far-flung former colonies with large Aboriginal communities and vast stretches of emptiness at the centre of who they are (Outback and Arctic, respectively). But these similarities aren't quite the close parallels they may seem. As comedian Dave Broadfoot put it, "Australia was settled by thieves and poachers and criminals. The Canadians never got caught."

Along with producer Merryn Hughes, David and Ignatius were seeking as much feedback as possible from as wide a swath of Canadian artists and commentators as possible. Hence, the symposia.

They moved us through in shifts, first to the VANOC offices and then to the stadium, where they explained the venue's limitations (an inflatable roof that made wire acts tricky) and its advantages (indoor, and thus removed from the vagaries of weather). In between these field trips, the round-table discussions plodded on as the usual competing agendas emerged: First Nations, Quebec nationalists, heartfelt environmentalists, sour-faced academics.

On our last night we all went out for dinner, and Ignatius came over to say hi. He's a very engaging individual, even though, with a name like "Ignatius Jones," he really should've been a 1970s private investigator. *Ignatius Jones, P.I.!* Either that or an X-Man villain.

We talked about Canada, his first impressions and how he'd noticed you couldn't "walk through the airport on arrival" without someone telling you that So-and-So was Canadian or that such-and-such was invented—right here in Canada!

I laughed. "It's true," I said. "What's even funnier is that Canadians themselves always—*always*—complain that the problem with Canadians is that we aren't patriotic enough."

"Really?" Ignatius had since crisscrossed the country, read extensively, and seen no evidence of Canadians being "unpatriotic."

"Oh, it's true," I said. "That's the perception. So whenever someone starts going on about how Canadians aren't patriotic enough, I ask them 'What? You aren't proud to be Canadian?' And they always say 'God no! Not me—*other Canadians.*' In all my years, Ignatius, I've never met this mythical 'other Canadian.' It's a bit like UFOs. You hear a lot about them, but you never actually see one firsthand. I'll tell you one thing, though. Whoever this 'other Canadian' is, he's got a lot to answer for, going around bad-mouthing us like that."

A magazine in Montreal once asked its contributors, "If you were a Canadian superhero, who would you be?" My response: "I would be Minor Hollywood Celebrity Man, spreading enlightenment by sidling up to strangers in movie theatres and whispering '*Y'know, he's Canadian,*' then disappearing into the night."

Ignatius thought this was very funny—though that may have been related to the amount of alcohol consumed at that point—and we joked about having a parade of Canadian superheroes in the Ceremonies, each one wielding an equally Canadian invention: poutine say, or giant earmuffs.

Now, I mention this rambling conversation because I think it may have had something to do with what happened next.

I flew back to Calgary, and was later asked to write a short piece about where I lived for an online "Cultural Olympiad" aimed at creating a digital portrait of the nation. The entries were meant to be thoughtful and succinct, and to provide a personal snapshot of one's own corner of Canada. I was feeling wistful the day I wrote it. Here's what I submitted:

I live in the shadow of the chinook, in a city of sandstone and steel. A city where even in the coldest grey days of winter, warm winds will arrive—spilling over the mountains, sweeping across the plains. These chinook winds turn the ice to slush, the slush to puddles. They loosen jackets, unwrap scarves, fill our chests with clean fistfuls of air, and we wander about feeling buoyant and grateful ... Then winter returns, the grey skies seal off the city again, and the meltwaters freeze. I live in a city of false springs.

And with that, I figured I was more or less done with all things Olympic. But then, many months later, I got a phone call asking if I'd consider coming back to Vancouver to discuss the Closing Ceremonies in more detail. I said sure. Even with another round of buttock-numbing blather, it would be good to see Ignatius again. So what the heck, I like Vancouver and I'm always up for a trip to the coast.

I'd expected another panel-group round table, but when I arrived there was just me. It was a very strange moment.

The atmosphere, for one, had completely changed. The days of endless round-table discussions were over, and the energy level had ratcheted up. There were people everywhere. It was like one of those old 1940s newsroom movies with extras hurrying every which way, carrying clipboards and stacks of paper, dodging each other with coffee cups in hand as orders were being barked out and phones were ringing. There were set designers and graphic artists, computer animators and engineers; there was even a full mock-up of the stadium, complete with miniature inflatable moose. And right in the middle of it all, David Atkins, looking like a man trying to rake leaves in a hurricane—and somehow succeeding.

The main elements of the Opening Ceremonies had largely been settled; they were now working on the Closing. Ignatius explained the difference in approach between the two. Whereas the Opening Ceremonies would be elegant and beautiful, the Closing Ceremonies would be more relaxed, more raucous, more fun. They would be a celebratory send-off for the athletes, complete with a concert showcasing Canadian music.

The Closing Ceremonies would highlight Canadian talent, innovation, and humour. And to that end, David and Ignatius wanted to include a scripted segment, with Canadian celebrities riffing on Canada, using the "I Am Canadian"–style rant of the beer commercials as a jumping-off point. Molson's was one of the sponsors, so there wasn't going to be a problem, but I did remain a bit apprehensive. And as you'll see, although I started off in that mode with my first attempt, I quickly tried to get as far away from that as possible.

Instead of "I Am Canadian," I suggested putting a spin on it.

"Canada is a Big Tent," I said. "And Canadian nationalism is very inclusive. Almost comically so. Basically, if you're good at something, we will claim you." I gave them an example. "Canadians always tell you that the telephone AND basketball are Canadian, right? But those two claims are based on completely contradictory criteria. Alexander Graham Bell was born, raised, and educated in Scotland. But we say the telephone is Canadian because he developed the idea over here. It doesn't matter where you were born, it's where you lived. Fair enough?"

They nodded.

"Basketball was invented in the States. We still claim basketball, though, because the inventor was *born* in Canada. Suddenly, it's where you're from that counts, not where you lived." I then broke the news to David and Ignatius as gently as I could. "You're Canadians now too. You've been living in Canada. You're working here, you've produced a world event—here in Canada. That makes you Canadian."

I have to say, they took it well, having their nationality confiscated like that.

"So," I said. "Why not make it 'YOU Are Canadian' instead? We could have the host of the Ceremonies address the athletes directly, tell them they're now considered Canadians. He could then claim all their medals for Canada."

David didn't miss a beat. "We could have a giant lever," he said. "Like a slot machine. We could pull it and have the medal count for the other countries spin down to zero as Canada's total soars."

That was the moment I realized we just might be on the same

wavelength. And so, like James Bond called before MI6, I accepted the assignment. There were even Bond-like gadgets, or the theatrical equivalent thereof: a state-of-the art system that could project anything we wanted onto the stage or even the audience. The visuals available were unlimited and—as the world would see in the Opening Ceremonies—magnificent. David showed me examples: the Trans-Canada projected onto centre stage, complete with traffic zooming by. A giant zipper opening up, allowing a cavalcade of iconic Canadian images to spill forth.

They wanted me to write monologues for the celebrities. Which celebrities? The list hadn't been finalized, but they would be internationally recognizable comedic actors who'd be comfortable performing live in front of the world.

"Have fun with it," they said.

So I did.

Little did I know that I'd dropped down the rabbit hole, had crossed over to the other side of the looking glass …

"Made in Canada": First Concept

This is the original concept I came up with.

A "Magical Mystery Tour"-slash-*Wizard of Oz*–type journey, it incorporates the required key elements of Canadian talent, innovation, and humour, and involves a fatherly William Shatner taking a vaguely confused Seth Rogen under his wing on a journey of discovery to teach him "the true nature of being Canadian"—only to leave Rogen more confused at the end than when he started.

I wasn't involved in selecting which celebrities would appear in the Closing Ceremonies: that was arranged entirely through DAE and was dependent on availability, scheduling, international recognizability, and a host of other considerations. So the names that appear in the following "Made in Canada" segment simply represent my own personal wish list from a wide range of possibilities.

I incorporated David's giant slot machine that changes the medal count, as well as a very sexy "dancing light bulb" costume the designers had come up with and which could be "popped" with a pin. Among the list of Canadian inventions was the Robertson screwdriver, and Ignatius had thought it would be funny to have someone shuffle out dressed as one, so I included that as well.

What I really wanted, though, more than anything, was to have the

306 THE VANCOUVER 2010 CLOSING CEREMONIES

Space Shuttle's Canadarm reach out to touch fingers with a hoser-clad Seth Rogen, replicating Michelangelo's Sistine Chapel; it would have become an iconic image of the Closing Ceremonies, I was sure. Alas, like almost everything else in the version that follows, it didn't make the final cut.

The echo of footsteps. A single microphone. SETH ROGEN, dressed in jeans and a plaid jacket, approaches. He has a backpack slung over one shoulder with a large prominent MAPLE LEAF sewn on it, upside-down. He clears his throat, then begins.

ROGEN

Um, hello. My name is Seth. I'm Canadian ... though I'm not really sure what that means exactly ...

His voice begins to trails off.

There is a BLINDING FLASH, and WILLIAM SHATNER appears, dressed in a shimmering tuxedo, all Hollywood and glitz.

SHATNER

Did I hear someone say ... Canadian?

ROGEN

(eyes wide in wonderment and awe)

Spock!

The Hollywood smile slides off Shatner's face, but just for an instant. He is soon back in full Shatner mode. He looks at Seth sympathetically.

SHATNER

Confused? Conflicted? Canadian? Come with me, young Seth.
Allow me to—*unzip*—the wonderful world that is Canada!

*On Shatner's cue a MASSIVE ZIPPER runs across the stadium,
releasing a tumbling array of images and inventions.*

SHATNER

The zipper. Invented right here in Canada. Earmuffs, too. And
frozen peas—*frozen peas, Seth!* But that's only the start.

*Lights reveal a FIGURE dramatically silhouetted, holding an ORB
aloft, looking like a Greek god or an Emmy Award. The figure is
revealed to be DAN AYKROYD holding up a bowling ball.*

ROGEN

Wow! Canadians invented bowling?

AYKROYD

No, Seth, not bowling. Five-pin bowling! It's like bowling—but
with five pins!

*Aykroyd winds up, but instead of a ball, the image of the TRANS-
CANADA HIGHWAY unrolls like a ribbon down the middle of the
stadium. Various national landmarks line the way—the CN Tower,
the Chateau Frontenac, the Rockies.*

*The asphalt does not have a centre line, though. Aykroyd stands in
the middle of the highway, with Shatner and Rogen beside him.*

AYKROYD

The Trans-Canada, Seth. Seventy-eight hundred kilometres
of highway, stretching from east to west, sea to sea. A feat of
engineering that stands among the—

The image of a TRANSPORT TRUCK roars past, narrowly missing Rogen, who leaps to one side.

AYKROYD

As the Age of the Automobile was dawning, and as the first long-distance roads were being built, it was chaos! Absolute chaos.

Two more vehicles pass, almost clipping Rogen.

AYKROYD

But one Canadian saw the light!

HALLELUJAH MUSIC builds and a shaft from heaven beams down, illuminating the image of … a SINGLE CAN OF YELLOW PAINT with a PAINTBRUSH leaning from it. The paintbrush rises, floats into the air a moment, and—swoosh, it adds a yellow line down the centre of the asphalt.

AYKROYD
(standing heroically astride the line)
That's right, Seth. It was a Canadian who put the yellow line down the middle of the road!

More traffic spins past on either side, nearly spinning Rogen in place.

SHATNER
(placing his hand on Rogen's shoulder)
Perhaps centre lane isn't the best place to do this.

PAINT ROLLERS appear, quickly painting over the image of the highway. The paint rollers get bigger and bigger, faster and faster, covering the entire surface of the stage, then moving on, painting the stands, the athletes, and the audience in washes of colour.

From centre stage a large GAME SHOW–STYLE ROULETTE WHEEL rises up, and beside it, in the sparkly gown of a 1960s game show host, CATHERINE O'HARA. Rogen is now unwittingly cast as a game-show contestant.

ROGEN

I'm starting to get the hang of this! The paint roller. Canadian, right?

O'HARA

Absolutely!

Loud CHEERS, images of CONFETTI.

O'HARA

The paint roller. The caulking gun. The electron microscope. Why, I get all flustered just thinking about it.

ROGEN

Did I win something?

O'HARA

Let's spin the Big Wheel of Canadian Inventions and find out.

She spins the wheel and images of various Canadian inventions flip past.

SHATNER
(hand gripping Rogen's shoulder, speaking almost to himself)
C'mon, electron microscope …

The images slow down and stop on—

O'HARA

Instant mashed potatoes! *(She reaches in, pulls out a box, poses like a 1960s commercial.)* Just add water … and stir!

SHATNER
(to Rogen)

Goes great with frozen peas.

The sound of a FOGHORN is heard as the lights dim. Rogen looks around, confused.

SHATNER

The foghorn. 1853.

The sound of the FOGHORN is replaced by that of a HEARTBEAT. It grows louder and louder, until its drumlike thump fills the stadium.

SHATNER

The pacemaker. 1950.

The heartbeat grows louder, faster, stronger until it changes into—the sound of a BASKETBALL BEING DRIBBLED. The image of a GIANT BALL appears, thumping into centre stage, startling Rogen. He ducks instinctively.

ROGEN

Basketball? I thought that was invented in, like, Massachusetts.

SHATNER

Yes, but James Naismith was born and raised in Canada. Canada shaped him. *(then, almost curtly)* So basketball is ours.

Shatner pulls out a large GLOWING NEON SPORK from his pocket. Rogen and Shatner gaze at it as though it were some rare treasure.

SHATNER
(speaking in hushed reverential tones)
Consider this small work of wonder. Neither a fork nor a spoon, but a crazy hybrid of both. It's ... a spork.

ROGEN
(in amazement)
The spork? That's Canadian too?

SHATNER
Oh, yes. *(then, with a gleam in his eye)* But we're just warming up.

Using the spork as a wand/baton, Shatner makes a gesture halfway between orchestral conductor and mad wizard as a burst of FIREWORKS lights up the stadium.

In a shower of glamour and glitz, PAMELA ANDERSON rises up in the LIGHT BULB COSTUME with an ELECTRIC BRA on.

Shatner reaches into his jacket, takes out a large PROP PIN, and pops the costume.

ROGEN
(with amazement, reacting more to this than any of the previous inventions)
No way! A Canadian invented the pin?

SHATNER
No. Not the pin—the Wonderbra! *(then, almost as an after-thought)* And also the light bulb.

ROGEN

The light bulb?

PAMELA ANDERSON

Henry Woodward in 1874. He then sold the rights to Thomas
Edison. It was a proud moment for Canadians everywhere.

ROGEN

Wow. The light bulb.

SHATNER
(quickly reminding him)
And the Wonderbra.

*The lights have grown softer, dimmer. Shatner puts his arm around
Rogen's shoulder.*

ROGEN

I never realized—

SHATNER

Shhh.

The mood has become very quiet.

SHATNER

Look up Seth, what do you see?

ROGEN

The inside of the stadium?

SHATNER

Beyond that ... The stars. Canada was the third nation in
space. We have crossed great distances, Seth. We have explored

the auroras. Launched telecommunication satellites. Built a space arm. As a nation, we have always looked—*to the skies.*

The CANADARM appears, extending slowly as Rogen reaches out, striking a Michelangelo pose ... touching fingertips with it.

As the Canadarm withdraws, EERIE MUSIC builds and a UFO arrangement of blinking lights appears. It's revealed to be not a spacecraft, but a tricked-out FLASH GORDON SKI-DOO with MICHAEL J. FOX astride it. He's dressed in a fighter pilot's ANTI-GRAVITY SUIT.

> **FOX**
>
> From the snowmobile to the anti-gravity suit, Canadian innovations have led the way. Mobile blood units. The Cobalt 60 treatment for cancer. Insulin. These have saved the lives of millions around the world. From the space age to the everyday, Canadians have been there.

There is an awkward pause. Someone has missed a cue. Fox repeats his line, looking with concern to an EMPTY SPOTLIGHT.

> **FOX**
>
> From the space age to the everyday ...

A begrudging EUGENE LEVY shuffles into the spotlight, dressed in a giant foam SCREWDRIVER COSTUME. He clearly does not want to be here.

> **FOX**
> *(to Levy)*
>
> Say the line ...

Levy holds his tiny costumed arms out in a half-hearted "tah dah" pose. When he speaks his voice is flat.

LEVY
I am the Robertson screwdriver. And I too am Canadian.

He turns and wuffles away, the foam rear-end wiggling. As he leaves, Levy passes MIKE MYERS on the way in. Myers is wearing a tuxedo and he gives Levy a staged smile, the way presenters at the Oscars do. But Levy just trudges past, head down. Myers shrugs it off, turns to the audience.

MYERS
Canadian talent and innovation has been at the forefront of—

He is interrupted by the SOUND OF A CELLPHONE.

MYERS
Sorry.

He reaches into his tux pocket, pulls out an OLD-FASHIONED 1880s TELEPHONE.

MYERS
(speaking into the phone, mugging slightly to the audience)
What's that you say? Why yes, as a matter of fact, the telephone is also a Canadian invention.

ROGEN:
Oh, come on! The telephone AND the light bulb?

Myers nods proudly.

ROGEN

I thought the telephone was a Scottish invention.

MYERS

Alexander Graham Bell. Born and raised in Scotland. But it's not where you're born and raised that counts. What's important is that later he moved to Canada.

ROGEN

But he built the telephone in Boston.

MYERS

Yes, but the idea was *formed* when he was visiting his dad in Canada. Which makes it a Canadian invention.

Myers now turns to the crowd, and as he speaks, the centre stage rises up to reveal a CIRCUS MERRY-GO-ROUND turning.

MYERS

Canada is a carnival! A Big Tent! We welcome everyone, from far and wide. It doesn't matter who you are or where you came from, if you're good at something—*we will claim you.*

If you were born here and moved away when you were five. If you spent time at one of our many airports. If you've passed through our airspace at any point—*we will claim you.*

You could be a superhero from another planet, or simply a Scottish inventor who summered in Cape Breton. It doesn't matter. Because *we will claim you.*

Leonardo da Vinci? Canadian.

As he speaks, HISTORICAL IMAGES OF THE PEOPLE NAMED appear, and each time Myers says "Canadian" a toque is added on.

MYERS

Michelangelo? Canadian. Aristotle? Plato? Canadian.

Myers is now addressing the ATHLETES directly, as various SPOTLIGHTS illuminate sections of the crowd. PATRIOTIC MUSIC rises in crashing bombast.

MYERS

And you, the Olympic athletes! You and you—even *you*. You too are part of this Big Tent we call Canada. You have come to Vancouver, you have spent time among us, you have competed on the world stage. And that makes you Canadian, too. All of you! *You are Canadian!!*

The music suddenly ends. A LARGE SLOT MACHINE with the Olympics medal tally displayed on it has now appeared.

MYERS

Which brings the actual home medal count to—

Myers pulls the lever and the numbers spin, reducing the other countries' medal count to zero while Canada's tally shoots up.

SHATNER

(putting a fatherly arm around Rogen's shoulder)
Do you see what a rich and complex tapestry Canada offers? A veritable cornucopia, if you will, of talent and innovation—

He is interrupted by the sight of EUGENE LEVY trudging back across the stage toward them. He is dressed in the same LIGHT-BULB COSTUME and ELECTRIC WONDERBRA that Pamela Anderson wore earlier.

SHATNER
(to Levy)

We already did the light bulb.

LEVY

Oh.

Levy turns, trudges back the way he came.

SHATNER
(turning his attention to Rogen again)

Still confused?

ROGEN

More than ever.

SHATNER

Ah. But that too is Canadian. It's a wonderful thing, isn't it?

ROGEN

It is. Thanks, Mr. Spock. (then, lowering his voice) I'm just glad it didn't, y'know, involve a bunch of Mounties and moose.

SHATNER
(looking uncomfortable)

Um ...

Shatner starts to say something, but changes his mind. THROW TO the singing Mounties and Busby Berkeley number complete with giant beavers and inflatable moose.

Celebrity Monologue Outtakes

When I presented that first concept, dubbed "Captain and the Slacker" (ironically so, considering Seth Rogen is one of the hardest working actors/writers/producers going today), David Atkins and the others read it over, thought about it. And then David said, in what has to be the deftest rejection any author could possibly receive, "This is good. Sometimes it's helpful to know what we don't want, so we can work toward what we do want." (I only wish I'd thought of that line back in my youthful single days. "Ladies, listen. Sometimes you need to find out what you don't want in man, so that later you'll know what you do want.")

Back to the drawing board.

For staging reasons, David and Ignatius asked for separate, stand-alone monologues without interaction between the different presenters. I narrowed these monologues down to four themes: "Big Dreams" (with Canada's Large Objects by the Road as a possible visual—I would have loved to have seen Vancouver's imperial Lions Gate statues perform a Chinese dragon dance or the Wawa Goose roll the Sudbury Nickel across the stage); "Sorry, Eh?" about Canadian manners and our reflexive apologies; a revised and reworked "Canadian Inventions"; and finally, the original "We Will Claim You!" idea.

After I wrote these, the monologues were rehearsed and rewritten, with a writer from the Jay Leno show brought in to further "punch up" the material. (The lines about peeing in the snow and trying to pronounce "The Strait of Juan de Fuca" without getting censored? I wasn't responsible for any of that.) I've always been wary about "comedy by committee," but I'm also cognizant of what a collaborative effort staged public events like these are. William Shatner's monologue in particular was hardly recognizable by the time it was done—beyond my original outline and concept and two or three lines that somehow survived the process.

An example: The original opening I wrote was

"My name is Bill, but you can call me Mr. Shatner. My name is Bill, and I am proud to be ..." He checks an index card in his hand. "Canadian."

Actual opening, after the vetting, rehearsals, and rewrites?

"My name is Bill and I am a proud Canadian."

No matter. It was a lot of fun, and it certainly provided my wife and me with the best date night ever, flying in for the Closing Ceremonies, sitting in DAE's private booth alongside assorted celebrities, drinking wine and watching the spectacle and the concert that followed—featuring Neil Young, Michael Bublé, and all the rest. They really were the best seats in the house, even better than the PM and dignitaries' booth that jutted out into the public eye next to us. (I could probably have hit the back of Stephen Harper's head with a peanut if I'd aimed carefully enough, and oh how I was tempted. Not for political reasons necessarily, but just to say I'd done it—especially having missed my chance with Bouchard and the blueberry pies.)

For broadcast copyright reasons, I can't include the final monologues as performed (though you can probably find them easily enough on YouTube). But what I can include is the material that didn't make it. Here, then, are three early versions of the monologues, starting with Shatner's, plus a song-and-dance number that got cut at the very last moment.

William Shatner: "We Dream Big"
"My name is Bill, but you can call me Mr. Shatner. My name is Bill, and I am proud to be ..."

He checks an index card in his hand.

"Canadian.

Oh, sure. I've never wrestled a bear or eaten a Beaver Tail, and I've never gone over Niagara Falls in a barrel. But my game is chippy. My deke is impeccable, and I take a personal and abiding pride in our mountains and our lakes.

We Canadians are passionate about our lack of passion. We boast about how humble we are. And we may not know all the words to our national anthem, but we mumble them with conviction.

We can translate cereal boxes into either official language. We wear wool socks to bed at night, not because it's warm, but because it's chic. And we know—in our hearts—that it *is* possible to make love in a canoe. Not advisable, but possible.

It was a Canadian who coined the phrase 'global village.' And it was a Canadian who thought to put cheese curds and gravy on top of French fries. Pure genius!

As Canadians, we know in our hearts that the Ogopogo is real. The Sasquatch is simply misunderstood. The toque *is* a jaunty fashion statement. And Santa Claus isn't Norwegian or Finnish. He's Canadian!

We Canadians built the world's largest Easter egg, its longest covered bridge, its tallest free-standing structure."

Images of these pile up, overlapping: the VEGREVILLE EGG, the HARTLAND BRIDGE, the CN TOWER, and so on.

"And right here in British Columbia, the world's biggest hockey stick! And, *right beside it*, the world's biggest puck, at no extra charge. We are Canadian! We dream big."

Martin Short: "Canadian Inventions"

For the reworked, rewritten "Canadian Inventions" segment, I turned it into a song-and-dance number tailored to Martin Short's manic energy. Sadly, a family health crisis forced him to pull out at the last moment, though he's still listed in the official program. (He missed the Oscars the following week as well.) Losing this segment was disappointing, partly because I saw it as the high point of the monologues, but mainly because Martin Short performs with such gusto that I would have loved to have seen him pull this off.

Short clears his throat, begins speaking.

"The telephone? Canadian. Basketball? Canadian. The complete works of William Shakespeare? Probably Canadian.

A Canadian invented the paint roller and a Canadian invented the foghorn. It was a Canadian who put the yellow line down the middle of the road. And did I mention the telephone?

My name is Martin. And on behalf of Canadians everywhere, I say to the world—You're welcome!"

He launches headlong into a show tune–style song-and-dance, with the first line in the "Over there! Over there!" mode.

"Frozen peas! Frozen peas!
  Canadian inventions, if you please.
Electric ovens, the goalie mask,
  Spiral nails, and since you asked—
The caulking gun, and Robertson screw
Five-pin bowling, the birchbark canoe.

Snowblowers, pacemakers, insulin.
Instant replay—everyone wins!

Time zones, foghorns, baggage tags,
Walkie-talkies—I hate to brag.

Space arms, G-suits, and radio too
Every one Canadian—yes it's true!

Electron microscopic views,
    Zippers, earmuffs, snowmobiles
The screw propeller—
    How good it feels!
To have invented everything under the sun,
From instant mashed potatoes to the Cobalt gun."

Dancing light bulbs appear. Short pops them, one by one.

"The Wonderbra, uplifting news!
Canadians invented the light bulb too—"

*The song and dance abruptly stops. Martin Short addresses the
audience in a solemn voice.*

"The inventors then sold the rights to Thomas Edison. It was a proud
moment for Canadians everywhere."

*He throws himself back into the song: Big finish, jazz hands, leg
kicks, the works.*

"Frozen peas! Frozen peas!
Canadian inventions if you please!"

Hurrying now to fit the final words in, he goes down on one knee, dragging the last syllables out soulfully.

"And let's not forget the internal-combustion self-propelled combine harvesteeerrr …

We are Canadian! We invented everything!"

Samantha Bee: "Sorry!"

I wrote the next monologue with Samantha Bee of *Daily Show* fame in mind, and have cast it here as it was originally conceived. I think Samantha Bee would have perfectly captured the smiling, passive-aggressive nature of Canadian apologies. It also incorporates an idea from one of the early brainstorming sessions—from Ignatius, I believe—to have footage of Canadian athletes apologizing to each other as they pass on the various courses. It also ends with an early suggestion for a way to use those giant inflatable beavers.

"Hi. My name is Samantha, and I'm sorry.

I'm sorry about—oh, so many things. I'm sorry about the weather, obviously. And I'm sorry I say sorry so much. It's part of a long Canadian tradition. The pre-emptive apology."

A montage of clips starts, beginning with scratchy B&W archival footage of Canadians in toboggans and woolly-toqued cross-country skiers saying "Sorry" as they pass competitors, ending with athletes from the 2010 Games smiling at the camera, holding up their medals, and apologizing.
Samantha turns back to the crowd.

"So, on behalf of all Canadians, I want to say—we're sorry. We're sorry we're so awesome at so many things. We're sorry we keep winning medals." (Stage whisper) "*No we're not.* We're sorry about poutine. We're sorry for hogging all the covers. And we're sorry we're sorry.

As Canadians, we believe in peace, order, and good government ... Well, two out of three ain't bad."

Addressing the PM's box.

"I'm looking at you, sir!

We Canadians are frontier-bred. Strong of jaw, pure of heart. But mostly, we're sorry. We're sorry about our national emblem, the mighty beaver. Oh, sure, we could have had a grizzly bear or a killer whale—or even the conveniently named Canada goose. But no. We chose a forty-kilogram, web-toed water rat whose most heroic trait is that he thinks to slap his tail to warn his buddies before he runs away. And for that we apologize."

Laughing.

"I mean, really. A beaver? As a national animal? What were we thinking?"

A rumble from the side ... and THE ATTACK OF THE GIANT BEAVER commences. Samantha flees, apologizing all the while.

Essay on Canada for
the Olympic Program

Having seen the celebrity monologues completely rewritten and distilled into four short pieces, I had one last duty to perform.

I'd also been asked to write an essay on Canada for the Closing Ceremonies program, a glossy, photo-album-style souvenir booklet presented to the audience and athletes at the Ceremonies. As you'll see, this allowed me one last chance to PUT BACK material that had been cut from the celebrity monologues, including Canada's contradictory claim to basketball AND the telephone. (And honestly, people, for the last time, we can have one or the other, but we can't have both.)

This essay was meant to be a general overview for visitors and Canadians alike, which is why it includes the story of how Canada was named, something that every Canadian schoolchild knows by heart, but which isn't common knowledge outside the country. It also allowed me to include one of my favourite Dave Broadfoot observations about Canada's position in the world. What can I say? The man has a knack for geopolitical analysis.

O Canada! Land of the silver birch, home of the beaver. Canada! Where the world's compass needles point.

The True North, the Magnetic North, strong and free: Canada

matters. As comedian Dave Broadfoot noted, "Without Canada, the Japanese could sail straight across and invade Denmark!"

According to legend, the early Portuguese explorers who probed the upper reaches of North America turned back, having scrawled on their maps "aca nada." *Nothing here.* From which came the name "Canada." A libellous tale to be sure! If anything, there is too much "here" here. Half a continent's worth of real estate, the second-largest nation on earth, Canada's greatest challenge has always been its size, the sheer scope of it. Not surprisingly, when Canada became the third nation in space, its communication satellites were skyrocketing heavenwards not for military or expansionist purposes, but in an attempt to cross the vast distance below.

No, the word "Canada" was not derived from Portuguese explorers but from Iroquoian guides, from a Native word, *kanata,* meaning village. And with a population of 33 million and a land that stretches from sea to sea to sea—from Atlantic to Pacific to Arctic—Canada is undoubtedly the biggest "village" on earth.

Even then, the country might have been known as EFISGA, a name suggested back in 1867 when the former colonies of British North America were coming together in Confederation, EFISGA being an acronym for "English, French, Irish, Scottish, German, and Aboriginal." Which is to say, Canada was already throwing a wide net, was already claiming as great a range of possibilities as it could.

Canada has given the world UN peacekeeping (for which its creator, Lester B. Pearson, won a Nobel Peace Prize) as well as such culinary delights as instant mashed potatoes, frozen peas, and prairie oysters (don't ask). The chefs of Europe are sick with envy about this, I assure you.

In keeping with this wide-net, inclusive approach, Canada also lays claim to inventions as disparate as the telephone and the game of basketball. Never mind that these claims are mutually contradictory. The telephone may have been invented by Alexander Graham Bell, who was raised and educated in Scotland and who built the first working model at his workshop in Boston, but he developed the principles for it in Canada. And it's not where you're born that counts, it's where you live. And basketball? Well, that was invented in the United States by James Naismith. But he was *born* in Canada. And, really, it's where you're born that matters, not where you live. Right? Such is the power of Canadian logic!

Other Canadian achievements include the foghorn, insulin, and the first voice-transmitted radio signal. (The opening message being typically Canadian as well: "Is it snowing where you are?") Even the light bulb was invented by Canadians who, in typically canny Canadian fashion, immediately sold the rights to Thomas Edison. A proud moment!

Canada: land of innovation and harmony! Where children—all the colours of the rainbow—frolic together under sun-dappled skies. A land of heroic compromise and death-defying acts of common sense. A sticky, maple-scented country. A barrel-chested northern land whose hearty inhabitants live as far south as humanly possible. A land of Mounties, moose, and mountains. And malls. Lots of malls.

A land of *habitant* and *voyageur,* of stalwart farmers and singing, toque-wearing, fur-trading lumberjacks and milk-fed hockey players who circle the ice gently driving other players into the boards.

It is a land that encompasses both the platitudinous and the profound, the silly and the sublime. A verb, not a noun. A journey, not a destination. Canada is an ongoing act of discovery, a leap of faith, an invitation. Oh, and the electron microscope? That's ours too.

Japanese
Encounters

The Great Weird North meets the Land of the Rising Sun. I spent five years in Japan, first on the Amakusa Islands south of Nagasaki and then later on the Kyushu mainland.

Every spring, a wave of flowers would move across the Japanese archipelago. They called it Sakura Zensen, the "Cherry Blossom Front," and one year I decided to follow the blossoms north, hitching rides from the southern end of Kyushu to the farthest tip of Hokkaido, a distance roughly equivalent to hitchhiking from Miami to Montreal. It was a journey that would take me from lush tropics to a snow-capped island off the coast of Siberia.

My pursuit of cherry blossoms would later become a travel memoir titled *Hitching Rides with Buddha* (published in the U.K. and U.S. as *Hokkaido Highway Blues*), but more importantly it gave me a chance to travel *with* the Japanese rather than among them, to meet them individually, one on one. Japan has always seemed to me to be a land of vignettes and small encounters, and this last section includes some of those encounters.

True Blue: The Ballad of Good Time Charlie

East is East and West is West and never the twain shall meet.
—Rudyard Kipling

Children, don't choose the cowboy life.
—Slim Williams

Saturday night. A smoky saloon. The band is playing hurtin' songs, and the barroom lights are dim. Texas licence plates line the stage. Lone-star flags adorn the walls. I kick back my fifth bottle of ice-cold Coors and stumble to the Li'l Cowpokes room, where I throw water on my face and try to clear my head. When I look up, I'm confronted by a poster for the Calgary Stampede.

It's all I can do to remind myself that I'm still in Japan.

If I were to walk out the front door of this cowboy canteen, I would find myself not in Texas, or even Calgary, but amid a cacophony of pachinko parlours and noodle shops. But here, in the dark cocoon of Good Time Charlie's, the world is forever Western.

I've come here to meet one of the most quixotic figures in Japanese pop culture: Charlie Nagatani, owner of this here saloon and lead singer in a band called the Cannonballs.

As I make my way back to my table, Charlie and the Cannonballs are up on stage, ripping through a down-home version of "Rocky Top Tennessee," and as my eyes adjust to the smoke and dark, details emerge like images on a photographic plate: Japanese salarymen, whooping it up, neckties loosened with reckless abandon.

The song ends, Charlie tips his cowboy hat to the crowd and, slinging his guitar down and letting it rest against a stool, he steps off the stage. He sees me, nods, and is heading toward my table when the salarymen beckon—and a startling transformation occurs. Charlie suddenly becomes the consummate Japanese host, pouring drinks, bobbing his head in obsequious bows, ingratiating himself with the guests.

Having placated the necktie rowdies, Charlie starts back toward me, and as he does his swagger returns, his gait loosens, his legs become lankier somehow. And by the time he reaches my table, the transformation from cowboy crooner to snack bar owner back to cowboy is complete.

"Welcome to Good Time Charlie's," he says—drawls, really—as he pulls

Charlie Nagatani at his bar in Kumamoto

up a chair beside me. He's wearing cowboy boots and Levi's jeans complete with a superfluously large belt buckle. His hat is pulled down low and he has a thin beard and tinted glasses; there is something—something about the way he's dressed that goes beyond simply Western attire. I can't put my finger on it, but it needles me during our conversation.

I begin with the obvious. "So how did this happen? How does a Japanese musician become a cowboy?"

He laughs. "Long time ago," he says. "Back in 1956. It was my twentieth birthday and—"

"In 1956?" I say. "That makes you"—I do the necessary calculations, which, in my Budweiser-addled state, takes some time—"That makes you sixty-four years old."

"That's right," he says.

Incredible. He doesn't look sixty-four. Even with his southern drawl and cowboy gait, he's got a lot of energy. He looks like someone in his forties, not someone about to start drawing a pension.

"It's the music," he says with a big ol' Texas grin. "Keeps me young."

Masateru "Charlie" Nagatani credits much of what's happened to him to country and western, as though the music were a mystical force of nature. And maybe he's right. Country music certainly changed his life—and it wasn't a slow, gradual change, it was a sudden transformation, the musical equivalent of Saul to Paul.

"One of my neighbours, he was working at an American military base here in Kumamoto City. Promised me a gift. You know, a happy birthday present. So there I was, waitin' to see what kind of stuff he'd bring. We were having a party and there was a knock on the door. I went to see who it was, and in came four musicians—all Japanese—in cowboy hats and boots."

The band played for U.S. servicemen, and Charlie's neighbour had invited them to Charlie's twentieth birthday as a surprise.

"They played for us, and I loved it. Back then," says Charlie, "my interest in music was mainly jazz, but after that night—" He leans back and smiles at me. "After that night, man, it was all over."

Charlie was in college at the time, but right there—that very night—he decided to drop out of school and devote his life to country-and-western music. The kid from Kumamoto City set out to reinvent himself as a cowboy.

"I joined their band and we did all right," he says. "Played at U.S. bases for homesick servicemen. But then Elvis Presley came along and everything went rockabilly. Across Japan, country-and-western singers switched to rock. But not me. I stayed true."

If nothing else, Charlie Nagatani is a stubbornly loyal man. He returned to his hometown of Kumamoto and formed his own band, the Cannonballs. "It's been forty years," he says. "And the Cannonballs are still around."

"Not bad," I say. "That's longer than the Stones."

Mind you, the personnel turnover has been high; eighty different Japanese musicians have been members of the Cannonballs at some point. Only Charlie has remained constant.

"When the Vietnam War began," he says, "I took the Cannonballs on the road. We toured Okinawa, Guam, Taiwan, Thailand, the Philippines—wherever the American troops were. Marine, Army, Navy, Air Force. I played 'em all. And in '76, I decided to take my music back to Japan. I quit touring U.S. bases, opened up this bar."

Since then, Charlie has become something of an institution in Japan. Fashions change and styles come and go, but through it all Charlie has remained steadfast and true, Japan's lonesome cowboy. Slowly, a Japanese country-and-western subculture has grown around him, especially here in southern Japan, and much of the credit goes to the senior statesman of twang, the elder prophet of hurtin' songs: Charlie Nagatani.

Charlie went on to launch his Country Gold Music Festival in the rolling hills of Mount Aso, a grassy volcanic caldera that forms a natural amphitheatre. It seemed a foolhardy venture at the time, but over the years, Country Gold has taken off and has attracted some of the biggest names in country music: Ricky Skaggs, Dwight Yoakum, Emmylou Harris, the Nitty Gritty Dirt Band. People come from across Japan and from Hong Kong and Korea; they come to Aso to don chaps and cowboy hats for a weekend-long jamboree.

It's easy to scoff at the image of Japanese men and women play-acting at being cowboys, riding horses in the Aso hills, tossing lassos and wearing Stetsons. But think of all those people in North America studying Japanese martial arts and donning karate outfits, bowing solemnly to their "sensei." Or think of our own Leonard Cohen, sitting cross-legged in his Japanese robes and shaved head, seeking Zen enlightenment atop Mount Baldy, California. It cuts both ways.

Indeed, Charlie Nagatani now has a cult following—in the U.S. of A. He recorded his first CD, *Good Time Charlie Sings Country Gold*, at a Nashville studio. It features a track with Emmylou Harris and backup by the Osborne Brothers, and with the help of songwriter Michael Woody, he turned his life into a country-and-western ballad titled "My Name Is Good Time Charlie":

> Kumamoto to Kentucky, Tokyo to Tennessee
> I dreamed one day I'd sing and play the Grand Ole Opry
> It's all I've ever wanted, all I've ever known
> My name is Good Time Charlie and I play that country gold

He played the Grand Ole Opry, too—not once, but six times—as well as TNN's *Nashville Now*.

"Backstage at the Opry, that first time?" he says. "Man, it felt like I was dreaming. It was not that far, you know, to the middle of the stage. But it seemed so far!" He laughs. "My heart was trembling and the microphone was too high. I pulled it down, played 'Walking the Floor Over You.'"

Charlie travels to the U.S. once or twice a year, and has friends and fans across North America.

"I've met a lot of good-hearted people through this music," he says. "There's something about it, something about country and western. It brings people together." He thinks for a moment and then, after a proper Texas pause, he says, "There's a lot of trouble between Japan and the West these days: political, economic, trade. I want to spread good feeling between the two instead. I want to bridge that gap."

And in that moment, it finally strikes me what it is about his getup that I find disconcerting. The large tinted glasses, the beard, the cowboy hat pulled way down low: it isn't so much a costume as a disguise. Everything about him—the clothes, the beard, the music, the persona—seems designed to mask his Japanese identity.

Charlie has been married to the same woman for almost forty years. His two sons have grown up and moved on. Neither son is a musician and neither has made a career in country and western. "Sure I'm disappointed," he says. "But it's a difficult life. Even now, country music isn't really understood by most Japanese people."

"So why not move on as well?" I ask. "Why not pull up stakes and settle in Nashville, say, or Austin, and open up a real country-and-western bar?"

"This *is* a real country-and-western bar," he says pointedly. And then, quietly: "Leave Japan? Leave this place?" He looks around the darkened interior of his bar as though for the first time, looks past the rowdy salarymen and beyond the rafters cluttered with cowboy paraphernalia, looks to where his guitar now sits idle on the stage.

"I love this music," he says. "And I love the lifestyle, but my heart? My heart is Japanese."

And softly in the background, as the crowds laugh and the beer flows, someone is playing hurtin' songs.

Renewing the Faith:
A Journey to Kinkazan Island

This is the first thing I ever had published, the first thing I ever wrote for publication in fact. It ran, along with some photographs I took, in the English-language edition of the Japanese national daily newspaper, *The Daily Yomiuri*, in July 1995.

Kinkazan Island is east of Sendai City and was directly in the path of the 2011 tsunami. The earthquake—and the tidal wave that followed—left more than 23,000 people dead or missing, and devastated entire communities along Japan's northern coast.

The scent of incense hangs in the air.

A young woman in a white robe and mask performs a slow-moving *kagura* dance to the rhythmic chants of the priests. The head priest steps forward to pass a wand of folded paper over the worshippers. We bow, foreheads almost touching the floor.

The ritual is repeated with a staff of small golden bells that jingle like coins in a cup. Kinkazan Island is dedicated to the gods of money circulation, and it's said that if you visit the island three years in a row your financial worries will be over. It's one of the three holiest places in northern Japan, and until just recently, women were not allowed here. (The deities enshrined are female and prone to jealousy.)

The island is east of Sendai, at the end of the Oshika Peninsula, and is an easy side trip from the famed pine-covered islands of Matsushima Bay. Kinkazan is a remarkably unspoiled place. Other than the ferry port, a few shops, and a *minshuku* inn, the only structure on the island is the impressive architectural complex of Koganeyama Shrine, set among the trees.

Free-ranging deer are everywhere on Kinkazan. Considered messengers of the gods, their main aim in life seems to be cadging handouts from visitors. In the mountains farther up colonies of wild monkeys roam free; unlike in other "wild" monkey parks in Japan, the monkeys of Kinkazan really are wild. They flee, screeching insults, when hikers approach.

The path to the summit begins behind Koganeyama Shrine, following a mountain stream for part of the way. I set off in the early afternoon and had the trail all to myself. Most of the visitors to Kinkazan are day trippers who have to catch the last ferry back, so few actually make the climb to the top. It's a one-hour hike from shrine to summit, without tour groups or crowds of schoolchildren to distract you. Only the wind in the forest, the cries of the monkeys, and—snakes.

No one said anything about snakes.

I was about to step over a long stick lying across the path when it suddenly came to life and slithered away. After that, the hike was less serene. Every stick and twig seemed poised to strike and I found myself longing for tour groups and schoolchildren.

At the top, a small shelter looks out onto a panorama of sea and shore. I'd become so accustomed to the usual tourist-intense zones that I'd assumed there'd be vending machines or even food stalls at the top. There were none, and I was panting with thirst after the climb. (The streams aren't safe to drink from because of possible monkey- or deer-borne parasites, to say nothing about snakes.)

That evening, as I soaked with fellow pilgrims in the shrine lodgings' magnificently located hot spring, I asked them about the snake I had almost trod upon.

"Did it have stripes?" they wanted to know. "Or did it have circles, like a five-yen coin?"

When I said I thought it was striped, and about a metre long, they said, "Don't worry. Only snakes with circles are dangerous, and Kinkazan doesn't have any of those." They laughed. "At least not that we know of. It was a good sign, crossing paths with a snake."

On Kinkazan, portents of good fortune abound. The island is imbued with gods and omens, with earthly desires given spiritual portent. After morning rites the shrine is silent and heavy with mist, and there is no doubting that the island is a holy place.

Westerners are understandably fascinated with Japanese Zen, but the spiritual depths of Shinto are often overlooked. Associated mainly with shrines and festivals, there is much more to it than that, and a night on Kinkazan offers Westerners a glimpse inside the living heart of the Shinto faith.

Lodgings

Koganeyama Shrine has its own lodgings, connected to the main shrine. A large *torii* gate marks the way and is impossible to miss. Note that this is a place of retreat and not an inn, so observe proper protocol. Bathe before supper, and make sure you understand where the morning rites will be held. Don't sleep in. Your name will be chanted during the morning blessings, so make sure you're there to receive them. Arrive at least ten minutes before services begin as well, because you'll probably need help putting on the pilgrim's vest. Sit up front, near the altar, so that the priest doesn't have to walk across the room to touch the bells to your shoulder and head. Watch the other pilgrims to know when and how to bow.

He Shoots, He Scores!
He Respects the Ref!

This was the second thing I ever had published. I sold it to an editor at *The Vancouver Sun* the same day I placed the article on Kinkazan Island with *The Daily Yomiuri*, and I thought to myself, "This writing gig is easy!" Oh, were it only so. My innocent past self, how I long to give you a hair tousle and headlock hug.

The references to an upcoming Olympics in Nagano date the piece a little, but I still find the story of the Dyck brothers abroad an engaging tale. It's also worth noting that in the 2010/2011 NHL season, the Edmonton Oilers added cheerleaders to their events. So the Japanese were ahead of the curve(s) on that one. They still haven't learned to swig beer and berate the ref, though.

Two players go into the boards. It's a good clean check. The glass rattles, and the sound echoes through the arena. The crowd is oddly silent. Then, as the two players separate, the inconceivable happens: they bow.

Welcome to the world of Japanese ice hockey.

The semi-pro JHL (Japan Hockey League) is about to celebrate its thirtieth anniversary, and with six full teams in competition, Japan has more hockey teams than Canada has baseball teams. In the last World

Hockey Championships, Japan came in fourth—second tier, but still. And in 1998, Japan will host the Winter Olympics.

After the Olympics, the JHL plans to go pro, and Japanese scouts are already scouring the Canadian junior ranks for potential foreign stars. They've sent hockey delegates to Vancouver, Calgary, Edmonton, and Quebec City, and have imported Canadian coaches and trainers as well, making hockey one of the few successful Canadian imports to Japan not involving lumber or fish.

On the surface, Japanese hockey seems bent on mimicry: players' names are written in English, and several teams have copied NHL uniforms right down to the colour schemes and stripe patterns. The Oji Corporation Hockey Team, for one, wears an exact replica of the familiar red, blue, and white of the Montreal Canadiens: all that's missing is the C in the centre. The Kokudo Bunnies—that's right, the Bunnies—are the reigning champions, and they wear uniforms based on the vintage gold and purple of the old Los Angeles Kings.

But beyond these surface similarities to North American hockey, the game is becoming something distinctly Japanese. Not only do the players refrain from fighting, they also refuse to go on strike. And as in Japanese baseball, the hockey teams are named not for their cities, but for their corporate sponsors. In Canada it would be like watching the Molson Canadiens take on the Burns Hot Dog and Luncheon Meat Oilers.

In Japan, where large corporations are accorded the highest respect, such blatant sponsorship doesn't strike the fans as distasteful, or even odd. The Nippon Paper Cranes, for example, are run by the Nippon Paper Company. The name has nothing to do with the Japanese art of paper folding.

For many years the JHL banned foreign players outright, but they have now opened the door to people of Japanese descent, so-called "heritage players." Among the first Canadians to take them up on this were a pair of brothers from the farmlands of Lethbridge, Alberta: Joel and Michael Dyck.

The brothers Dyck are both in their twenties and they both play defence for the Cranes. With a family name like Dyck, they would appear to violate the Japanese heritage-only rule, but as Joel explains, their mother is of Japanese descent: "Her maiden name is Oshiro."

Joel, the younger brother, played hockey with the Mount Royal Cougars before getting a phone call from hockey coach Dave King asking him if he was interested in playing overseas. It was Joel's first time in Japan, and he didn't speak the language. The Cranes also have two Russian coaches on staff, with their own Russian–Japanese interpreter.

Russian to Japanese to English, then back to Russian, and then to Japanese. Communication can be difficult. "But basically it's still hockey," says Joel. "If you can show it on a chalkboard, you can understand it."

Michael arrived in Japan a few months later, having played hockey with the Regina Pats for three years and then later with the Lethbridge Proghorns. He'd retired from the game to finish a degree in political science, was coaching amateur hockey, and had recently married when he heard from Joel that there was an opening with the Cranes.

"It was a rapid transition," he says. Within a week he'd left his old job, signed on with the Cranes, and was on his way to Japan.

"In Canada, things are left more to the individual player's initiative," says Michael. "In Japan, everybody trains together, all the time. It can get to you after a while."

Practices are longer and harder than they are in Canada, and the schedule can be gruelling. Players begin training twice a day, every day, months before the first game is played.

Joel and Michael commend the Japanese players on their conditioning and their skating skills, but the Japanese players are also more cautious than Canadians. Fewer risks are taken, fewer hits, less clutch-and-grab, do-or-die hockey.

Fighting, a fine Canadian tradition, is not tolerated in Japanese hockey. Fair enough. But in Japan, even clean checks are called if the referees consider them excessive or too "enthusiastic." For players like Michael Dyck, this can be a frustrating experience.

"Joel inherited the Japanese traits," jokes Michael. Joel is 5'9" and 180 pounds. "I'm 6'4", 214 pounds. When I came over, I was the biggest player in the league."

A hard-hitting defenceman, Michael spent a lot of time in the penalty box last season, often for plays that would never have been called back in Canada.

To make matters worse, players in Japan—bizarre as this may sound—are actually expected to show "respect" to the referees. In Canada, linesmen and refs are much-abused figures of authority, with everyone from the players to the fans to the coaches openly questioning their calls, as well as their sanity, character, intelligence, family lineage, and ophthalmologic deficiencies—often in the same one-breath run-on-jeer. *"You call that an offside, you stupid crazy half-blind son of a bitch!"* Almost an art form, really.

Not so in Japan. "You have to control your temper when you're over here," says Michael. "Even on a bad call, you say nothing and just go to the box. They won't hesitate to call a ten-minute misconduct."

Japanese players will often reflexively bow to referees—or even to players they've just checked. Just a small bob of the head, but very telling. In the higher ranks of the JHL the hockey is faster and more precise, but it's also a tighter and much lower-scoring game. The excitement level is definitely muted in Japan, which may be one of the reasons they added "cheergirls" to the roster.

Miniskirts and tank tops may not seem the most sensible choice of clothing in an air-conditioned hockey arena, but the cheergirls of the JHL, in the stands, complete with pompoms and set choreographed moves, are now an irreplaceable part of Japanese hockey. Like the players, the women involved are company employees. *"Go Oji Corporation Hockey Team! Go!"*

The crowds do need to be prodded at times, if only because the fans in Japan tend to be a bit subdued. There are few of the primal screams and cries of anguish that fill the Pacific Coliseum on a Saturday night. Gone too is that other proud Canadian tradition, the post-championship urban riot.

The Japanese, you see, are attempting the impossible. They are attempting to tame ice hockey. The beer-swilling, testosterone-driven anarchy that *is* Canada's game is being rewritten.

"I think one of the things Canadians can take pride in is their intensity," says Michael. "Canadians show up at game time ready to give 100 percent every time. Canadians rise to the game."

Or as a Japanese player noted, "Canadians play to win. We play not to lose."

And so, when all is said and done, do we as Canadians have anything to fear? Will the Japanese ever conquer that all-Canadian chaos we call ice hockey? Can they master a sport that has been likened to playing chess at two hundred miles an hour? Can they learn to yell at barroom TV sets and get involved in heated arguments over inane statistics with people at the next table?

Will Japan ever beat Canada at its own game?

"I think the Japanese may surprise a lot of people," says Michael. "Give it ten years and I think you're going to see some very competitive hockey being played here."

Asked how he'd feel if he were to compete against Canada in the Winter Olympics, Joel says, "I'm not eligible. I'd have to get my Japanese citizenship first. But if I did have the opportunity to play for Japan in the Olympics, I would."

Would he have mixed emotions, seeing the Canadians line up across from him in opposition? "I have ties to both," he says. "But I'd do my best, whether it was for Canada or for Japan. I always play to win."

East Meets West

The articles on Kinkazan Island and the Dyck brothers may have been the first things I ever had published, but my first regular writing gig was with the Charlottetown daily newspaper, *The Guardian* (actual masthead motto: "Covers the Island like the Dew"). I was working for a tour company, and I pitched an idea for a column on Japanese culture and customs aimed at a PEI audience to Gary MacDougall, the paper's managing editor. Titled "East Meets West," the column ran from 1996 to 1998, first in weekly instalments, then later monthly. Here are just a few samples, starting with the debut.

Yes, We Have No Bananas

There's a tale often told, apocryphal perhaps, of an American businessman giving a presentation to a Japanese client. At one point the American remarks, "This is a whole new ball game," and the Japanese client, offended by the reference to its being a "game," decides they aren't taking the venture seriously, and he kills the deal. An important business opportunity was lost simply because of a cultural misunderstanding.

Mistakes cost money. They waste time and energy, they lead to mistrust and frustration on both sides.

Cultural differences, social customs, even basic grammar can result in unintentional but serious problems. An example is the Japanese use of "yes" *(hai)* and "no" *(iie)*. The English language has a fetish about mixing negatives and positives in the same statement, but not the Japanese. In Japanese, *hai* does not exactly mean "yes"; rather, it means "that is correct." Just as *iie* suggests "that is not correct."

It is quite acceptable in Japanese to answer the question "You didn't go to Summerside?" with "Yes. I didn't go." For speakers of Japanese, the sentence "Yes, we have no bananas" is a perfectly reasonable response.

This would seem to be a minor linguistic difference, but it can have unfortunate consequences. A tour operator in Charlottetown almost stranded a Japanese tourist recently after asking him, "So you don't need a ride to the airport?" The man answered "No," meaning "No, I do need a ride."

Tourism in Prince Edward Island is now the province's second largest industry, just behind agriculture. We can't go stranding tourists over a small quirk of grammar.

In PEI, the two solitudes aren't French and English but rather Islander and Japanese. And thus (prepare yourself for the mandatory Confederation Bridge metaphor), in much the same way that Strait Crossing bridges the Northumberland Strait, "East Meets West" hopes to bridge a cultural gap. This column will cover everything from manners to social taboos, hand gestures to holidays. We'll even learn some Japanese along the way: common greetings, questions, tips on pronunciation.

About my background. I'm based in Charlottetown and work in PEI's tourism industry. Before that, I lived in Japan, where I taught English to Japanese students (or rather, English was taught in their presence. It remains one of the dread courses in the Japanese curriculum. You know things are bad when students perk up for algebra).

The Japanese teachers I worked with were forever rushing up to me and asking questions like, "Mr. William! In the sentence *When*

EAST MEETS WEST 347

five minutes have passed, she will have been playing the cello for one hour longer than I would have been, had I not stopped, is 'playing' a past present subjunctive gerund or a qualifying reflexive vowel movement?"

To which, I would straighten my shoulders, look them in the eye, and say, "I'm a little busy right now. I'll get back to you on that." Then I'd sneak out the side door when they weren't looking.

Point being: I've always felt cultural context was more important than grammar and syntax. The gaffes and errors reported in "East Meets West" come from firsthand experience. Learn from my mistakes; you'll be glad you did.

"Is it true?" I hear you ask. "We won't have to worry about cross-cultural confusion anymore?"

To which I reply, with the utmost sincerity, "Yes, you won't."

Emily and Anne Battle It Out

A delegation from Prince Edward Island left for Japan last Thursday for the Kanata Conference, intent on better promoting the Island to Japanese visitors. My invitation was apparently lost in the mail, but no matter. With all the various schemes and ideas being bandied about, I thought I would offer my own insightful, profound, and vastly under-appreciated views on the matter.

What is the secret to expanding the Japanese market? The answer is Emily.

I don't mean that in the theological sense. I mean it in a we-have-taken-Anne-just-about-as-far-as-we-can sense. When ol' Carrot Top starts showing up on licence plates and bags o' potato chips, you know the market is pretty well saturated.

Emily of New Moon is Lucy Maud Montgomery's *other* young, sensitive orphan girl. She's very different from Anne. For one, she's quiet. Also, she has black hair, not red. That last point may seem minor, but in the world of L.M. Montgomery, even something as inconsequential as hair colour becomes an important character trait.

Like Lucy Maud, the Japanese are acutely aware of personality types and social niches. In Canada we focus on ethnic niches, but in a country as homogeneous as Japan the question is not "What's your ethnic background?" but "What *type* are you?" This applies especially to Japanese women, who are such a key demographic in the PEI tourism market.

When I first went to Japan, the questions women were asking themselves were: Are you "body-conscious" *(bodi-kon)*? Or are you a spoiled post–economic miracle Daddy's girl *(ojo-sama)*? Or a tough-minded, hard-living woman *(oyaji-gyaru)*? Are you cartoon-cute *(kawaii)*? Full of life *(genki)*? Or international and sophisticated *(kokusai-jin)*? The specific categories will have changed, but the "what type of personality are you" fascination remains.

By comparing and contrasting Emily to Anne, Tourism PEI could pose the question directly to Japanese women: What type are you? Are you an Emily or an Anne? Are you quiet and sensitive or outgoing and talkative? (In much the same way that women of my generation used to ask each other, "Are you a Betty or a Veronica?")

This might increase repeat visits as well, with Japanese visitors coming first for an Anne Tour and then later for an Emily. We could even turn the Emily vs. Anne dichotomy into a rivalry of sorts, with Anne the reigning undisputed heavyweight champion and Emily the up-and-coming underdog. Opposing musicals, Anne vs. Emily fan clubs, duelling potato chip sponsors, contrived tabloid scandals, Indian leg wrestling, knife fights, petitions to give Emily her own licence plate: the list is long, as Emily and Anne duke it out to decide once and for all the coveted title of Cutest Fictional Character in PEI.

Will young Emily ever surpass Anne in the hearts of the Japanese?

Anne is plucky and cute, the Island is beautiful, and a love of childlike innocence—along with an affinity for nature—is central to Japanese sensibilities. Emily, meanwhile, appeals to that quieter, more stoic, almost melancholic aspect of the Japanese character.

Is the average Japanese woman an Emily or an Anne?

A friend of mine from Fukuoka put it best: "We wish we were Anne of Green Gables, but deep down inside we know we're more like Emily of New Moon."

It is this tension between the reality and the dream that draws Japanese visitors to the Island, year after year, and it's a point that people in the travel business should keep in mind. You have to appeal to both the Emilys and the Annes.

Next up? Cherry blossom viewing vs. lupins. Sushi vs lobster rolls. Sashimi vs. Malpeque oysters. Karaoke vs. ceilidhs. And so on ...

"I Am a Carrot!"

I woke suddenly, yanked from an already fitful slumber by a vicious muscle cramp in the bottom of my right foot. As I leapt out of bed in agony, my long-suffering wife, still groggy from sleep, called out, "Pull your thumb! Pull your thumb!"

Assuming this was some sort of ancient Japanese secret *shiatsu* technique, I began frantically pulling on my thumb even as I continued to hop about on one foot.

"Not your thumb!" she said. "Your other thumb! Your foot thumb."

I stopped. "Would you mean my toe, by any chance?"

My wife is fluent in English, but every now and then she still stumbles.

I know how she feels. Learning a second language is tricky. Once, as a speaker at a teachers' conference in Tokyo, I confused the Japanese word *nin-gen* (human) with the word *nin-jin* (carrot). An easy enough mistake to make, but it still caused a lot of puzzled looks among my Japanese audience when, reading from my notes in phonetic Japanese, I declared, "I am a carrot! You are a carrot! We are all carrots! We must work together in the spirit of our common carrotness to build a brighter tomorrow!"

Not my proudest moment, and something my so-called friends never tire of bringing up. *"Ich bin ein carrot!"* they'll say by way of greeting or, in more sympathetic moments, "Hey, don't worry about it. None of us are perfect. We're all just carrots." (And if nothing else, I now have the utmost sympathy for Anne when she yells at Gilbert, "Don't call me Carrots!")

Not that my linguistic misadventures were limited to Japan. As a youth volunteer in rural Quebec, I once blithely described my francophone boss as *"le gros fromage."* Unfortunately, this is an idiom that doesn't translate very well into French. The man thought I was making some sort of veiled reference to his body odour and he didn't speak to me for several days.

It cuts both ways of course. Travellers to Japan often find it difficult sitting on tatami-mat floors for extended periods. Even with the cushions, it can become painful. You end up with anaesthetized legs, limbs so numb you stagger drunkenly when you try to get up. This is especially true with the formal *seiza* position: knees bent together, bum resting on heels. The Japanese are aware that Westerners are not always at ease sitting on the floor, and they prefer to see you sprawled out and comfortable. Kay Harding, an Englishwoman who studied classical Noh theatre in Yatsushiro City, was taken aback while visiting a Japanese home when the father of the family, noticing that she was kneeling in the *seiza* position, leaned over and whispered to her, "Please ... spread your legs. I understand this is something you English women like to do."

How do you respond to something like that?

My wife, meanwhile, has mastered most English idioms, but still makes the occasional slip-up. Once, while talking about a colleague of ours, she confided, "To be honest, I don't really like his guts." I tried to explain to her that in English the only thing you can do with someone's guts is hate them. You can't dislike them, feel ambivalent toward them, or have mixed feelings about them. You can only hate them. Which is why I arched an eyebrow later when my wife sidled up beside me and cooed, "Honey, I love your guts."

Who knows, maybe she does love my guts. After all, around our place, I'm *le gros fromage.* At least, in the French sense of the word.

Shortcuts and Magic Words

So today I'm going to teach you twenty thousand words in Japanese.

We'll start with three. These are the "magic" words: *domo, dozo, sumimasen.* With these three you can express gratitude, friendliness, regret, and apology; you can even invite customers in. I've had entire conversations consisting of little else. Their meanings are as follows: *domo:* "thanks" (can also be used as a friendly form of "goodbye"); *dozo:* "please," as in "go ahead" or "help yourself" (if you're offering samples to a Japanese tourist, or holding the door for them, you can simply say "dozo"); and *sumimasen:* "I'm sorry" or "excuse me."

Japanese is classified as a "syllabic language," with consonants generally separated by vowels and vowels pronounced without running them together as we do in English. (Spoken Japanese sounds very similar to Spanish in this way, though flatter in intonation.) You can see it in the way foreign place names are shoehorned into Japanese pronunciation. The "Prince" in "Prince Edward Island" becomes *pu-rin-su.* And though "Canada" poses no problem, because it neatly divides into three Japanese-sounding syllables *(ka-na-da),* Australia becomes *oo-su-to-ra-ri-a.*

Even the most familiar words can become unrecognizable. I was about to board a Japan Airlines flight once when I noticed the word UIRIAMU printed in large letters across my boarding pass. When I couldn't find this word in my Japanese–English dictionary, I began to fret. What if it meant something like "SEND VIA ALASKA"? I hurried to the flight desk and asked them what the Japanese word *uiriamu* meant in English. The lady looked at me in a strange way and said, "Don't you recognize your own name, Mr. William?"

To make matters worse, the Japanese have borrowed all kinds of "loan words" from English. Normally, this would be helpful for non-native speakers. But in Japan, English words are often given an unexpected twist. Consider the word "snack." First-time visitors to Japan—and I was one of them—often make the mistake of assuming that a place advertising "snacks" will be selling, well, snacks. But in Japan the word doesn't mean "light repast," but rather "overpriced hostess bar where salarymen go to have their egos fondled and their wallets lightened." Many an English speaker has wandered into a bar with the word SNACK in the name only to stumble out, hours later, dazed and confused, poorer but wiser.

Other English words have been altered just enough to confuse you. For example, in Japan the word *koppu* refers not to a cup, but to a glass. And a *feminist* isn't someone who believes in equality of opportunity between the sexes. In Japan a "feminist" is simply any man who is kind to women. The most antiquated, old-fashioned male can be considered a "feminist" in Japan if he thinks to open doors for ladies or give them a seat on a crowded bus. A feminist in Japan is what we would call a gentleman in the West.

When I first arrived in Tokyo, I remember my excitement when I found out I'd be staying with a friend at "Fujiview Mansion." I'd expected nights of luxury, only to discover that in Japan *mansion* doesn't mean "opulent abode," but rather "tiny apartment." Something always gets lost in translation. (Also, Mount Fuji was about as viewable as "ocean front access" is in Florida.)

During my stay in Japan, I became frustrated at the long, roundabout journey I had to take to get to work. I asked a Japanese colleague of mine—an English teacher, no less—to show me a shortcut. "You want a shortcut?" he said, looking puzzled. "Yes, yes, a shortcut!" So he bustled me into his car and drove me to a barbershop where they gave me a dorky crewcut that took weeks to grow out. In Japan, it turns out, *shortcut* refers to a close-cropped hairstyle.

More than nine hundred Japanese words have entered the English language. Words like *tofu, karate, kimono, sushi, banzai, kamikaze,* and—of course—the social plague that is *karaoke.* (Karaoke, I've always maintained, is not so much performed as perpetrated.)

Japan's contributions to English pale compared with the number of words the Japanese have taken from us, though. Estimates range as high as twenty thousand terms. Everything from *terebi* (television) to *uisukii* (whisky) and *tabako* (cigarettes), and so on. Which is to say, if you can master the altered pronunciation, adding vowels between consonants and keeping the vowels from slurring together, you can instantly learn thousands of "Japanese" words.

So next time someone asks if you're bilingual, you tell 'em "Well, I did read Will's column the other day, so I now know about twenty thousand words in Japanese."

That's it for this week. I'll see you later at the snack. I'm taking a shortcut, so I may be late.

How to Lose Your Job in Japan

Japan is a land of lifetime employment. It takes a lot of work to get fired in Japan, but I came close. And I did it in record time, first day in fact.

It began when I arrived for what I thought was my first day of work at the local high school, only to find the staff room and hallways deserted. I wandered about looking for other teachers, but the only other person I met was the school clerk in the front office.

"No one's around," I said. "I must have the wrong school. Or maybe the wrong day."

"Okay," she said.

"Is it all right if I go home?"

"Okay," she said.

So I left. (Later I discovered that "okay" was the only English she spoke.)

Having assumed I'd properly informed the office that I was leaving, I headed out, only to hear someone shouting my name as I crossed the schoolyard. It was the principal. He was waving at me. So I waved back.

"See you tomorrow," I said.

As I passed the auditorium, I saw an entire line of teachers waving goodbye to me. That was one mystery solved; the teachers were hiding in the auditorium. But why all the waving?

"It's a bit much," I thought. After all, I was just going back to my apartment; it wasn't like I was leaving for good or anything. Still, it was nice of them, so I waved back.

When I got home the phone was ringing.

It was my supervisor. "William, are you all right?"

"Sure," I said.

There was a long pause. "We are waiting for you."

Waiting for me?

"In the auditorium. Your welcome presentation. Everyone is looking forward to meeting our new Canadian teacher. They are still waiting."

Which is how I found out that in Japan, a wide overhand wave means "come here" and not "goodbye."

Gestures matter.

The Western hand signal for okay is understood and even used in Japan, with the extended fingers held high. But if the fingers are more cupped, and the circle not as tight, it doesn't mean okay, it means "money" or "expensive." Confusing "okay" with "expensive" could cost you a lot of yen.

"Let's go for a drink" is signified by tipping a thimble-sized drink toward your mouth, mimicking the tiny cups used for saké. In the West we make a giant, mug-sized gesture. And in Japan, holding up your big thumb means either "boss" or "husband." (No comment.) A little finger, usually wiggled suggestively, means "girlfriend." Holding two fingers to your temples, like a bull about to charge, signifies either anger or jealousy. And so on. (Folklore has it that the high arc of silk that Japanese brides wear on their heads is meant to cover their "horns of jealousy." Grooms, apparently, are immune to such feelings, as they wear nothing on their heads except pomade.)

Our middle-finger gesture, considered so taboo that it's often pixilated on TV in North America, is only vaguely understood in Japan. They seem to think it's simply a youthful, carefree, cool thing to do. Which may explain why the entire graduating class of Kawaura Senior High School in Amakusa—including their homeroom teacher!—is featured in their yearbook photo smiling up at the camera and cheerfully giving us the finger. Needless to say, this is among my most cherished mementoes from my time in Japan. I have that yearbook on my shelf even now. I show it to people when they ask, "So what was Japan like?"

Elections Are a Noisy Affair—but Tidy

With election fever now upon us, it may be helpful to consider the Japanese approach to winning votes and influencing the masses. It differs radically from our own.

If you're unfortunate enough to visit Japan during an election, you will find yourself surrounded by bedlam. Japan must have the noisiest election campaigns in the developed world. Loudspeaker vans drive up and down every street, all day, blaring out amplified electoral messages. The din is so loud, so frenetic, you'd think something important was going on, a protest perhaps or a vigorous debate on the issues of the day. No such luck. All that the candidates are doing is repeating their names again and again and again and again and again: "My name is Taro Suzuki, please remember me at election day. My name is Taro Suzuki, please remember my name. My name is Taro Suzuki …" and so on, endlessly.

I have never understood the thinking behind this strategy. Annoying potential voters doesn't seem like the wisest approach a politician could take. The strange thing is that they *know* how annoying they are. The loudspeaker trucks begin at the bleary-eyed crack of dawn, and the message usually starts with an apology: "I'm sorry to bother you so early in the morning, but my name is Taro Suzuki, please remember me." *Oh, I'll remember you, buddy …*

For a while I thought maybe it was their opponents who were doing this. That is, Taro's rival in the election was driving around bugging people and ruining Taro's good name. But no, you'll see the candidate inside the van, waving as though he were the Pope Himself and not, say, some minor pork-barrelling politician. So why do they do this?

I discovered the answer when a friend of mine named Tatsuhiro Hiramatsu, a local *mikan* farmer, ran for city council. Tatsuhiro invited me along on the opening day of the campaign, and it was then that I learned the truth: the candidates drive around all day waving at people and broadcasting their names because *it's fun*. It's like leading your own personal parade. The candidates often don't even use the loudspeaker themselves but hire pretty ladies called "nightingales" instead, who do the announcing for them in high-pitched, squeaky voices. (For some reason, high-pitched, squeaky voices are considered the acme of ladylike allure in Japan.)

When two of these noisy vehicles pass each other, the effect is an uproar that would lead to an exchange of gunfire in the United States, but is tolerated with hostile indifference by the general public in Japan. What's worse, in rural areas, when the politicians and their supporters see an exotic, butter-smelling foreigner (i.e., *you*) they go into a frenzy of waving and grinning, apparently unaware that foreigners are not technically allowed to vote in Japanese elections.

The good news? In Japan, candidates can't go running around slapping up posters and lawn signs wherever they please. They must use designated poster boards at designated sites, with spaces allotted equally to every candidate. Highly civilized, I think, plus it saves on litter and cuts back on the eyesore clutter we get over here. In Canada, our elections may be quiet, but they're messy. (If we could combine the best of both systems—the Japanese rules about no wasteful postering and the Western rules restricting noise pollution—we might finally come up with the perfect system of electioneering, one that's both quiet *and* clean.)

Noise is used as a weapon in Japan in other situations as well. Whenever there's a scandal involving political corruption, the black buses of the ultra-right movement will swoop in. What follows is a divinely Japanese form of harassment. The loudspeaker buses will surround the home of the politician involved and will loudly, endlessly, praise him. In modesty-conscious Japan, this is a terrible thing to do. *"What an honourable person is Taro Suzuki, so pure, so wonderful, a prince of a politician! Surely he would never accept bribes to secure public-works contracts!"* It's a very effective tactic. Were they to insult the man publicly, it might generate sympathy—and certainly legal action; the Japanese have libel laws just like anyone else—but by heaping praise on him instead they turn it into a form of public ridicule.

Maybe we could adopt this in Canada as well. *"Mr. Chrétien is an honourable man! He kept his promise to kill the GST. He is an honest person, a prince of a politician!"* And so on, endlessly.

New Year's

In the West, we have the Seven Deadly Sins, which are, if I remember correctly, Greed, Avarice, Insincerity, Parking Illegally in a Handicap Zone, Slowing Down to Merge, Saying "Disinterested" When You Clearly Mean "Uninterested," and Running for Public Office.

The Japanese, however, are far more creative when it comes to sinning. Not content with a mere seven sins, they've come up with no fewer than 108. (Even with my own imaginative approach to vice, I find it hard to think of 108 truly unsavoury acts.) Not only that, but the Japanese manage to commit all 108 sins in a single year, which is why Buddhist temples across Japan start the New Year with a gonglike ringing of the temple bell 108 times. This is said to cleanse the soul, wipe the slate, reset the odometer, etc.—giving everyone a fresh start at moral transgressions after January 1. You wonder if Catholic priests in Japan ever get weary of this. *"Forgive me Father, for I have sinned. How? You may want to get comfortable, we're going to be here awhile ..."*

One year, I decided to count the tolling of my neighbourhood bells, just to see if they missed any, when lo and behold, the bells rang right up to two hundred times and beyond. I was dumbfounded. Had they invented even more sins? A breakthrough in depravity! But no, as I found out, anyone making a small donation was allowed to ring the bell at New Year's, and with all the laughing and shouting going on, no one seemed overly concerned with the actual number of sins tabulated, venial or otherwise.

New Year's is a joyous celebration in Japan, and most of it centres on the local Buddhist temple or Shinto shrine, where throngs of people crowd in after midnight. They buy lucky arrows, an allusion to the unwavering course an arrow takes (the same image found in the English idiom "a straight arrow"). Last year's arrows are then burned in a bonfire lit by the priests, which is a darn clever way of ensuring that everyone buys a new arrow every year. Sort of a spiritual version of planned obsolescence.

The first dream of the new year is also an auspicious event, with the three luckiest images being Mount Fuji, an eagle, and an eggplant. Why an eggplant, I couldn't tell you. The food of choice during the holidays, meanwhile, is an innocuous but loathsome substance called *mochi*. Mochi is—and this has been scientifically proven—evil. Pure, unadulterated evil.

Undoubtedly the product of at least one of the 108 deadly sins, mochi is made by taking perfectly good cooked rice and then pounding the daylights out of it until it turns into a glutinous, phlegm-like mass of dough. This is then rolled into gag-sized balls and forced upon unsuspecting guests. Eating mochi is a lot like eating partially congealed rubber.

As a teacher in Japan, I was expected to make the rounds of my students' homes at New Year's, where green tea and mochi balls were inevitably offered. Refusing it would have been rude, so I ended up choking down wads of the stuff over the years. I suspect I still have a large mass of undigested mochi in my stomach even now—and all in the name of international goodwill. Don't thank me. I was only doing my duty.

When Japanese students asked if we had mochi in Canada, I said "No. With only seven sins to work with, we don't have any time to spare for the serving of mochi." When they asked what traditional foods Canadians did eat at New Year's, I replied, with a certain pride, "Leftover turkey and soggy stuffing."

Anything else would be a sin.

Valentine's Day

Saturday is Valentine's Day, and we know what that means. Chocolate-covered everything! Chocolate-covered kisses, chocolate-covered hearts, chocolate-covered livers, kidneys—the works! I once lived a short drive from the Ganong factory in St. Stephen, New Brunswick, where the first heart-shaped Valentine's Day boxes were sold, making

St. Stephen the Official Last-Minute Unoriginal Romantic Gift Idea Capital of the World. *"Here you go honey, a box ... shaped like a heart! Didn't see that coming, did ya!"*

Which brings us to today's topic: the interplay of love and duty, and of chocolate and gender roles.

In Japan, Valentine's Day is a completely one-sided affair: women do all the giving. They're expected to present chocolates not only to their husbands and lovers (often, but not always, the same man), but also to their colleagues, co-workers, supervisors, and any other male they come in contact with on a regular basis.

The term for this is *giri choco,* literally "duty chocolates." It's become such an acknowledged ritual that companies in Japan have even begun marketing chocolates under this name, calling a spade a spade. But it does seem to diminish the spirit of gift-giving. "Here's your damn *giri choco.* Happy friggin' Valentine's."

The unfairness of this system has been noted, and men are now expected to reciprocate with return gifts on March 14, a holiday the Japanese seem to have invented out of whole cloth to complement Valentine's. They call it White Day, because men are supposed to give the women in their life something white, usually white chocolate, but it could be anything from silk scarves to panties. White Day has been a bit of a bust, though, largely because it happens *after* Valentine's, when the men have already scored their annual haul of chocolates and see little need to bribe the women in their life. Meaning, women still give more than they receive. (I know, I know, marriage in a nutshell.)

When my wife asked me why White Day wasn't marked on calendars in Canada, I had to explain we don't have White Day.

"But when do women receive gifts from men?" she asked.

"They don't," I replied.

"They don't?"

"Nope."

"Well, what about Valentine's Day?"

"Oh, that," I said. "We celebrate it pretty much the same way you do in Japan. Women give men chocolates."

"Really?"

"Absolutely. Why would I lie to you about something like that?"

Alas, somebody spilled the beans and my wife found out the truth. So now I have to go out in the cold and rain and spend my hard-earned money buying her something romantic. I can't get to St. Stephen for a heart-shaped box, so I'm hoping I can convince her that in Canada two tickets to the AHL hockey finals in Saint John are considered a romantic gift. Scoff if you like, but I almost had her convinced at one point that in Canada it was bad luck for a husband to pick wet towels off the floor. Wish me luck!

Ghost Stories Keep You Cool at Night

August is a scary month around our place. The Japanese mid-summer Festival of the Dead, Obon, takes place around this time. In Japan, families visit their ancestral graves to welcome the spirits back for a visit. Family altars are lit, priests chant Buddhist sutras, and in the evening slow-moving circle dances are held.

At the end of their spectral soirée, the ancestral spirits are sent off with fireworks and small lantern boats set adrift in the sea. These boats are designed to sink, and as the lanterns disappear one by one into the water the effect is ineffably sad.

Obon resonates on several levels. It's a time for family get-togethers and hometown nostalgia, a religious observance that is both neighbourhood festival and an acceptance of the impermanence of things. It's also a terrific time for ghost stories.

In the hot humid days of August, ghostly tales are valued for the chilling effect they create in their listeners. The creatures involved include a frog-like water spirit, a cyclops-like beast that hops around on one foot, a woman who turns into a snake, a snake who turns into a woman, and a haunted umbrella. Really. I have a theory about the umbrella. From my own experience I know that in Japan, when umbrellas are left unopened, leaning beside the front door during rainy season, they provide an ideal venue for spiders to take refuge in. And we're talking Japanese spiders, which are of the Mothra vs.

Godzilla variety. More than once, as I hurried outside, I flung open an umbrella above my head only to have a piñata of arachnids tumble down. I believe my girlish shrieks are still echoing somewhere over the mountains of central Kyushu.

Near my wife's hometown is Mount Nakaoyama, site of an ancient battle between samurai armies; the hillsides were drenched with blood and the souls of the dead are said to have seeped into the very soil. The battle itself was hard-fought but indecisive, and the ghosts of the samurai continue to battle for supremacy down through eternity. A large rock, visible from my wife's home, is said to contain the footprints of a stallion leading up and into the sky. Just a story of course, but locals avoid the mountain after dark anyway and few have ever ventured to Horse Print Rock.

During Obon, television networks in Japan feature ghost stories, and when I was living with a family we watched an Obon tale about a taxi driver who picks up a pale young woman by the side of a bridge. Her dress is tattered and soaking wet, and after she tells the taxi driver the address, she lapses into silence in the back seat.

As the driver eyed her warily in the rear-view mirror, I realized I'd heard this tale before.

"We used to tell this story at camp!" I said excitedly. "Turns out the address is a graveyard, and when the driver turns around she's gone. She drowned in the river years before and her body was never found."

I'd ruined the ending for them, admittedly, but I was so caught up in the moment and so fascinated by the universal nature of ghost stories that I hadn't been able to stop myself. Sure enough, the story played out just as I'd described. Amid eerie Japanese music—and Japanese music can be really eerie—the taxi pulls up to … a cemetery.

The driver is confused. *"The address. There—there must be some mistake."*

"No," says the girl in the back seat. *"There is no mistake."*

But here the story changes, in a way so subtle I almost missed it. In the Canadian version, the girl simply vanishes. But in the

Japanese version she pays for the ride and collects her change, and *then* vanishes.

The significance of this should be noted: in Japan, even ghosts behave properly. Even the undead do not go around stiffing taxi drivers.

This social cohesion—a result of samurai ethics, Shinto origin myths, Confucian morality, and ethnic homogeneity—is what makes Japan one of the safest societies on earth. It also makes it a nation of courteous ghosts and polite ghouls. Not the most terrifying creatures on earth. (Umbrella-dwelling spiders aside, of course.)

The next time I need some mid-August chills, I think I'll invest in an air conditioner.

For the Love
of Sumo

Personally, I think it's the hair.

They oil it back in a long ponytail and then flip it forward, creating a slick, fan-shaped rooster crown. When the Tokugawa Shogunate modernized Japan in the late nineteenth century, only sumo's *rikishi* were allowed to keep their samurai topknot. Today, these distinct hairstyles give them a certain medieval allure.

The hair is also a source of their strength. When a rikishi ("wrestler" doesn't quite describe what they do) retires from the ring, his topknot is ceremonially cut away with a pair of golden scissors.

It's gotta be the hair.

Why else would ladies swoon and young girls scream? Why else would top models and high-flying stewardesses pursue them, marry them? Why else would people get so excited about flabby, half-naked men dressed in elaborate wedgies?

When I moved to Japan, I spent the first few months in a daze of culture shock and constant bewilderment. Plastic food in restaurant windows. Corn on pizza. Slippers in the toilet room. But strangest of all was the bizarre spectacle that invaded my living room every two months like clockwork: Japan's never-ending sumo tournaments.

At first, it seemed more slapstick than sport.

Two men enter a ring; the first one to hit the ground or leave the ring loses. Simple, right? But pulling back one layer of meaning only revealed another. It was like trying to understand Japan as a whole, it was like trying to peel an onion.

Sumo bouts rarely last thirty seconds, but the buildup is almost unbearable. Procrastination rather than preparation, it seemed to me. The rikishi stretch their shoulders, rinse their mouths with water, toss salt into the air (as part of a purification ritual), stomp their feet, glare at their opponent, then go back and wipe their armpits with hand towels. Everything except actually fight.

"Get on with it!" I would shout at my television.

Sumo bouts are like springs, *slooooowly* compressed. The tension mounts and mounts, and then—finally!—in a sudden clash, the victor is decided.

There was a definite rhythm and pace to it, but damned if I could figure it out. Not that my Japanese friends were any help.

"How do they know when it's time to charge?" I would ask.

"You mean the *tachiai*? When the time is right, they will know."

"How?"

"Oh, they will know."

"How will they know?"

"They will know."

"But—but—"

The tide began to shift when I saw Kyokudozan in action. Sumo has no weight divisions whatsoever. The smallest rikishis are routinely pitted against the largest, and no one finds this unfair or lopsided. And, sumo stereotypes to the contrary, Kyokudozan was not obese. If anything, he was a little on the scrawny side, weighing in at 223 pounds. The first time I watched him fight, he was up against a 420-pound giant named Onokuni. "This is going to be good!" I thought, and I settled back to watch the massacre.

What happened next sent shivers down my spine. To use the proper Canadian hockey terms, lithe little Kyokudozan deked Onokuni out of his shorts—figuratively speaking, thank God.

He faked right, stepped left, then jumped backwards like a cat, letting the larger man's momentum work against him. This wasn't burlesque. This was poetry in motion.

These guys weren't simply grappling at each other like overly amorous hippos, I realized; they were using bona fide techniques: feint, leverage, bursts of speed, misdirection and, when need be, sheer strength.

I began to recognize certain fighters: Kirishima, an older, muscular rikishi who used the difficult "lift and carry out" approach. Mitoizumi, a big goofy-looking kid known as the Salt Shaker because he threw massive handfuls of salt into the ring before every fight (to the appreciative roar of the crowd). Terao, "the Typhoon," whose blistering arm-thrust attacks terrified his opponents. Mainoumi, the smallest rikishi fighting, who'd secretly injected a pad of silicon under his scalp in order to meet the minimum height requirements. (No weight restrictions, only height.)

In a land where team play and group consensus are crucial, sumo was unabashedly individualistic. Fighters stood and fell on their own merits, and each had his own style, his own strengths, his own weaknesses.

By my fifth tournament, I'd become the sumo equivalent of a Deadhead. I pored over the standings, clipped magazine articles, collected sumo handprints, sumo playing cards, sumo T-shirts, and limited-edition commemorative sumo mugs.

I loved sumo the way some people loved their country. It is— and I think I'm being objective in my assessment—the absolutely greatest sport in the history of the universe. What's not to love? It has everything you could possibly want in public entertainment: conflict, tension, pomp and pageantry, and big sweaty half-naked men.

I was a particularly big fan of a fighter named Chiyonofuji, better known as "the Wolf." Chiyonofuji was the son of a Hokkaido fisherman. He was short, stocky, and solid muscle. While other fighters used sheer mass to win, Chiyonofuji employed physics. Using his smaller size to his advantage, he would act as a human fulcrum, powering his opponents out of the ring. If Chiyonofuji got hold of an opponent's belt, inside and on the right, the fight was pretty well over. He would lean in, legs low, shoulders rigid, and—suddenly— these giant men would flip upside down, ass-over-teakettle, leaving Chiyonofuji still standing, alone and unchallenged, at centre ring. It was a religious experience to see the Wolf in action.

Alas, just when I'd decided to quit my job and devote my life to Chiyonofuji, he retired. He was only one win shy of the all-time victory record, in a sport with a 1200-year-old history. My eyes teared up when I watched his topknot-cutting ceremony on television.

Like any devoted/rabid/irrational fan, I wanted to become the object of my affection. Who wouldn't want to be a rikishi? They're massive, strong, arrogant men. They drink heavy, play hard, and giggle like kids. A scent of perfumed oil and sweat surrounds them like an aura of, well, perfumed oil and sweat. Women throw themselves at rikishi, and rikishi get to eat as much as they want. I want to be reborn as a rikishi so badly.

For some reason, a disproportionate number of them come from the geographic extremes of Japan—Hokkaido in the far north and Kagoshima in the south—and even their styles of fighting have been described as "hot" or "cold," with the smaller southern rikishi known for their rapid-fire arm attacks and the heavier northern rikishi tending more toward slow, walrus-like holds. The Wolf was from the north, but his style was always described as "southern" in its intensity.

The Wolf is long gone, however, and the two reigning superstars of sumo, known affectionately as Tak and Wak, are a pair of brothers spoon-fed for stardom. Their father was once a grand champion and their uncle was president of the Sumo Association. Or maybe it was the other way around. It doesn't matter, I hate them both, especially pouty-faced Tak, who became a media darling. After the last tournament Wak got promoted to *yokozuna* (grand champion) alongside his brother Tak, making them the first pair of brothers ever to attain sumo's highest rank.

Tak and Wak's arch nemesis was an American, the Hawaiian rikishi Akebono. Akebono stands 6'8" and tips the scales at five hundred pounds, but is built awkwardly. With his high round stomach and skinny stork legs he looks like a grapefruit on a pair of chopsticks. And yet, oddly constructed though he is, Akebono managed to climb to the top of the sumo world. Of course, his name isn't really Akebono; every rikishi adopts a florid *nom de plume* while active in sumo. You'll see great bloated whales of humanity waddling about with names that translate as Small Brocade or Morning Sunrise. Akebono's real name was Chad Rowan, and he became the first foreign-born yokozuna in the history of sumo, something that sparked racially tinged tensions and nasty editorials by commentators who didn't want to see their sport tainted with foreign blood.

I asked my Japanese work supervisor—a fellow sumo aficionado—what he thought about the Great Akebono Debate. He couched his opinions in diplomatic terms. "I would prefer a Japanese grand champion, but Akebono has made a sincere effort. He learned to speak Japanese, and he is trying very hard to adapt to the Japanese lifestyle. I think he will be a very hard-working yokozuna." Not good. Not great. Hard-working. Sincere. In Japan, these are the higher compliments.

In a way, I understand Japanese reservations about oversized foreign rikishi. If you had an ancient sport intimately tied with the culture and religion of your native land, would you want some dude named Chad surfing in from Honolulu to become exalted grand champion?

Sumo is the official national sport of Japan. It began as a religious rite, staged at Shinto shrines to entertain the gods (even now, sumo officials are more Shinto priests than referees), and the original bouts often went to the death. Part religion, part ritual, part spectacle, sumo transcends contradictions. It's silly. And solemn. Explosive, yet restrained. Awkward at times, yet filled with moments of breathtaking grace.

I eventually made a sacred pilgrimage to Fukuoka City (which is a great place to fly into, by the way, because the international airport code for Fukuoka is FUK. All your baggage tags and claims stickers are stamped FUK, FUK, FUK). I went to Fukuoka for the final day of the Spring Tournament. I checked into a space-age-capsule hotel and then went for a stroll through the neon and noodle shops of the city's famed Nakasu nightlife zone, a shimmering *Blade Runner* labyrinth of light and noise.

And that's when I met the Wolf.

I was walking down a garish side-alley when I ran right into him. Chiyonofuji. He and his entourage were coming out of a bar and I excitedly informed him of who he was. *"Hey! You're Chiyonofuji!"* He concurred. And that was pretty much it. He brushed past and was gone. (Years later, Chiyonofuji, now known as Kokonoe, came to Prince Edward Island to play golf. He stayed at the CP Hotel in Charlottetown and my wife asked him for an autograph on my behalf. Didn't seem to remember me, though.)

Fortunately, a few minutes after humiliating myself with Chiyonofuji, I ran into several other rikishi, including one named Kotonishiki. He was getting into a cab and I ran over in the assumption that he'd be thrilled to shake my hand.

I said, "Do your best in tomorrow's bout!"

He said he would, and son-of-a-gun if he didn't go out and win the very next day! Needless to say, I am now a *big* Kotonishiki fan.

When I told my Japanese colleagues about my encounter, they agreed that Kotonishiki had been very polite to have stopped to chat. (It helped that I had a hold of his hand and wasn't prepared to let go until he acknowledged my existence.) Kotonishiki himself would later get caught up in a love-triangle sex scandal, complete with a pregnant mistress and vengeful wife, all of which the newspapers covered with an incredible eye for journalistic detail.

The life of a rikishi. You just can't beat it …

The wrestlers named in this article have all since retired, and the higher ranks are now dominated by Mongolian wrestlers. More recently, the sumo world has been rocked by accusations of "match fixing" between rikishi—I'm sure you heard about it; it was in all the papers—but the competitive core of the sport, with all its drama and thousand-year-old pageantry, remains.

The Last
Kamikaze

It begins with a photograph.

A black-and-white image turned sepia over time, it shows five young boys laughing. The focus of their attention is a puppy. A heart-warming scene, but for one detail: the boys, barely in their teens, are wearing combat flight uniforms. They are kamikaze and they are about to die. It's one of the saddest photographs I've ever seen.

I came across it while living in Minamata City on the Japanese island of Kyushu. South of Minamata is Chiran, a quiet town of sidewalk canals and garden villas tucked in among forested hills and rolling fields. Chiran is renowned for its *chiran-cha*, a soft, understated green tea with no aftertaste, prized among connoisseurs. Rows of thick tea-bush shrubberies form caterpillar contours across the landscape. Chiran was also the site of a World War II airfield training ground, and it now houses a museum dedicated to the kamikaze. It was there that I first came across the photograph on display.

In Japan the kamikaze are national heroes, and the square-shouldered statue of a pilot in front of the museum, with the double-speak inscription inside depicting the kamikaze as "men who gave their lives for peace," are testaments to this. In the West, on the other hand, they're generally portrayed as either foam-at-the-mouth zealots

Five young kamikaze pilots play with a puppy prior to their flight

or brainwashed pawns of an imperial war machine. Nowhere are they portrayed simply as young boys, swept up in something they never really understood.

Radio logs and private journals confirm that the kamikaze pilots did not die yelling "Long Live the Emperor!" They died crying out instead for their mothers; the last word from their lips, as their planes plunged into fire and steel, was most often *"Okaasan!"* I want my mom.

The photograph of those boys haunted me. I returned to the museum several times and finally asked if I could purchase a copy. There were none for sale, but the lady behind the counter gave me one of the museum's poster-size versions. I took it back to Minamata, had it framed and put behind glass. It cast a pall across my small room and became the focal point of my own growing anger over the dark side of Japanese history. "Dead, dead, dead, dead, dead," I would say, belligerent on saké and beer, pointing to each of the boys in turn as my Japanese colleagues sat, still as stone Buddhas, in the tension-filled silence of my tatami-mat living room. I kept bringing up the past like a child picking at a scab. "This is your Emperor's Army," I would say. "Just boys."

And then—a remarkable thing happened. I'd ordered food from Isshin Taisho, my neighbourhood pub. The man who owned the shop had delivered the meal and was chatting with me when he noticed the photograph on my wall. He smiled and pointed to the boy in the upper right-hand corner of the picture, the one looking off-camera. "My father," he said.

"Your father?"

"Yes. Would you like to meet him?"

Thus began my unlikely friendship with Eiji Imazato, the shopkeeper's dad.

As it turned out, one of the boys in that photograph had *not* died, had survived, was still very much alive, was, in fact, my neighbour. I'm not sure what I expected, really. A bitter ex-solider, perhaps. I was greeted instead by a tanned, elderly man brimming with energy, his face creased as much by laughter as by life. His handshake was stronger than mine will ever be.

Mr. Imazato's life cuts a remarkable arc, one that parallels the story of modern Japan: from imperial militarism to crushing defeat and slow recovery, from wartime aggression to redemption, from pariah to international competitor, from outcast to victor.

And like Japan, Mr. Imazato survived the war by the slimmest of margins.

The Mission

Eiji Imazato remembers the last day of his life. A clear, cloudless dawn. Wind from the south-southeast. April 27, 1945.

"I'd been sent north, to be trained as a pilot. The Battle of Okinawa was underway and the situation was very bad. We then flew south to Chiran, to prepare for a suicide mission. Our flight path took us right over Minamata, my hometown. We were flying low above the same rice fields and riverbanks where I used to play as a little boy. My heart felt very heavy. We passed right over my home, and in the yard I could see my mother. She looked up as we passed. I was an only child, seventeen years old. She didn't know that the plane above her was carrying her son. She didn't know I was up there looking down. When we got to Chiran, I wrote a last testament and farewell letter, informing her of my death."

History books describe the kamikaze as "fearless in the face of death" and even "cavalier." More than one has described them as sleeping soundly the night before their mission. But these works rely more on Japanese wartime propaganda pieces than firsthand accounts.

"We couldn't sleep," says Eiji. "We were awaiting our fate. It's— it's difficult to explain in words how we felt. It was a long night. I remember the sound of a clock ticking as I lay there."

The next morning, one of the schoolgirls who volunteered at the base served the pilots their morning meal. Her hand was trembling when she poured the tea.

"I thought to myself, 'This is the last meal I will ever have.' Rice. Miso soup. Two eggs. Three bitter pickles. I remember that girl. I remember how her hand trembled."

The photograph?

"Ah, yes," he says. "The photograph. Some local kids had found this abandoned puppy, and we asked if we could hold it. I showed the puppy a small doll I was carrying. It had been made for me by a friend named Chii-chan. She lived in my neighbourhood, and she'd given me the doll as a protective charm. I held it up for the puppy to see, and I whispered, 'Please take my life. Please take it and live for a long time, because I am soon going to die and I want to live on in you.'"

In Japan, life is often thought of as something tangible that can be poured from one being to another. Folk legends and children's fairy tales are replete with stories of lives being poured into cherry trees or contained in mountains or forests or sky.

"We were laughing and playing with the puppy, passing it around so each of us got to hold it, and an army reporter took our picture."

The other boys in the photograph?

"We were all around the same age. We'd only known each other for a short time, but we became very close. Their names?" He points to them each in turn. "This is Hayashi. His name was Utsunomiya. And this boy, his name—his name was ..." but Eiji can't remember. Their names have dissolved with the passing of time.

"At 0500 we started our engines. We saluted the ground crew, and they saluted back. I was shaking, I couldn't stop shaking."

Eiji leans forward and looks directly into my eyes. "We were ready to die, you understand? Once your plane leaves the ground, once the mission is underway, you are not expected to return."

Wind of the Gods

The kamikaze were formed in the final months of the war, even as the American juggernaut was rolling back the Emperor's Army from island to island. Although born of desperation, the idea of suicide bombers was not an aberration in Japanese thought. Rather, it was consistent with the beliefs of Japan's militaristic regime, which were built around the core samurai values of *bushido,* the Way of the Warrior. Bushido stressed obedience and sacrifice; the use of suicide pilots was the logical extension of this way of thinking.

The correct term is Tokkotai, an abbreviation of "Special Attack Force." The name *kami-kaze* means "Wind of the Gods" and refers to the typhoons that twice scattered Kublai Khan's invasion forces in the thirteenth century. Just as these winds had turned back an imminent Mongol invasion, so too would waves of suicide pilots and underwater human torpedoes turn back the American hordes. In three thousand years of recorded history the Japanese had never been conquered by an invading army. Like Macbeth, they believed they lived "a charm'd life." Like Macbeth, they were wrong.

The kamikaze were volunteers, true. But the seduction of wartime mythology and the pressure from their peers were overwhelming. In several cases a commander would volunteer his entire unit.

Lives, tossed away like random mortar shells. Worse than desperate, it was self-defeating. As one historian dryly notes, the pilots "were not allowed to learn from their experience." The Mitsubishi planes they flew were outdated and usually stripped down to the bare essentials. Some were little more than bombs with wings attached, motorless gliders to be released from mother planes with boys on board to aim them into enemy ships.

The main target was to be aircraft carriers, but the young pilots, confused and flying in a state of sustained panic, often dive-bombed escorts and scout ships by mistake. American servicemen at first mocked them, dubbing the gliders *baka bombs,* from the Japanese word for "idiot," and at one point the servicemen on board an American perimeter ship, tired of being mistakenly targeted by kamikaze, painted a huge sign with an arrow reading CARRIERS THIS WAY.

The humour soon turned to horror, though, as wave after wave of kamikaze planes swooped down on the American fleet. Most were taken down in the sky, many crashed harmlessly, some skimmed the very surface of the carriers. And when one did get through, the results were devastating. A single kamikaze pilot could cripple a large ship and kill four hundred servicemen—or more.

Although hard to tally, records show that there were between 2000 and 2500 suicide flights. They took out 71 ships, damaged 292 others. The kamikaze attacks killed more than 6600 Allied servicemen, but they didn't sink a single fleet carrier or battleship—their prime targets— and for all their postwar glory and near-mythic stature, they did not affect the outcome of a single battle in which they were engaged.

Their impact was psychological more than strategic, and in this they did score an ambiguous victory. The kamikaze saved Japan from a full-scale invasion—and led instead to the nuclear annihilation of Hiroshima and Nagasaki. American forces had waded through blood and shrapnel to take the tiny island specks of Okinawa. But faced with mainland Japan—a nation larger than Great Britain and with twice the population, faced with a country capable of producing kamikaze pilots and an army that would rather be burned out of coral caves than surrender—the U.S. High Command was determined to avoid a full-scale invasion at all costs. And so it was that a single plane appeared over the skies of Hiroshima. Bodies melted. Shadows were seared into sidewalks.

Three days later, a second plane appeared over Nagasaki.

On a Runway, Long Ago

Eiji Imazato is playing with his granddaughter. Behind him is the family altar, which honours the memory and spirit of the Imazato ancestors. On display beside it is a collection of medals, a selection of photographs. Not wartime medals, but athletic ones. Not photographs of pilots, but of a man, running.

Eiji's wife enters, proffering green tea and cookies amid a flurry of polite apologies and set phrases. She giggles at my heavy accent when I speak Japanese. A beautiful woman. A grandmother. Fifty years ago, she would have preferred suicide over meeting my gaze.

April 27, 1945.

That day.

I am asking Mr. Imazato about That Day again. As he prepared to board his plane, was there a feeling of exhilaration? Sadness? Or fear?

"Sadness, more than fear. I was nervous, like before a school exam. It's difficult," he says. "What happened on that runway—it's difficult to explain the emotions I felt. How did I survive? *Why* did I survive? I think maybe it was fate, or just luck. I was climbing into the cockpit of my plane when I heard someone shout 'Wait!' It was Shinichi, my flight leader. He was very upset. Ground crew were crowded around his plane. The engine wouldn't start and he got out and ran across to me. He had tears in his eyes and he yelled 'Get out! I'm taking your plane!' I think he just chose me at random. 'You can have my plane once it's repaired,' he said. There was nothing I could do. It was an order. So I climbed down. As the others taxied down the runway, I stood there feeling sick. I was clenching my teeth in shame. I stood there—on the runway—as my friends flew up into the sky, one by one. None of them came back."

Eiji was rescheduled to fly as soon as repairs to his flight leader's plane could be made, but parts were in short supply and by the time Eiji's turn in the flight rotation came up, Hiroshima and Nagasaki had been obliterated and the war was over.

His last-minute escape on the very runway of a suicide mission is a remarkable tale in itself. But Eiji's story doesn't end on that runway. It begins there.

Ruin and Redemption

After the war, Eiji returned to his mother's house in Minamata.

"I was in a state of shock," he says. "I'd been raised my whole life in a military society. When peace came, I didn't know what to do. I'd already sent my will and final farewell to my mother. I'd told everyone that I would not be back, that I was going to die for Japan. My friends and I had vowed to perish together, and now? Now there was only me. I felt like I'd betrayed them. I felt like I had lied. Even now, I feel guilty for my friends who died, while I survived. I didn't tell anyone about what happened on that runway, how I'd been just about to fly. It felt like a crime to come that close and not complete the mission. It felt like a crime just to be alive."

Eiji suffered an emotional breakdown and spent several months recuperating. Slowly, he put his life back together. He married. Found work in the postwar reconstruction. And he began to run.

He ran first in solo marathons, alone through the hills and fields, and then later on proper tracks. His training with the armed forces, the drills and obstacle courses, had first revealed his athletic prowess, his stamina. And through his running, Eiji found a renewed sense of focus. The 100 metre. The 200 metre. The 400 in 47.8 seconds. The 800 in 1 minute 49.7. At his peak in 1957 and 1958, Eiji was unstoppable.

He chuckles and says, with no small amount of pride, "Other athletes were afraid of me. I was running for my life. I'd been given a second chance; I knew how—how *precious* life is." He laughs at his own sentiment, and then strives to put his experiences in a larger context. "Our world had ended. Each of us had to rebuild our lives, just as we had to rebuild our country."

For years, Eiji was one of Japan's top-ranked runners, and at the age of seventy-two, he shows no sign of slowing down. A few years ago he ran—and won—the 400-metre event at a track meet for Japanese and American war veterans. Old enemies, now friends and competitors.

Eiji running the 400-metre in his seventies

As an Olympic judge, with a medallist

It was through amateur sport that Japan's own redemption was recognized internationally. In 1964, Japan hosted the Olympic Games as a democratic nation only nineteen years after being devastated by a war of its own making. People were calling it a miracle, and it was. Eiji kept pace. At Tokyo in 1964, the former kamikaze pilot was now an Olympic judge.

The Olympics provided a chance to recoup lost pride. It also provided an opportunity to mend fences. Japan had occupied Korea for fifty years prior to World War II and during the occupation had treated the Koreans brutally. In the 1936 Olympics, Korean athletes had been forced to march under a Japanese banner, their nationality and language officially censored. In 1988, when South Korea played host, Japan sent a delegation of athletes to Seoul, and Eiji Imazato was among them as a trainer with the Japanese team.

Mr. and Mrs. Imazato today

Now an elder statesman of amateur sport, Eiji Imazato was invited to Atlanta in 1996 (for personal reasons he could not attend) and to Sydney in 2000.

It's late in the evening and Eiji is showing me family photo albums. Children and grandchildren, sporting events. It's only near the end that I make the connection. "Your eldest son," I say. "His name is Shinichi."

"That's right."

"Your flight commander."

"That's right. I named my son after him. The one who took my plane, the one who died in my place. You know, I kept that a secret for a long time, why I had chosen that name. It's because of Shinichi that I'm alive. And it is through Shinichi, the son, that I will continue." And then, with a great deal of pride, he says, "I have five grand-children. Five."

He smiles.

It's the same smile that was captured in a photograph more than fifty years ago, the same smile that has turned to sepia over time. The same smile framed behind glass on the wall of my room: a young boy, looking off-camera, as though seeing something no one else can.

It's the most triumphant photograph I have ever seen.

Prairie Zen

"Hide and reveal, hide and reveal."

Mr. Hironaka points to a path that curves off into a shade pool of trees. It draws you in, this path, but only when you follow it do you see the destination, hidden from view: a small well made from unvarnished wood.

You might be in Kyoto or Nara, but the sky above is pure prairie blue, the air is dry, not humid, and the trees—so painstakingly pruned along Japanese principles—are Canadian: crabapples for spring flowers and maples for autumn, with spruce and pine, dogwood and juniper woven in.

These are the grounds of the Nikka Yuko Garden in Lethbridge, Alberta, and the choice of locale is not as strange as one might think. Japanese farmers first settled in the Lethbridge area in the early 1900s. Which is to say, they had been well established for several generations and had been integrated into the community long before the start of World War II, when a second wave of Japanese settlers arrived, those forced inland during the Japanese evacuation of the West Coast.

The story of B.C.'s dispossessed Japanese, stripped of their property and sent into exile, has often overshadowed more positive stories of Japan in Canada. The deep and abiding roots of the Japanese

Canadian experience in southern Alberta is a case in point, and it is this heritage that is honoured at Nikka Yuko—the name being derived from the *kanji* characters for "Japan Canada Friendship."

The garden began with the fortunate convergence of a local Buddhist minister, a progressive newspaper publisher, and an energetic tourism officer all conspiring to bring about a Japanese oasis in the Western plains.

It was launched as a 1967 centennial project, with its design overseen by a respected Japanese landscape architect after an extensive tour of the Lethbridge area to study the local climate, plants, terrain, and culture, with the final plans drawn up by one of his students. The structures in the garden—from the tea house pavilion to the bell tower, from the wooden gates to the curved bridges, right down to the hidden water well—were built in Japan using handcrafted traditional methods, then disassembled and shipped to Lethbridge to be reassembled by master tradesmen.

Canadian trees were planted and trimmed to exact Japanese specifications, creating a blend of Canadian solidity with Japanese elegance, something that's reflected in Mr. Hironaka as well.

Born and raised on a farm in southern Alberta, Robert Hironaka is a member of the original centennial committee that worked to bring about the garden. A man of science—Mr. Hironaka has a Ph.D. in animal nutrition, has worked as an agricultural adviser in Ottawa, and has served as chancellor of the University of Lethbridge—he is also attuned to the aesthetics of Japanese gardens. His background in science doesn't preclude spirituality, either. Mr. Hironaka is co-author of the book *Garden of Serenity* and author of a meditation on modern Buddhism titled *Now Is the Moment*.

When George Hall, the director of the Lethbridge Community Foundation, heard that I was coming to Lethbridge to visit the garden with my homesick wife and dual-citizen sons in tow, he arranged a tour of the garden with Mr. Hironaka.

Now in his eighties, Mr. Hironaka's enthusiasm for Nikka Yuko has hardly dimmed: if anything, it has grown stronger. "I come two or three times a week," he says, pointing out favourite spots and hidden views he feels best capture the serenity of Nikka Yuko.

The garden includes elements of three classical Japanese forms: the dry rock garden (popularly known as "Zen gardens"); the tea house garden, which evokes the quiet elegance of the tea ceremony (tea ceremonies are held by trained hosts every Sunday during the summer); and the wider "stroll garden" with its curving paths and flowing streams.

"Sometimes people refer to the gardens, plural. But that's not correct," Mr. Hironaka explains. "There is only one garden, combining all three in harmony. Take away one element and it doesn't hold together."

The large stones in the Zen garden were chosen and placed with great care. Looking for rocks that contained the proper lichen-stained sense of age, the designers travelled as far as the Crowsnest Pass to find the perfect pieces, millions of years old. Stark white gravel was then raked into circles around them, like waves emanating from islands, or like prairie winds through summer grass, inviting reflection, meditation, perhaps even that flash of insight known as *satori*.

The tea house pavilion offers a view of the pond and waterfall, and Mr. Hironaka points out the many nuances at play. "You see the stone pagoda, just visible behind that tree? It was hidden intentionally, so that it wouldn't compete with the waterfall."

He also points out the smooth, stream-flattened stones along the water, which were gathered from the natural rock polisher of the Oldman River. "We held a rock-gathering day," he says. "A few bottles of beer were involved. Maybe more than a few. We collected all the river stones in a single afternoon. It was like a community picnic."

The Nikka Yuko Garden also employs the Japanese technique of *shakkei,* or "borrowed landscape," framing the garden with Henderson Lake on the other side and extending Nikka Yuko—aesthetically, at least—beyond its original boundaries. The lake forms a continuation of the view, and, in effect, brings the garden into a wider context.

Having passed through the central pavilion, with its tatami-mat tea room and *ikebana* flower arrangements and kimonos on display, having caught the scent of pine and prairie sky, having seen the stone pagoda slip in and out of view as we walk along the path, having heard the low toll of a bronze bell cast in Japan specially for Nikka Yuko, my wife is almost in tears.

The path at Nikka Yuko forms a circle that doesn't quite close, and that too is intentional. Even here, there is a distinctly Japanese touch: the path ends in a series of stepping stones that lead down to the pond. They are placed irregularly so that one has to be careful—mindful—watching where one steps, and in doing so to become aware of the textures and shape of each rock.

At water's edge, the path ends and one must turn back, retracing the entire route, seeing everything again but from a different angle. What seemed like flat land on the way down is now revealed to be a rolling undulation. And under a bridge we crossed earlier, we now spot a second waterfall, which was sheltered from view on the walk down and is now showing itself.

When we notice this, Hironaka-san smiles. "Hide and reveal."

CREDITS AND ACKNOWLEDGMENTS

Material in *Canadian Pie* was adapted from the following:

The Beaver: Canada's History Magazine
"Encounter: Agnes Macphail" June/July 2004
"Duncan Campbell Scott: Worst Canadian?" August/September 2007

Canadian Living
"True Patriot Love" February 1997

Charlottetown Guardian: "East Meets West"
"Yes, We Have No Bananas" August 29, 1996
"Three Magic Words and a Carrot" September 5, 1996
"Sumos Pack a Certain Sex Appeal" September 12, 1996
"Gestures Generate Considerable Confusion" September 19, 1996
"Emily and Anne Battle It Out" October 17, 1996
"Ghost Stories Keep Japanese Cool in Summer" October 31, 1996
"Japanese Holidays a Time to Discover New Sins" December 12, 1996
"Elections Noisy Affair in Japan" May 15, 1997
"Giving Chocolates a Duty in Japan" February 12, 1998

Elm Street
"A Poem for Canada's Poet Laureate" Summer 2002

En Route
"Ich bin ein Carrot!" May 1999
"The Lost Art of Crank Calls" September 1999

Esquire UK
"Worlds Apart: Canada in the Aftermath of History" October 2002

Financial Times Magazine
"Once Upon a Time: Stone Soup" January 26, 2008

Flare
"An Open Letter to Women" November 2001
"What's Your Sign: How to Pick Up Girls (or Not)" November 2003

The Globe and Mail
"Bookmarked: The Writer in the Greenroom" January 16, 2001
"After Survival" June 30, 2001
"Ohmygawd! Just What I Didn't Need" December 22, 2001
"How's the Book Going?" September 5, 2009
"The Burden and Glory of Being Dad: Reading the Hardy Boys" June 19, 2010
"Prairie Zen" August 7, 2010

Maclean's
"To Pierre, with Thanks" December 13, 2004

Maclean's: "Will Ferguson's Canada"
"Size Matters: Large Objects Beside the Highway" July 22, 2002
"Mythic Isle: PEI" August 12, 2002
"Love and Loss: Quebec City" September 30, 2002
"Sandstone City: Calgary" October 7, 2002
"Ode to Virility: Toronto's CN Tower" October 21, 2002
"The King of Tides: Fundy" November 18, 2002
"City of Vignettes: Montreal" January 27, 2003
"A Golden Nugget: Yukon" October 6, 2003
"Ghosts of a Nation: Batoche" November 17, 2003

Maclean's Backpage
"The Founding Scoundrel" January 14, 2002
"Ulster? Not Us Thanks" March 18, 2002

Maisonneuve
"An Open Letter to Montreal" Fall 2006

The New York Times
"Canada's Black Heart" July 18, 2007

New Brunswick Reader (Telegraph-Journal)
"Lessons My Fayther Taught Me" April 4, 1998
"Unintentional Beauties" June 6, 1998
"Naked in New Brunswick" September 12, 1998

Ottawa Citizen
"Preston Came A'Wooing" May 30, 1998
"Those Danged Right Wingers: Shootout at UA Corral" March 25, 2000
"An American, a Canadian and a Brit Walk into a Bar" March 11, 2001
"My Lunch with Preston" March 24, 2001

The Citizen's Weekly
"The Last of the Kamikaze" February 1, 1998
"The Ballad of Good Time Charlie" March 15, 1998
"A Kiss in the Dark" May 24, 1998
"For the Love of Sumo" June 28, 1998
"Voyage of the *Uchuck*" September 23, 2001

Outpost
"Bulls, Baseball, and a Strong Thumb" December 1998

St. Croix Courier
"A Small but Powerful Mastermind" July 28, 1998
"William Shakespeare: A Great American" August 11, 1998

Toronto Sun
"Myth or Reality? Sometimes PEI Seems Too Good to Be True" August 10, 1997
"A Round of Bridges" September 13, 1998

The Vancouver Sun
"He Shoots, He Scores—He Respects the Ref!" August 5, 1995

The Walrus
"Buzz and Bastards: An Encounter with Jean Chrétien at BookExpo" October 2007

World & I
"The Last Kamikaze" May 1997

The Daily Yomiuri
"Renewing the Faith" July 27, 1995
"A Bridge Too Far for Timeless Island of Anne of Green Gables" February 17, 1996

YorkU Magazine
"What's in a Name?" Fall 2003
"The Art of the Con: Pedigreed Pooches and Spanish Prisoners" Summer 2007

* * *

"Me vs. My Wife" adapted from "Pots and Pans" in *Mixed Messages,* edited by Paul Knowles (English Garden Publishers, 2007).

"Dead Politicians" adapted from the Introduction to the new edition of *Eye Opener Bob* by Grant MacEwan (Brindle & Glass, 2004); used by permission.

"Mind the Gap!" adapted from the Introduction to the Penguin Black Classics Edition of *Sunshine Sketches of a Little Town* by Stephen Leacock (Penguin Canada, 2006); used by permission.

"The Mad Trapper of Rat River" expanded from *100 Photos That Changed Canada* edited by Mark Reid (Canada's National History Society in arrangement with HarperCollins Canada, 2009); used by permission.

* * *

Although generally ascribed to John Lennon, the expression "Life is what happens when you're making other plans" goes back much further than Lennon and has been attributed to various authors, journalists, and comedians over the years.

Quote by playwright Eugene Stickland at the start of "So How's the Book Going?" used by permission.

"As the Irvings Turn Theme Song" by Steve Stackhouse © 1997 Steve Stackhouse; used by permission.

Lyrics to "My Name Is Good Time Charlie" by Charlie Nagatani with Michael Woody © 1992 Fuji Music; used by permission.

Photo of Mr. and Mrs. Imazato © 1997, 2011 Will Ferguson.
Photos of Eiji Imazato running the 400-metre and with Olympic medallist courtesy of Mr. Imazato.
Photo of Charlie Nagatani © 1997, 2011 Will Ferguson.
Photo of "The Mad Trapper, 1932," NA-1258-119, courtesy the Glenbow Archives.
Photos of the Shediac Lobster, the Campbellton Salmon, and the Nackawic Axe courtesy the New Brunswick Department of Tourism and Parks.
Photo of Jumbo the Elephant by Carol Beechey courtesy the City of St. Thomas.
Photo of Ernie the Turtle courtesy the Town of Turtleford.
Photo of the O'Leary Potato by Donna Rowley courtesy the PEI Potato Museum.
Photo of Ms. Claybelt by Lois Weston-Bernstein courtesy the Temiskaming Shores & Area Chamber of Commerce.
Photo of the Happy Rock by Monica Radford Ferguson courtesy the Town of Gladstone.
Photo of The Big Nickel at Dynamic Earth, a Science North Attraction, courtesy Science North, Sudbury.

* * *

The author would like to thank editorial director Andrea Magyar, copy editor Karen Alliston, production editor Sandra Tooze, and everyone else at Penguin Canada who helped make *Canadian Pie* possible. Any eccentricities of style or errors in grammar and quirks of punctuation remain the sole responsibility of the author and should not in any way be ascribed to a lack of editorial input.

The author would also like to thank the following people for their assistance in providing images and information on their local attractions: Carol Beechey in St. Thomas, Ontario; Stephanie Deschenes at Science North in Sudbury, Ontario; Monica Radford Ferguson in Gladstone, Manitoba; Kim Gartner in Macklin, Saskatchewan; Kelly Harle at Tourism Saskatchewan; Deanna Kahl Lundberg in Turtleford, Saskatchewan; Donna Rowley in O'Leary, PEI; Diane St. Amour at Tourism New Brunswick; and Lois Weston-Bernstein in New Liskeard, Ontario.